The Globalizing Legal Sector in Korea

Korean Communities across the World

Series Editor
Joong-Hwan Oh, Hunter College, CUNY

Korean Communities across the World publishes works that address aspects of (a) the Korean American community, (b) Korean society, (c) the Korean communities in other foreign lands, or (d) transnational Korean communities. In the field of (a) the Korean American community, this series welcomes contributions involving concepts such as Americanization, pluralism, social mobility, migration/immigration, social networks, social institutions, social capital, racism/discrimination, settlement, identity, or politics, as well as a specific topic related to family/marriage, gender roles, generations, work, education, culture, citizenship, health, ethnic community, housing, ethnic identity, racial relations, social justice, social policy, and political views, among others. In the field of (b) Korean society, this series embraces scholarship on current issues such as gender roles, age/aging, low fertility, immigration, urbanization, gentrification, economic inequality, high youth unemployment, sexuality, democracy, political power, social injustice, the nation's educational problems, social welfare, capitalism, consumerism, labor, health, housing, crime, environmental degradation, and the social life in the digital age and its impacts, among others. Contributors in the field of (c) Korean communities in other foreign lands are encouraged to submit works that expand our understanding about the formation, vicissitudes, and major issues of an ethnic Korean community outside of South Korea and the United States, such as cultural or linguistic retention, ethnic identity, assimilation, settlement patterns, citizenship, economic activities, family relations, social mobility, and racism/discrimination. Lastly, contributions relating to (d) transnational Korean communities may touch upon transnational connectivity in family, economy/finance, politics, culture, technology, social institutions, and people.

The Globalizing Legal Sector in Korea: Legal Education, Legal Profession, and Jury System, edited by Jeong-Chul Kim and Joong-Hwan Oh

Korean Collaboration in the Shadow of Japanese Rule: Negotiating Nationhood, by Jeong-Chul Kim

Korean Immigrants in Latin America: Home Away from Home, edited by Kyeyoung Park

Social Work Practice, Research, Empowerment, and Education for Koreans in the United States, edited by Anderson Sungmin Yoon, Suk-hee Kim, Mingun Lee, and Juye Ji

Korean Migration and Mobility in the Global South, edited by Yonson Ahn and Jihye Kim

Korean Nuclear Diaspora: Redress Movements of Korean Atomic-Bomb Victims in Japan, by Yuko Takahashi

Korean Kirogi Families: Placemaking, Belonging, and Mothering, by Young A. Jung

Cross-Border Interactions and Encounters between Germany and Korea in the New Century, edited by Yonson Ahn and Jihye Kim

The Making of a Smart City in Korea: The Quest for E-Seoul, edited by Hoejeong Lee, Jaehyeon Jeong, and Joong-Hwan Oh

Korean Immigrants from Latin America: Fitting into Multiethnic New York, by Jin Suk Bae

From Sweatshop to Fashion Shop: Korean Immigrant Entrepreneurship in the Argentine Garment Industry, by Jihye Kim

Korean Wild Geese Families: Gender, Family, Social, and Legal Dynamics of Middle-Class Asian Transnational Families in North America, by Se Hwa Lee

The Globalizing Legal Sector in Korea

Legal Education, Legal Profession, and Jury System

Edited by

Jeong-Chul Kim and Joong-Hwan Oh

BLOOMSBURY ACADEMIC
NEW YORK • LONDON • OXFORD • NEW DELHI • SYDNEY

BLOOMSBURY ACADEMIC
Bloomsbury Publishing Inc, 1359 Broadway, New York, NY 10018, USA
Bloomsbury Publishing Plc, 50 Bedford Square, London, WC1B 3DP, UK
Bloomsbury Publishing Ireland, 29 Earlsfort Terrace, Dublin 2, D02 AY28, Ireland

BLOOMSBURY, BLOOMSBURY ACADEMIC and the Diana logo are
trademarks of Bloomsbury Publishing Plc

First published in the United States of America 2026

A catalog record for this book is available from the Library of Congress.

ISBN: HB: 979-8-216-27769-9
ePDF: 979-8-216-27771-2
eBook: 979-8-216-27770-5

Series: Korean Communities across the World

Typeset by Integra Software Services Pvt. Ltd.

Contents

Figures

Tables

Acknowledgments

This book has been a journey—one made possible only through the generosity, collaboration, and encouragement of many people.

First and foremost, we thank the chapter authors, whose scholarship, creativity, and persistence brought this volume to life. Each contributed not only their expertise but also their passion for understanding how Korea's legal sector is adapting—sometimes uneasily—to the forces of globalization. Working with such thoughtful and committed colleagues has been both an honor and a joy.

Our sincere thanks also go to the editorial and production teams, whose careful attention to detail, responsiveness, and steady guidance made the complex process of bringing an edited volume to publication feel manageable—and at times even enjoyable.

Finally, we owe the deepest gratitude to our families. You patiently endured the long hours, shifting deadlines, and countless conversations about law schools, legal professions, and jury systems. Your love and support have been our anchor.

This volume is dedicated to everyone who believes that thoughtful scholarship can illuminate the complexities of reform and, in some small way, help build a more just and inclusive legal system.

Jeong-Chul Kim
Joong-Hwan Oh
Co-editors

Preface

When Korea began opening its legal sector to the world in the late twentieth century, the goal seemed clear: modernize institutions, strengthen the rule of law, and prepare a new generation of legal professionals for a global stage. Yet, as the chapters in this book reveal, the journey has been anything but straightforward.

The Globalizing Legal Sector in Korea: Legal Education, Legal Profession, and Jury System tells the story of a legal system in transition—where new ideas meet old structures, and where reforms meant to democratize access sometimes end up reinforcing familiar hierarchies. It is a story of convergence and resistance, of hybrid institutions that are neither fully "Korean" in the old sense nor fully aligned with the Western models that inspired them.

The volume is organized into four parts, each exploring a critical site of change. Part 1, "Legal Education in the Era of Global Convergence," examines how the adoption of American-style law schools promised to produce more practical, globally minded lawyers, but collided with entrenched exam culture and elite gatekeeping. Part 2, "Restructuring the Legal Profession: From State Monopoly to Market Competition," looks at how liberalization and foreign law firm entry have reshaped the profession, opening opportunities for globally credentialed lawyers while deepening inequalities. Part 3, "Democracy and the Jury: Citizen Participation as Legal Reform," explores the introduction of Korea's jury system—a bold experiment in participatory justice that remains bounded by judicial authority. Finally, Part 4, "Law in Transition: Legal Norms, Justice, and the Contradictions of Global Reform," turns to substantive legal change, from insolvency law to the abolition of statutes of limitation in cases of illegal international adoption, where demands for justice push against procedural and institutional constraints.

These chapters show that legal globalization in Korea is not a one-way importation of foreign models, nor a simple success story. Instead, it is a process of adaptation, negotiation, and contestation—shaped by Korea's unique political history, social structures, and aspirations for global standing.

We offer this volume to scholars, practitioners, and policymakers interested not only in Korea but in the broader dynamics of legal change in a global era. In its pages, you will find case studies, comparative insights, and critical reflections that illuminate the promises and paradoxes of legal reform in a rapidly globalizing society.

Jeong-Chul Kim
Joong-Hwan Oh
Co-editors

1

Introduction

Contradictions in Korea's Globalizing Legal Sector

Jeong-Chul Kim and Joong-Hwan Oh

Over the past three decades, South Korea's legal sector has experienced significant transformation. From education and professional training to institutional reform and citizen participation, the legal field has evolved in response to internal demands and external pressures. Yet the full scope of these changes—how they intersect, conflict, and reshape one another—remains underexplored.

The 1997 financial crisis marked a turning point. It exposed deep political and institutional vulnerabilities, prompting calls for greater transparency, accountability, and rule of law. Simultaneously, South Korea adopted aggressive neoliberal reforms under IMF guidance, liberalizing markets and restructuring industries to align with global capitalism (Chang 2002). These shifts placed intense pressure on the legal system—not only to modernize and meet international expectations, but also to restore public trust and institutional legitimacy (Wade 1998; Kim 2015).

Legal education was overhauled, new categories of legal professionals emerged, and reforms such as the limited introduction of jury trials were enacted to reflect democratic ideals. South Korea soon became one of East Asia's most litigious societies, straining long-standing Confucian values of harmony and deference (Lee 2012). As the legal system expanded, it became a site where tradition and innovation collided. Recent analyses have highlighted how the shift from a state-regulated legal profession to a market-driven system has created new hierarchies, particularly in how globalized legal networks influence job placement and career progression (Moon 2021; Lee 2019).

Now, nearly three decades later, it is an opportune moment to reevaluate Korea's legal transformation. While initial reforms were shaped by crisis and a drive for international competitiveness, subsequent developments reveal deeper contradictions and enduring challenges. Persistent inequality in legal education, fragmentation in the profession, and ambivalence about democratization reflect unresolved tensions in Korea's evolving legal landscape. In particular, ongoing research stresses the continued influence of "elite capture" in legal education and the profession, which has obstructed the democratizing potential of legal reforms (Kwon 2021; Kim 2018).

These transformations are best understood as a dialectical struggle between two forces: on one side, external pressures to adopt global legal standards, and on the other, internal efforts to preserve national legal traditions and institutional frameworks. As David Harvey (2014) argues, contradictions are the engine of transformation in capitalist systems. They do not resolve neatly, but continually reproduce and reshape themselves. Korea's legal globalization is no exception.

Efforts to align with American or international models—such as US-style law schools or liberalized legal markets—have produced hybrid institutions. These reflect not seamless convergence, but ongoing tension between global norms of efficiency and competition, and domestic legacies of hierarchy, state-centrism (Ginsburg 2004), and civil law tradition. Rather than linear modernization, Korea's legal development is characterized by friction, ambiguity, and contested legitimacy. Research by Steele and Taylor (2009) has emphasized that this "hybridization" of legal systems, especially in East Asia, often leads to outcomes where global norms are selectively adopted, filtered through local institutional power structures, and reinterpreted to align with national interests.

Understanding these dynamics through the lens of contradiction allows us to see reform not as a smooth trajectory but as a space of negotiation, resistance, and reconfiguration. Whether in legal education, the legal profession, or judicial reform, Korea's experience demonstrates how transnational norms are filtered through local institutions, social hierarchies, and political strategies. Global legal norms are often "localized" or resisted in ways that defy idealized forms of legal globalization (Antons 2013; Dezalay and Garth 2011). Imported legal frameworks in East Asia often clash with local values and produce uneven, contested outcomes. In Korea, these contradictions are especially salient across four core domains: legal education, the legal profession, citizen engagement via jury trials, and rule of law.

This book situates Korea's legal transformation within this contradictory global context. It explores four interconnected dimensions of legal globalization: (1) legal education and training, (2) the legal profession and market, (3) institutional reform including the jury system, and (4) the practice of law. The chapters in this volume examine how Korean legal institutions have adapted, resisted, or selectively integrated global norms—while continuously negotiating their own national legal identity.

Legal Education in the Era of Global Convergence

Across many Asian countries, legal education has become a central focus of reform, often linked to national projects of modernization and global integration (Steele and Taylor 2009). In South Korea, this momentum culminated in the 2009 introduction of American-style graduate law schools, replacing the older system dominated by the highly selective National Judicial Examination and centralized training at the Judicial Research and Training Institute (Kim 2006). The reform promised to produce legal professionals with practical skills, global competence, and interdisciplinary awareness.

Yet structural reform does not automatically yield democratization or a broadened legal imagination (Steele and Taylor 2009). In Korea—as in Japan—many students remain focused on bar exam preparation rather than developing critical thinking or applied legal skills. Admission procedures still favor applicants from elite universities, limiting diversification and internationalization. What was framed as a transformative reform quickly became enmeshed in long-standing institutional logics and cultural norms.

Legal reform in Korea has typically been initiated through top-down, state-led processes, often in response to international pressures or moments of political vulnerability (Ginsburg 2004). The restructuring of legal education was no exception. It served broader state goals of enhancing Korea's global competitiveness while retaining administrative control over entry into the profession.

Rosa Kim's chapter examines this reform in depth, showing how the new graduate law school system created both opportunities and complications. While it increased the number and diversity of law graduates, it also raised concerns about cultural fit, institutional resistance, and the limited capacity of Korea's legal market to absorb new entrants. Kim emphasizes that the change was not a simple transplant of the US model, but the product of a protracted national debate, reshaped by domestic legal, political, and educational realities. The resulting system—neither fully foreign nor purely domestic—illustrates the hybrid nature of Korea's legal education reform.

Moon's chapter adds a longer historical perspective, tracing how US legal education gained prominence in Korea during the 1990s amid debates over reforming the insular, exam-centric system inherited from Japanese colonial influence and German legal traditions. The American model promised to produce well-rounded, globally fluent professionals, but bar exam requirements continue to dominate curricula and student priorities, undermining the original goals of fostering practical competence and critical analysis.

As Moon notes, Asian legal reforms often involve selective borrowing of Western "ideal types" that are unevenly integrated into local contexts (Antons 2013). In Korea, law schools have become arenas where global prestige, social capital, and foreign credentials are converted into professional advantage (Dezalay and Garth 2011). This dynamic reinforces new hierarchies without dismantling old ones.

Taken together, these chapters show that Korea's legal education reform—while modernizing in form—has in practice reproduced entrenched inequalities. The "Americanization" of Korean legal education is best understood as a contested, hybridized process shaped as much by internal constraints as by external pressures. Importantly, the consequences of these reforms extend beyond the classroom. The way law schools are structured, the credentials they privilege, and the networks they cultivate all directly shape who enters the profession, what roles they occupy, and how the profession itself evolves. This direct link between educational change and professional restructuring provides the bridge to the next part of the volume.

Restructuring the Legal Profession: From State Monopoly to Market Competition

Globalization has profoundly reshaped South Korea's legal profession as well. Historically, the field was small, state-regulated, and tightly controlled by an elite trained through the National Judicial Examination and the Judicial Research and

Training Institute (JRTI). However, the liberalization of the legal services market—alongside the entry of global law firms and the expansion of quasilegal professions like patent attorneys and judicial scriveners—has disrupted this traditional structure and introduced new complexities.

These professional reforms were often pursued by the state not simply to liberalize the market, but to enhance its own strategic capacity in a globalizing economy (Ginsburg 2004; Moon 2021). Globalization in legal sectors across Asia is frequently part of broader state strategies aimed at attracting investment, modernizing institutions, and cultivating global legal talent (Steele and Taylor 2009; Wilkins, Trubek, and Fong 2020). However, the results are rarely straightforward. Instead of convergence toward a unified global model, what emerges are "hybridized outcomes," where foreign institutional forms are grafted onto domestic structures, producing uneven and sometimes contradictory transformations (Steele and Taylor 2009).

In Korea, the opening of the legal market to foreign firms and attorneys has revealed persistent tensions between liberalization and professional resistance. Domestic lawyers have often opposed these changes, citing risks to professional autonomy, cultural dilution, and market saturation (Ahn 1994; Silver, Lee, and Park 2015; Song 1994). Even as formal regulations shifted, entrenched informal hierarchies—based on elite firm preferences, client loyalties, and university prestige—have continued to restrict access to the most desirable positions (Lee 2019).

Globalization has also stratified the profession along new lines. Lawyers with "global capital"—foreign degrees, English fluency, and international internships—enjoy significant advantages, while those without such credentials have been increasingly marginalized (Steele and Taylor 2009; Kim 2018). As Dezalay and Garth (2011) note, a new class of corporate lawyers and legal technocrats now acts as brokers between global legal norms and domestic institutions. Their legitimacy is derived not only from legal expertise but also from ties to elite global networks, particularly US law schools and corporate law firms, reinforcing professional stratification and privileging cosmopolitan elites over domestically trained or regionally based practitioners (Dezalay and Garth 2011; Moon 2021; Dinovitzer and Garth 2025).

This preference for global credentials has further deepened internal hierarchies. Foreign-trained lawyers—especially those with US qualifications—are highly sought after by top Korean and international firms for their bilingual fluency, cross-border expertise, and familiarity with international standards (Silver, Lee, and Park 2015). Yet such hiring practices have also created new barriers, elevating those with prestigious foreign qualifications while sidelining others. In effect, market liberalization has expanded opportunities for some while entrenching asymmetries that mirror and amplify existing inequalities in Korea's legal profession.

Kwon's chapter offers detailed empirical insight into these contradictions. She explores how the introduction of twenty-five law schools in 2009 aimed to democratize legal education and broaden participation. The reform attempted to reduce the dominance of young, male graduates from elite Seoul universities by requiring law school graduation for bar exam eligibility. Kwon's findings indicate that while diversity in gender, age, and professional backgrounds improved, the reform ultimately failed to dismantle structural elitism in the profession. SKY universities (Seoul National, Korea, and Yonsei) continue to dominate bar passage rates and top legal employment outcomes, while regional law schools struggle to compete. She also highlights how financial barriers—such as high tuition and limited scholarships—restrict access for students from underprivileged backgrounds, thereby reproducing socioeconomic stratification under the guise of educational reform.

Empirical research by Lee in this volume (2019) explores the rapid growth and transformation of Korea's legal profession, particularly since the introduction of the law school system in 2009. This reform aimed to produce competent legal professionals capable of addressing both domestic and international legal demands, while also increasing diversity within the legal profession. The study compares law school graduates with those trained under the previous system (JRTI trainees), analyzing their socioeconomic backgrounds, career paths, work environments, and job satisfaction. The findings provide insight into the impact of legal education reforms and the progress toward achieving more diversified legal careers in Korea.

Lee (2019) highlights that the law school system, designed to modernize legal education and expand the legal profession, was not a one-size-fits-all solution. Although the reforms have diversified the legal community to some extent, they have also perpetuated systemic inequalities. Graduates from top universities, particularly those from Seoul's prestigious institutions, continue to dominate Korea's legal profession, in terms of both job placements and career advancement. Lee's research documents how these graduates tend to secure higher-status positions, especially within large law firms or in government roles, while graduates from regional universities face more limited opportunities in the legal market.

Moreover, Lee discusses the dual challenges that emerged with the law school system: on one hand, it increased the accessibility of legal education to a broader demographic, but on the other hand, it reinforced the professional dominance of elite legal networks, creating a new kind of educational hierarchy. The continued dominance of certain institutions, which are still seen as "gatekeepers" to the profession, undermines the democratic intent behind the reforms. Lee's findings emphasize the hybrid nature of Korea's legal education reform, which, despite its goal to modernize and globalize, simultaneously deepens existing professional divisions, highlighting the contradictions inherent in Korea's legal modernization efforts.

These reforms, though designed to modernize Korea's legal profession, have created a fragmented and hierarchical field. As globalization opens new spaces for legal practice, it simultaneously deepens divides—between global and local professionals, metropolitan and regional actors, and high-prestige and peripheral career paths. In short, Korea's legal profession today is not defined by convergence toward a liberal or global ideal. Instead, it is shaped by layered contradictions—between state strategies, global pressures, and national hierarchies. These tensions are structural features of legal globalization. They are not transitional anomalies but persistent dynamics that this volume seeks to examine in depth.

Democracy and the Jury: Citizen Participation as Legal Reform

Among the most symbolically potent yet institutionally contested reforms in South Korea's legal globalization is the introduction of the jury system. Enacted in 2008 through the *Act on Citizen Participation in Criminal Trials*, the reform was designed to promote transparency, build public trust in the judiciary, and align Korea with international norms of participatory justice and the rule of law (Choi 2014). Rooted in Anglo-American legal traditions, this innovation marked a dramatic departure from Korea's historically bureaucratic and judge-centered legal culture.

However, legal reforms in East Asia often serve dual purposes: they address international demands for legitimacy while simultaneously preserving domestic institutional authority (Ginsburg 2004; Antons 2013). Korea's jury system exemplifies this dynamic. While it signals a commitment to democratization and citizen engagement, its actual implementation remains cautious and limited. Jury verdicts are advisory rather than binding, and judges retain the final authority—revealing the reform's symbolic dimensions more than a wholesale embrace of participatory adjudication (Kim 2015).

Steele and Taylor (2009) emphasize the *contextual complexity* of legal transplants in Asia, where global norms must navigate deeply rooted bureaucratic traditions. Korea's jury system has been rhetorically celebrated as democratic reform, yet institutionally circumscribed—reflecting ambivalence about surrendering adjudicatory power to ordinary citizens. What emerges is a form of managed participation, where citizen involvement is carefully channeled rather than fully empowered (Woo, Rhee, and Lee 2021; cf. Lee, Lee, and Han 2025).

This volume's empirical chapters unpack how these tensions manifest in practice. Chapter by Lee (2016) traces the system's early goals and persistent challenges. A 2013 revision attempted to encourage binding verdicts and clarify evidentiary standards, yet actual usage rates remain low, and constitutional debates over due process continue. Without sustained judicial buy-in and deeper public trust, Lee argues, the jury system risks stagnating as a symbolic gesture rather than a transformative institution. Nonetheless, comparative findings suggest that lay jurors frequently render more lenient and community-sensitive decisions than professional judges, reflecting shifting cultural attitudes about justice (see also Kim, Yoon, and Oh 2020; Lee, Lee, and Han 2025).

Lee and Woo's chapter explores deliberative dynamics between judges and jurors. In the Korean system, jurors begin deliberations independently but may consult the judge if they fail to reach consensus. Their study finds that these interactions can enhance legal understanding and reinforce the legitimacy of outcomes—particularly when judges clarify key legal standards such as "beyond a reasonable doubt" and the presumption of innocence. The process demonstrates that judicial involvement need not undermine juror autonomy and can instead foster collaborative legal reasoning.

Chapter by Woo and Levinson examines how diversity affects jury deliberations. Drawing on data from thirty-two shadow juries across nineteen trials, the study finds that demographic diversity—especially in age and gender—can suppress deliberative participation due to hierarchical cultural norms. However, "speech diversity," or the equitable sharing of voice, was strongly associated with more evidence-based and reasoned decision-making. Their findings suggest that procedural equity in deliberation may be more important than representational diversity alone for achieving deliberative justice in East Asian settings.

Taken together, the Korean jury system exemplifies a selective adoption of foreign ideals, filtered through domestic institutional legacies and cultural conservatism. While the reform expresses aspirations toward democratization and transparency, it also reflects long-standing anxieties about citizen competence and judicial legitimacy.

Ultimately, Korea's jury system underscores the contradictory logics of legal globalization: the external imperative to adopt democratic norms versus the internal drive to retain bureaucratic control. Reforms of this kind serve as both symbolic performances and sites of negotiation, where legal authority, public perception, and international credibility are continuously contested. Far from being merely transitional, these tensions are structural—and their analysis is central to understanding the evolution of legal reform in Korea.

Law in Transition: Legal Norms, Justice, and the Contradictions of Global Reform

Globalization has left a profound imprint on South Korea's legal system, extending beyond structural reforms in education and the legal profession into the domain of substantive law and justice. In this sphere, Korea's legal transformations reflect not only the possibilities but also the limitations of global legal reform. The success or failure of law reform in East Asia often hinges not on the content of legal change itself, but on its capacity to navigate "creative norm destruction"—the strategic rejection, adaptation, or domestication of global legal norms by local actors (Antons 2013). Korean legal development, therefore, is best understood not as convergence with Western legal systems, but as a process shaped by enduring institutional legacies, power dynamics, and contested notions of justice and legitimacy.

Chapter 9 by Choi uses contract and insolvency law to illustrate this tension. Focusing on proposed amendments to Korean insolvency legislation that would allow creditors to terminate contracts based on nonperformance during insolvency proceedings, Choi critiques the erosion of collective procedures in favor of creditor self-interest. Such reform, he argues, would disrupt equitable asset distribution and procedural integrity. Instead, the chapter proposes a legal alternative grounded in the principle of "discontinuity," reinforcing the trustee's right to reject ongoing contracts in order to avoid unjust enrichment and preserve efficiency. In doing so, Choi challenges assumptions rooted in global commercial practice and highlights how insolvency reform must be calibrated to Korean institutional realities—particularly the need for collective fairness over market-based individualism (cf. Rhee 2020).

Edelson's chapter explores a radically different facet of law in transition: the retroactive removal of statutes of limitation in cases involving illegal international adoptions. Between the 1950s and 1990s, up to 200,000 Korean children were sent abroad—many through coercive or fraudulent means. These adoptions often involved false documentation, forced separation of birth mothers, and legal misrepresentations of the adoptees' status. Today, many adoptees seek legal redress from the Korean government and adoption agencies. However, procedural time bars often prevent their claims from being heard.

Edelson argues that in cases of systemic child rights violations and human trafficking, the legal system should prioritize justice and accountability over strict adherence to limitation periods. Drawing on international legal developments—including decisions from European courts and UN treaty bodies—he calls for retroactive legal reform as a means of aligning Korea with evolving global human rights standards. Similar debates are ongoing in jurisdictions such as Australia, the Netherlands, and the United States, where limitation statutes have been lifted in cases involving child abuse and state complicity (see also Loibl 2021).

Together, these chapters illustrate the contested terrain of substantive legal reform in the age of globalization. Whether in commercial regulation or human rights adjudication, Korea's legal evolution reveals the friction between formal legal harmonization and the practical realities of justice and institutional legitimacy. These cases also underscore the political stakes of global legal borrowing: even ostensibly neutral reforms carry normative assumptions that may clash with domestic cultural expectations and power structures.

Rather than portraying Korea's legal system as converging toward a Western liberal ideal, this part emphasizes its hybrid and contradictory development. Both Choi's critique of insolvency reform and Edelson's advocacy for retroactive justice demonstrate how legal modernization often involves deep tensions—between efficiency and equity, global legitimacy and local authority, and formal procedure and substantive justice.

Such contradictions are not anomalies but constitutive features of Korea's legal globalization. They reveal how the transplantation of global legal norms, far from creating uniformity, generates sites of resistance, contestation, and reinterpretation. Understanding Korean law in this light requires moving beyond doctrinal analysis toward a contextual, critical approach that attends to institutional constraints, legal culture, and the evolving demands of justice in a global era.

Concluding Remarks: Law in Motion, Reform in Context

This volume does not offer a simple narrative of legal convergence or Westernization. Instead, it approaches Korea's legal transformation as a dynamic and contested process—one shaped by globalization, but mediated through deeply rooted institutional legacies, state strategies, professional interests, and cultural constraints. Rather than focusing narrowly on theoretical frameworks or domestic case law, the chapters collected here explore how Korea's legal education, legal profession, services market, and institutions have been reconfigured through their encounter with global norms.

As emphasized in this introductory chapter, the legal reforms in Korea over the past three decades—spanning from the restructuring of legal education and the rise of corporate law professionals to the experiment with jury trials—highlight not only innovation but contradiction. Each reform reflects both external pressures for global alignment and internal responses shaped by local legal culture and bureaucratic conservatism. What emerges, then, is a hybrid legal order, where global models are adopted, resisted, or transformed through negotiation and selective implementation.

We invite readers to view Korea's legal experience as a window into the broader landscape of legal globalization in East Asia. Through this lens, law appears not merely as a set of technical norms but as a space of power, identity, and ideological struggle—where actors compete to define legitimacy, authority, and access. Legal professionals, state institutions, and civil society actors are not passive recipients of globalization but active participants in the construction and redefinition of legal norms.

The empirical studies featured in this volume—on legal education reform, market liberalization, professional hierarchies, participatory justice, and evolving legal norms—offer critical insight into how law is continually remade at the intersection of state power, global capitalism, and professional ambition. These chapters draw on and contribute to ongoing debates in legal transplant theory, the sociology of professions, and the political economy of legal institutions.

This volume is intended for scholars and students in fields such as legal studies, law and society, comparative law, sociology of law, and East Asian studies. It also speaks to policymakers, legal practitioners, and reformers across Asia and beyond who are grappling with the implications of legal globalization. At a time when global legal standards are often invoked as benchmarks of reform, yet their local implementation remains fraught, this book offers timely and critical perspectives on how globalization is both embraced and resisted on the ground.

We also anticipate that this book will resonate beyond academic circles. Informed readers interested in legal reform, governance, professional development, and justice in Korea and East Asia will find in these pages a rich and empirically grounded analysis of how global legal change unfolds in practice. By situating Korea's legal transformation within broader global dynamics, this volume contributes to a deeper understanding of how law functions as both an agent of globalization and a reflection of national struggle.

Bibliography

Ahn, Kyong-Whan. "The Growth of the Bar and the Changes in the Lawyer's Role: Korea's Dilemma." In *Law and Technology in the Pacific Community*, edited by P. S. C. Lewis, 123–8. London: Routledge, 1994.

Antons, Christoph, ed. *Law and Society in East Asia*. London: Routledge, 2013.

Chang, Ha-Joon. *Kicking Away the Ladder: Development Strategy in Historical Perspective.* London: Anthem, 2002.
Choi, Jong-Sik. "Korean Citizen Participation in Criminal Trials: The Present Situation and Problems." *International Journal of Law, Crime and Justice* 42, no. 2 (2014): 83–102.
Dezalay, Yves, and Bryant Garth, eds. *Lawyers and the Rule of Law in an Era of Globalization.* London: Routledge, 2011.
Dinovitzer, Ronit, and Bryant G. Garth. "Law, Empires, Legal Professions, and Status Hierarchies: Comparative Perspectives." *Annual Review of Law and Social Science* 21 (2015): 343–58. https://doi.org/10.1146/annurev-lawsocsci-062124-121908.
Ginsburg, Tom, ed. *Legal Reform in Korea.* London: Routledge, 2004.
Harvey, David. 2014. *Seventeen Contradictions and the End of Capitalism.* Oxford: Oxford University Press, 2014.
Kim, Chang-Rok. "The National Bar Examination in Korea." *Wisconsin International Law Journal* 24, no. 1 (2006): 243–60.
Kim, Jong-Cheol. "The Rule of Law and Democracy in South Korea: Ideal and Reality." *East Asia Foundation Policy Debates* 26 (2015): 1–6.
Kim, Rosa. "A Benchmark in Asian Judicial Reform: The New Korean Jury System." *Suffolk Transnational Law Review* 38, no. 2 (2015): 281–323.
Kim, Rosa."Globalizing the Law Curriculum for Twenty-First-Century Lawyering." *Journal of Legal Education* 67, no. 4 (2018): 905–48.
Kim, Seong-Kyoon, Bong-Joon Yoon, and Jeungil Oh. "A Study on the Decision-Making Behavior of Judge in the Criminal Trial: The Effect of Sentencing Guideline in South Korea." *International Economic Journal* 34, no. 4 (2020): 599–612.
Lee, Gyooho. "Attorney Fee Arrangements Really Matter in Terms of Access to Justice in Korea." In *Cost and Fee Allocation in Civil Procedure*, edited by Markus Reimann, 201–9. Dordrecht: Springer, 2012.
Lee, Inyeong, Jungwon Lee, and Yuhwa Han. "Cultural Differences in Jury Deliberations and Jury Decision Making between South Korea and the United States." *Psychology, Public Policy, and Law* 31, no. 2 (2025): 181–203.
Lee, Jae-Hyup. "The Introduction of the Law School System and the Structure of the Legal Profession in Korea: Status and Prospects." *Journal of Legal Education* 68, no. 2 (2019): 460–90.
Lee, Jae-Hyup, and Jisuk Woo. "Judge-Jury Interaction in Deliberation: Enhancement or Obstruction of Independent Jury Decision-Making?" *Oñati Socio-Legal Series* 6, no. 2 (2014): 179–96.
Lee, John Sanghyun. "Transplanting Jury Trials in South Korean Legal Soils: Comparative Analysis with Jury Trials in the United States." *Asian Journal of Criminology* 11 (2016): 111–33.
Loibl, Elvira C. "The Aftermath of Transnational Illegal Adoptions: Redressing Human Rights Violations in the Intercountry Adoption System with Instruments of Transitional Justice." *Childhood* 28, no. 4 (2022): 477–91.
Moon, Jaewan. "The Influence of U.S. Legal Education on South Korean Legal Education." *Waseda Bulletin of Comparative Law* 39 (2021): 13–22.
Rhee, Robert J. "The Political Economy of Corporate Law and Governance: American and Korean Rules under Different Endogenous Conditions and Forms of Capitalism." *Wake Forest Law Review* 55 (2020): 649–714.
Silver, Carole, Jae-Hyup Lee, and Jeeyoon Park. "What Firms Want: Investigating Globalization's Influence on the Market for Lawyers in Korea." *Columbia Journal of Asian Law* 28, no. 1 (2015): 1–40.

Song, Sang-Hyun. "Challenges to Legal Education in Korea." In *Law and Technology in the Pacific Community*, edited by P. S. C. Lewis, 285–94. London: Routledge, 1994.
Steele, Stacy, and Kathryn Taylor, eds. *Legal Education in Asia: Globalization, Change and Contexts*. London: Routledge, 2009.
Wade, Robert. "The Asian Debt-and-Development Crisis of 1997-?: Causes and Consequences." *World Development* 26, no. 8 (1998): 1535–53.
Wilkins, David B., David M. Trubek, and Bryon Fong. "Globalization, Lawyers, and Emerging Economies: The Rise, Transformation, and Significance of the New Corporate Legal Ecosystem in India, Brazil, and China." *Harvard International Law Journal* 61 (2020): 281–351.
Woo, Jisuk, and Justin D. Levinson. "Diversity, Dialogue, and Deliberation: An Empirical Investigation of Age, Gender, and Meaningful Decision-Making in Korean Juries." *Asian-Pacific Law & Policy Journal* 19, no. 1 (2017): 23–48.
Woo, Jisuk, June Woong Rhee, and Jae-Hyup Lee. "The Effects of Trial Procedure Factors and Deliberation Factors on Shadow Jurors' Perceptions about the Fairness of Jury Trials in Korea." *Journal of Korean Law* 20 (2021): 413–28.

Part One

Legal Education in the Era of Global Convergence

2

The "Americanization" of Legal Education in South Korea

Challenges and Opportunities

Rosa Kim

Introduction

In 2007, the South Korean government voted to adopt an American-style three-year law school system, and effected a radical change in the legal education process.[1] The event marked the end of decades of debate about how best to transform a national bar exam system that averaged below a 5 percent passage rate, yielding too few practitioners to provide affordable legal services, and failing to produce professionally skilled lawyers who could be competitive in the global market. In a country that currently vies for the title of "most wired" in the universe and figures prominently as a major player in the world economy, the legal education system established during the Japanese colonial period had fallen far behind these economic and societal changes.[2] Like other countries that have engaged in legal education reform in recent times, Korea[3] had recognized that the global legal market is headed toward standardization based on the US model of law education and training.[4] Though nominally "American" in style, the newly created education system is the culmination of much national debate and compromise, reflecting the realities of Korean politics and economics, rather than a literal duplication of a foreign system.[5]

While this wholesale transformation of legal education from an "exam system" to an "education system"[6] holds much promise for the future of Korean law, it is already facing serious challenges in the transition. In February 2012, the first class of graduates from the new three-year law schools will have entered the marketplace. The most immediate hurdle for the new graduates is that they are facing a legal job market that has not yet been diversified and expanded enough to accommodate the sudden rise in the number of legal job seekers, even with a quota in the number of students permitted to pass the new bar exam.[7] Another major challenge of the transition is determining how best to adopt a new curricular and pedagogical approach to law teaching that may not be compatible with Korean culture. Moreover, with the old system in the process of being phased out during the transition, the tension between the existing bar and the new law schools and their proponents continues to grow and threatens to erode the public confidence in the new system.[8]

As with any radical change on a big social scale, successful transformation of the legal education system in Korea will require overcoming these and other challenges and setbacks. As difficult as the transition might be, to have it occur at a time when American law schools are engaging in their own self-assessment and discussing possible significant changes to the American system creates a unique opportunity for Korea to learn from the American experience and "get it right" from the outset. By taking advantage of this opportunity and integrating the key lessons from American legal education, Korea can develop a new legal education model that best suits its needs.

The first section of this chapter will provide background on the history of legal education in Korea to give some context for understanding the magnitude of the reform. The second section will examine the law instituting the reform, its stated mission and key provisions. The third section will discuss the economic, cultural, and pedagogical challenges of adopting an American-style three-year law school system. The last section will explore the opportunities afforded by Korea's large- scale reform to fashion a new forward-looking legal education model. The last section will offer some brief concluding remarks.

History of Legal Education in Korea

Prior to the reform, law education in Korea consisted of undergraduate education with a law concentration, "cram" school to prepare for the national bar exam,[9] and two years of government-sponsored training for the small numbers of bar passers to become judges, prosecutors, and private practitioners. Considered the most difficult standardized exam one can take in Korea, the national bar exam has held an "open" process, in that an undergraduate education is not a requirement to take the exam, though the low passage rate makes it a risky career choice.[10] For the small minority who passed the exam, the students completed a two-year apprenticeship and training at the Judiciary Research and Training Institute (JRTI) run by the Supreme Court. Graduates of the JRTI receive bar licenses and are qualified to be judges, prosecutors, and private practitioners.[11] The JRTI has historically emphasized training and education for judges and prosecutors with only limited courses for private practice, as its original purpose was to train future judges and prosecutors, making the bar exam in effect an entrance exam to the JRTI.[12] Training at the JRTI is under the instruction primarily of experienced judges, prosecutors, or private practice attorneys, and teaching by university professors is minimal.[13] In recent years, the gradual increase in the number of JRTI entrants due to the quota increases for bar passers has changed the composition of the trainees, such that the majority of JRTI graduates are becoming private attorneys, and a minority, approximately one-fifth, judges or prosecutors.[14] Thus, the focus of the education on training for judges and prosecutors has been increasingly misplaced.[15]

Due to the quota system for bar passage that has strictly controlled the number of lawyers in Korea since 1949, there are relatively few lawyers per capita in Korea; compared to the 1 to 300 ratio in the United States, in Korea it is approximately 1 to 5000.[16] By 2008, the total number of lawyers in Korea reached 10,000, with women accounting for approximately 10 percent.[17] The small size of the legal profession has helped to enhance its prestige and makes lawyers the most privileged class in Korean society.[18] The resulting shortage of lawyers means that ordinary citizens may not have access to legal services due to high fees.[19] Moreover, the elitist nature of the profession is magnified by the reality that the Korean bar tends to be dominated by graduates of the top universities in Korea, especially Seoul National. Thus, historically, practicing lawyers in Korea have formed a "virtual oligarchic monopoly."[20]

To some, however, the national bar exam has served as a symbol of fairness and opportunity to achieve the career dream without formal education, as historically none was required to take the exam.[21] Beginning in 2006, however, the Supreme Court did impose a new requirement that only those who have taken more than thirty-five credits of law-related college-level classes were able to apply for the exam.[22] There has also been no limitation on the number of times applicants can take the exam.[23] In fact, many people devote years attempting to pass the bar because of this no-limit policy and low passage rate.[24] A related criticism against the bar exam system in Korea is the presence and success of bar preparation or "cram" schools.[25] Almost all Korean students studying for the bar spend time and money at cram schools.[26] University course study on law subjects is perceived as inadequate preparation for the exam, as the cram schools also provide much-coveted shortcuts and test-taking techniques.[27] About 90 percent of successful bar exam takers attended cram schools.[28]

Another major problem with the national bar exam system has been the lack of connection between legal education at the undergraduate level at universities and the content of the exam itself.[29] Because the exam is not geared to measuring practical knowledge and professional technique and is designed to test legal theory and doctrine, which could be learned through memorization, formal education was not required.[30] The lack of a real link between institutional legal education and the judicial exam meant that the primary focus of undergraduate law education was the theoretical subjects that would help with passage of the exam, rather than any practical education that would prepare them for practice.[31] With its emphasis on memorization rather than problem-solving, the bar exam, according to some, has not helped to prepare Korean lawyers to serve as legal professionals in settings that are complex and diversified, including international transactions.[32]

It is interesting to note that although many Korean universities had undergraduate law programs prior to the reform, the vast majority of students who graduate from the programs do not enter law practice.[33] Because the pass rate for the bar exam is so low, many choose to forego pursuing a legal career in favor of nonlegal careers in corporations or government.[34] Those who aspire to become university law professors typically pursue graduate studies, often abroad, rather than prepare for the bar examination, so a minority of professors are admitted to practice, and there is relatively little exchange between the practicing bar and academia.[35] It is ironic, then, there are so few law professors who are licensed as lawyers, yet they are responsible for teaching and preparing students for careers practicing law.[36] Unlike the United States, only a small number of graduate students pursue careers as scholars, and graduate law programs have served to provide a means for some students to defer military service until they pass the bar exam.[37]

In 1987, the Korean government instituted a new Constitution, marking the beginning of a transition from an authoritarian style of government to a democratic system.[38] Democratization meant that the judiciary, the branch responsible for administering the national bar exam, would have to undergo significant reform and establish itself as an entity independent of undue influence from the executive branch.[39] Interestingly, the push for judicial reform came from the executive office, first in 1995 by President Kim Young-sam, who advocated the adoption of a US-style law school system to create more globally competitive legal professionals.[40] While this first proposal met with opposition and failed to materialize, President Kim did successfully institute a more open approach to the bar passage quota by increasing the annual cap from 300 in 1995, and gradually thereafter to 1,000 in 2002.[41] The quota increases began the trend that inevitably led to full-scale reform.[42]

In 2003, President Roh Moo-Hyun began his term with firm initiatives to reform the judicial system to ensure that the democratization process would occur in the judiciary in a manner parallel to the reforms that were taking place in government.[43] The Judicial Reform Committee was created with a stated mission, among others, to improve the judicial system, enhance democratic legitimacy and public trust, provide easy access to justice, and produce qualitatively and globally competitive legal professionals.[44] The proposal to create an American-style law school system again generated a great deal of public debate, with opponents emphasizing the "American" aspect of the reform, suggesting that Korea was compromising its national character to pursue a popular international trend.[45] The Committee's proposals led to several reforms of the judicial system, culminating in the adoption of the new law school system in 2007.[46]

Opposition to legal education reform, then and now, seems to have originated from the existing bar and a minority of law professors who had every incentive to retain the status quo, as they enjoyed the social privileges and benefits of being part of the most elite social group in Korean society.[47] These opponents argued that the new system would devalue the bar exam and create a rapid rise in the number of lawyers, both consequences that hold little advantage for the existing lawyers.[48] Moreover, the reform would necessitate a shift in the power and influence over training new law students from the Supreme Court, which has run the two-year mandatory training for bar passers, to professors and universities.[49]

There was also opposition to the reform from judges and practicing attorneys arguing against abolishing the JRTI, dramatically increasing the size of the practicing bar, thus creating more competition, and possibly lowering the quality of legal practice.[50] Underlying the debate is also the tension between academics, many of whom did not take or pass the bar, and those who passed the bar exam and were trained at the JRTI, highlighting the divided interests between the two constituencies.[51] Perhaps a more compelling argument against reform has been that the new system would discriminate against those who cannot afford the cost of education in the new law schools.[52] Some, however, have pointed to the cost associated with cram schools and the opportunity cost of the time spent, often years, on bar preparation, to rebut this notion.[53] Moreover, the opponents also argued that the new system would go against the notion of fairness that the bar exam symbolizes, in that anyone is eligible to take it, though both the passage rates and the percentage of passers who do not have a university education are very small, not to mention the considerable cost of attending cram school.[54] These concerns, while still voiced by some members of the Korean bar, ultimately gave way to the momentum of the pro-reform movement.

The New "American-Style" System

In adopting an American-style law school system, Korea has resolved to establish an entirely new model for educating and creating lawyers. Under the US system, the law school is a graduate-level school responsible for training legal professionals, and the bar exam is a means to confirm and validate the mastery of law school curricula—a system that is the opposite of the pre-reform Korean system.[55] The objective of this major overhaul of the legal education system has been to address the need for professional legal education, the need for legal specialists and training for them, the concern with professional ethics, and the relatively small size of the legal profession.[56] Thus, the transition would shift Korean legal education away from high status but generalist training to specialized professional education aimed at producing practicing lawyers.[57]

In July 2007, the legislature passed the bill governing the creation and operation of the new law schools, called the Graduate Law School Act (GLSA).[58] To plan for the opening of the new schools in 2009, the Ministry of Education set a quota of 2,000 students per class.[59] In January 2008, the Legal Education Committee selected twenty-five schools that would be permitted to establish a three-year law school of the forty-one schools that applied after a competitive selection process, and each school was assigned a maximum number of 40–150 students per class.[60] Fifteen universities in Seoul and ten universities in other provinces were chosen in an effort to promote regional representation.[61] The application and selection process involved many interested schools frantically preparing for site visits and vying to be chosen.[62] The chosen universities were required to close their existing law colleges or departments, while others that were not chosen for the new law schools would keep their existing law departments.[63] The new schools may recruit only students who have completed a four-year undergraduate program, and at least one-third of the new recruits must be non-law majors to ensure diversity among the students within the programs.[64]

A Korean version of the law school admissions test was created, called the Legal Education Eligibility Test (LEET), and administered for the first time in August 2008.[65] As with the LSAT, students are required to take the LEET to apply to one of the new law schools.[66] There is also an emphasis on English-language skills for admission to the new law schools, indicating the importance of the ability to work and communicate in a global context.[67] The new bar examination, the Lawyer Admission Test, was created for the first graduating class in 2012 and is expected to replace the old state bar exam in 2018.[68] By then, it is expected that most of the role of the JRTI will shift to the new law schools.[69] Law school attendance is a prerequisite for sitting for the bar exam, and the number of attempts to pass is limited to three within five years.[70] Similar to US bar passage rates, the bar passage rate under the new system was expected to be 70–80 percent, and those who successfully complete law school will have little difficulty passing the exam.[71]

In fact, in 2010, the Ministry of Justice established a passage quota of 75 percent amid protests from current law school students who advocated for a higher quota, for instance, between 80 and 90 percent.[72] Though the source of much debate during the reform discussions, the view prevailed that limiting the enrollment numbers would enable this high bar passage rate and minimize the reliance on cram schools.[73] The prediction was that smaller student bodies at the new law schools would allow the development of curricula that include lawyering skills courses and clinical education.[74] With the bar exam taking on less importance relative to the old system, students would be able to focus more on their coursework and pursue a more diversified curriculum and practical learning opportunities.[75] The hope was that greater opportunities for practical training and specialization would allow for a more globally competitive legal workforce.[76]

The GLSA states as its Ideals of Education "to cultivate lawyers … possessing knowledge and capabilities that enable professional and efficient settlement of complicated legal disputes, with the objective of providing good legal services that meet the diverse expectations and demands of people."[77] To achieve these ideals, both the content of the curriculum and the pedagogical method employed at the law schools must be altered; there must be a transition from the lecture format with an emphasis on memorization, to more interactive teaching with the use of the Socratic method,[78] and a change in the curriculum to become more globalized and diversified, including offering courses taught in English and covering foreign legal systems and international law.[79] A main objective of the new system is to emulate what US law schools typically explain as their goal in educating students, "to think like a lawyer."[80] Thinking like a lawyer means learning skills such as research and writing, analysis, and the use of hypotheticals.[81] The new emphasis on coverage of international law reflects the understanding that Korea needs to produce lawyers who have the skills to deal with a globalized economic and legal community.[82] A more diversified curriculum will allow graduates to work in a wide range of sectors, such as international organizations and NGOs.[83]

Finally, the reform will also address what its proponents have referred to as a problem with legal ethics.[84] Allegations of unethical practices among judges and prosecutors, including preferential treatment to recently retired judges from the same court who then represent private parties in that court, have fueled the demand for changes in legal education and emphasis on ethics and professional responsibility.[85]

The makeup of the faculty will also change such that 20 percent of all faculty at the law schools must have at least five years of practical experience.[86] This provision is a clear statement of intent to make the curriculum more practice and skills-oriented. The GLSA also requires the schools to provide professional training and the integration of theory and practice; specifically, the schools must provide the following courses: professional responsibility, legal research, legal writing, moot court, and a practical internship.[87] Most schools will offer skills courses that cover civil, criminal, constitutional, and tax litigation, while some plan to offer courses in contract drafting, negotiations, tax planning, and clinical courses.[88] Training lawyers to be professionals, rather than "functional bureaucrats" requires emphasis on ethics and practical skills, hence the requirement of practical courses at the new law schools.[89] As the new schools settle into the changed curricula mandated by the GLSA, they will face considerable challenges in both the content and method of teaching.

In addition to instituting a new pedagogical approach, legal education reform also forces Korea to face the economic challenge of employing more than double the number of new lawyers each year at a time when the nature of legal employment in Korea is changing in any event, due to the opening of the legal market to foreign businesses. Underlying these many layers of challenges is the question of cultural compatibility between the two systems and the best ways to ensure that any clashes do not impede the success of the reform. Consequently, the reform will test Korea's ability to adapt and modify not only the way lawyers are educated and employed, but also the role they play in Korean society.

Challenges Posed by the Reform

Korea's adoption of an American-style legal education system will no doubt run into various short- and long-term challenges—economic, cultural, and pedagogical. While these challenges have already begun to test Korea's will to persevere with the reform, they are only natural, given the scale of systemic changes that are being instituted. Staying committed to the reform's goals and being open to finding effective ways to resolve these challenges will be essential in the transition.

Economic Challenges

The immediate problem facing the first class of graduates seems to be economic, as the increased numbers of legal job seekers is already facing heightened competition for jobs, and tension between the interests of traditional JRTI students and new law school students continues to grow.[90] Understandably, those who became lawyers under the old system will feel territorial and even resentful of those who took the "easier" route and are now competing for the same positions. However, once the old bar exam and the JRTI are completely phased out, these tensions will subside. The greater challenge is to normalize the marketplace quickly to accommodate the higher number of professionally trained lawyers. The more efficiently this process can occur, the greater the likelihood that the new system will take hold and preserve the public confidence.

Arguably, the single most powerful incentive for Korean policymakers to take on legal reform has been the globalizing trends in the marketplace and the recognition that Korean lawyers are not properly trained to handle international business transactions. Just as other countries responded to economic and cultural globalization by reforming their legal education systems,[91] Korea is also dealing with the reality of the growing number of transnational law firms in Seoul, as well as global NGOs.[92] Under the 2007 Free Trade Agreement between Korea and the United States, the Korean legal services market began a three-stage process of opening in 2008.[93] Part of the challenge of the new schools is to provide effective training for lawyers to function and compete against non-Korean legal service providers in an open legal market.[94] Prior to the reform, some changes were underway in anticipation of the market opening. For example, since 2000, Korean schools have increasingly adopted American law school courses such as clinics, ethics, and specialized courses in international business.[95] In 2004, English became a required subject on the Korean bar exam and the JRTI added International Contracts and other international subjects to its curriculum.[96]

One way to achieve a synergy between the education framework and the Korean market forces would be to diversify the legal market through expanding the realm of legal employment beyond the traditional areas of criminal and civil litigation.[97] Legal jobs must take root in sectors previously not occupied by lawyers in Korea, such as in government and corporations. Moreover, while the newly opened Korean legal market promises to create more jobs for the new graduates, an infrastructure for hiring and facilitating such placements must be prioritized.[98] These initiatives should stem increasingly from a combined effort between law schools and the prospective employers in both the private and public sectors, rather than from the Ministry of Justice. Ultimately, Korean lawyers need to be able to work in a variety of sectors, serving many different functions, rather than be limited to the three traditional types of legal jobs—judge, prosecutor, or private practitioner. Achieving diversification of legal jobs to support the new legal education system seems critical for the Korean bar to flourish in its new form.

Cultural Challenges

A key issue in adopting an American-style legal education system is the ability to reconcile the institutional and cultural differences between the two countries. The influence of US-educated Korean lawyers and law educators on the trend toward adopting an American-style system has been considerable. An increasing number of Korean lawyers, including judges, prosecutors, academic, and practitioners, have been coming to the United States in recent years for advanced law degrees or visiting scholar positions.[99] The heavy influence of US law on Korean law, particularly in the areas of corporate, international trade, bankruptcy, maritime and insurance, intellectual property, banking and securities, and antitrust law has propelled the increase in Korean law students studying at US law schools.[100] The Korean government and private sector employers commonly provide one- or two-year paid sabbaticals for study in the United States for judges, prosecutors, government bureaucrats, and corporate employees.[101] Most large law firms also allow associates the opportunity to study in the United States and often to obtain practical training in a US law firm.[102] Many Korean students acquire an LLM in American Law degree, and sit for a state bar, most notably the New York bar, as a means of gaining important experience and knowledge of US law and adding prestige to their resumes.[103] For most Korean students, their experience at US law schools is the first time they are introduced to the Socratic Method.[104] Thus, by sheer exposure, US-educated Korean law students and professors have gained a broader global outlook and technical knowledge of US-style legal analysis.[105]

Achieving cultural compatibility between the Korean and US systems will require bridging the gap between the two educational systems and the cultures they reflect. The problem is one of reconciling the cultural differences between a civil law system based on Confucian values that emphasize hierarchy and inequality, and a common-law system based on fundamental belief in social equality.[106] For instance, in the law school context, Confucian values translate to a highly unequal relationship between professor and student, arguably making the lecture method, not the Socratic or interactive methods, the natural format for teaching. Resistance to a new, more "horizontal" relationship between professor and student can be expected in the short term, but over time, it will become normalized.

Moreover, the Korean legal system has a code-based civil law system instituted under Japanese colonial rule and based on the German system.[107] Given the basic differences between the two systems, one critique of the reform has been that emulating the American common law system was ill-advised because the lecture-style method is the only way to learn the large body of code-based law required by Korean law, and the differences in legal culture would make it impossible to make this transition.[108] While some argue that civil law systems generally require more lecture-based courses to enable teaching a greater quantity of substantive law, others maintain that the overall quantity of content taught is comparable between the two systems and that there is an increasing trend of each method being integrated into the other.[109]

Proponents of reform in Korea maintained that US law and practice influence international transactions related to Korean businesses, that the methodologies used in American law schools are transferable, and that common law countries are as broad and diverse as the law in Korea and other civil law countries.[110] There is also active discussion regarding moving toward an integrated approach to teaching, so that doctrine, theory, and skills can coexist in the teaching of a single course to more accurately reflect what it means to be a good lawyer.[111] While ultimately a type of civil law–common law hybrid legal education system may be the most fruitful consequence of Korea's adoption of the American system, to make the three-year law school model work in Korea, there must be a willingness to adopt the broader legal culture, not just the education framework.

Pedagogical Challenges

A practical challenge for implementing the GLSA's new curricular mandates is to identify educators who have the ability to put these changes into practice. For example, there will be difficulty finding full-time faculty who can teach skills-oriented courses, as full-time professors are barred from practicing law under the GLSA and practicing attorneys may not have the necessary teaching skills.[112] Some have suggested that faculty at the Korean law schools need to become more diversified by having more foreign professors teach at the Korean law schools.[113] Moreover, forging ties with foreign law schools through exchange programs will allow students to understand legal issues in a global context and be better able to serve those needs.[114] Greater presence of foreign professors will be helpful early in the transition, but in the long term, Korean educators must be the ones to teach the skills-oriented and specialized courses and these courses must be integrated fully within the curriculum. In this regard, it may be beneficial to provide systematic training for Korean law professors and hire additional faculty members who are practitioners.[115] One method of gaining expertise on subjects that are new to the curriculum, such as first-year legal writing, is to have US faculty teach workshops to train their Korean counterparts.[116]

Korean law schools can learn from the experience and research already performed in the United States to implement curricular strategies that will produce lawyers who are more practice-ready. For example, integrating skills into traditional "doctrinal" courses across the curriculum, an idea that US law schools are currently considering and implementing, can be a priority from the outset, thus establishing a new "norm" for law school curricula. While Korea has the seemingly daunting dual task of transforming both the content and method of teaching law, it is in a unique position to build the curriculum "from scratch" and find the best path for meeting the goals by utilizing the research and studies the United States has already produced. With the new law schools in operation since 2009, Korea should seize the opportunity at this early stage of the transition to integrate the skills and values US educators have identified as being essential for good lawyering.

Opportunities to Integrate Key Skills and Values

A major overhaul of the legal education system in Korea has created major challenges but also a unique opportunity for Korean law schools to define and integrate the skills and values desired in a law school graduate. It also affords the chance to address the problem areas that the United States has identified in recent studies on its own legal education system.[117] The mission and goal provisions of the new law make clear that the reform is designed to emulate not only the American structure of law schools, but also the underlying skills and values. Undertaking the legal education reform at a time when the model American system itself is reevaluating the direction of law school curricula presents the opportunity develop and modify some of the existing aspects of the US system. Three specific areas that Korean law schools should target for consideration are as follows: (1) greater emphasis on skills and their integration throughout the law school curriculum; (2) modified application of the case method and Socratic teaching; and (3) expansion of assessment methods to include more formative assessments.

Skills Integration

The American Bar Association has described fundamental lawyering skills as follows: problem-solving, legal analysis and reasoning, legal research, factual investigation, communication, counseling, negotiation, litigation, alternative dispute-resolution procedures, organization and management of legal work, and recognizing and resolving ethical dilemmas.[118] These are skills that are common to all lawyers, regardless of the particular legal tradition of their respective countries.[119] Because of their importance, the recommendation of the Task Force regarding the faculty employed to teach these skills and values is to have full-time faculty teach skills and values, as they have the time and expertise to devote to teaching and developing new pedagogical methods, while maintaining the use of skilled practitioners as adjunct faculty.[120] As discussed in the previous section, the GLSA mandates the inclusion of skills courses in the law school curriculum in recognition of their importance in training law students as professionals.[121] This is a fundamental aspect of US law training, and has been central to the US curriculum, but the challenge for both US and Korean law schools now is to establish the best ways to integrate more skills into the law school curriculum to better train students for practice. Many US law schools are currently trying to institute this integrative model for law schools based on the recommendations of the Carnegie Report in 2007.[122] One option is to introduce skills earlier in the curriculum to encourage student engagement through greater classroom rigor.[123] Furthermore, skills can be integrated into the curriculum such that both theory and practice are taught in the same course in recognition that skills and doctrine are not, and should not be treated as, separate or mutually exclusive.[124]

Korean schools can also look toward including experiential learning through internships and externships at private law firms, governmental agencies, and judicial clerkships.[125] More applied practice skills such as contract drafting and negotiations should also have a place in the curriculum.[126] Instituting clinical programs would also greatly enhance practice skills, as they have in US law programs, though there would have to be a change in the current rules under the GLSA barring faculty members from practicing law.[127] Just as the US schools are looking to remedy the lack of skills integration in the curriculum, Korean law schools can both integrate skills into doctrinal courses and integrate skills classes throughout the three-year curriculum and hold them to the same importance and status as doctrinal courses.

Modified Case Method

The second area Korean schools should consider as they establish the new pedagogical norm for their law schools is to shift the teaching methodology from lectures delivering a large quantity of substantive information to one that is aimed at engaging students in an interactive and academically rigorous environment.[128] The American case-dialogue method, with the focus on teaching students how to "think like a lawyer," stresses a way of thinking rather than a kind of knowledge and is designed to actively engage the student.[129] It teaches students to theorize from natural contexts based on a defined set of facts, apply specified rules and procedures, and then draw conclusions.[130] One critique of this method is the absence of connection to actual situations that involve real people and matters of social need, justice, and morality.[131] Further, it limits the ability to teach how to use legal thinking in the complexity of actual law practice and also fails to take into account sufficient emphasis on the ethical and social aspects of the profession.[132] The value of this method, however, in actively engaging students in the classroom, is one that Korean law schools should adopt.

Even if it could be established that civil law based on codes requires teaching a greater quantity of substantive law, this would not preclude the inclusion of Socratic or interactive components in classroom instruction. The exclusive use of the Socratic method in the US law teaching has been criticized as being overused and ineffective in cases where other teaching methods would expose students more effectively to the practice of law.[133] For Korean law schools, the Socratic method, and other interactive and engaging methods, could be employed as a component of the overall methodology, rather than supplanting the lecture format entirely. Korean law educators, for example, should take an expansive approach to the traditional case method by integrating doctrine and skills to reflect the civil law system and its particular characteristics and to incorporate more practical, real-world applications.

Formative Assessments

The third area of focus for Korean law schools in drawing from the American experience is the methodology for assessments in the classroom. The Carnegie Report takes to task the notion of summative assessment as the primary mode of assessing law students' performance, namely, the end of semester final exam.[134] Conversely, formative assessment offers opportunities to improve learning as the course proceeds and allows the instructor to make adjustments in teaching based on the results.[135] If, according to the Carnegie Report, assessment is a tool to make students aware of what it requires to become competent in their field,[136] this is an area that Korean schools should consider carefully, since historically the basic method of testing has been overwhelmingly of the summative type. Assessing students on their practical skills as well as their mastery of legal doctrine should also promote classroom engagement. Moreover, assessing students on the full breadth of their knowledge and skills on the new bar exam would help enhance the connection between law school education and the bar exam.

In striving to filter out the weaker aspects of American law school education, Korean law educators and administrators should be mindful of the issues that have dominated the conversation on legal education reform in the United States and find ways to bypass them. The effectiveness of legal education generally, and legal reform in Korea specifically, will depend on whether the new system can honor and implement these skills and values of good lawyering in a meaningful way that reflects the realities of Korean law. The risk attendant to adopting a new method and system of teaching law by a country with a distinct history and culture should not be underestimated.[137] The real challenge for Korea is to incorporate the aspects of the American system that best suits its needs and recognize the cultural limitations of employing new pedagogical methods.[138]

Conclusion

The legal education system of Korea has a deeply rooted history that should inform the current adoption of an American-style three-year graduate school system. A radical change in the process of educating law students will necessarily involve the types of economic, cultural, and pedagogical challenges Korea is currently beginning to face. While evidence of the difficulties of the transition fuels the national debate about the wisdom of taking on the reform in the first place, the motivation to reform should remain undeterred.

The assumption that the American three-year graduate school model is the "gold standard" as far as its ability to produce effective lawyers[139] has been the foundation of Korea's legal education reform. Ironically, Korea's overhaul of its legal education process is occurring at a time when American law schools are reassessing their system and revamping their curricula to meet the demands of the current marketplace and create more practice-ready lawyers. Going forward, Korean educators and administrators should recognize the unique opportunities afforded by the timing of the reform. Specifically, Korea should take advantage of the knowledge gained by the self-assessment the US legal education community is undergoing to identify aspects of its system that need improvement and modification. In this regard, Korea can incorporate the improvements and modifications from the outset and create a more effective legal education model that will yield a greater number of well-trained lawyers.

A bigger supply of qualified lawyers able to compete with their United States and other foreign counterparts will help Korea meet the demands of an increasingly globalized legal community, as all signs indicate that lawyers everywhere should have practical training and professional skills to bring to the table. Beyond meeting the demands of a more globalized world, legal education reform should be motivated by the desire to produce lawyers who can simply provide competent legal representation to every client.[140] If Korea can keep its resolve to achieve both of these goals, its legal education reform will prove to be a major achievement in its modern history.

Notes

1 The author thanks her colleagues, Associate Professor Leigh Mello and Professor Stephanie Hartung, for their helpful comments. Thanks also to Andrés Reyes for his valuable research assistance.

2 *See generally* Dai-kwon Choi, "A Legal Profession in Transformation: The Korean Experience," in *Reorganisation and Resistance: Legal Professions Confront a Changing World*, ed. William L. F. Felstiner (Oxford: Hart Publishing, 2005), 193–4.

3 All references to "Korea" in this chapter mean South Korea.

4 *See* Stephen Zamora, "The Cultural Context of International Legal Cooperation," *Journal of Legal Education* 51, no. 3 (2001): 462, 463. While historically foreign legal models, especially from Europe, heavily influenced the United States, it has become an exporter of legal models due to its predominance in the world economy and the

interest of foreign lawyers in engaging in graduate legal studies in the United States. *Ibid.*

5 *See* Tom Ginsburg, "Transforming Legal Education in Japan and Korea," *Penn State International Law Review* 22, no. 3 (2004): 433, 439. The use of quotation marks in the title of this chapter acknowledges the reality that Korea's reform cannot be summed up by the word "Americanization" alone.

6 *See* Park Se-Il, "The Value of American-Style Law Schools," *The Chosun Daily*, September 7, 2007, https://www.chosun.com/english/opinion-en/2007/07/09/Q5UT3WFD2QJPOPG5WUMY3MBZGI/.

7 *See, e.g.*, Suh-young Yun, "Law School Students Sing Job Blues," *The Korea Times*, November 23, 2011, http://koreatimes.co.kr/www/news/include/print.asp?newsIdx=99420; Jae-min Lee, "Bleak Job Prospects for Law Grads," *The Korea Herald*, January 10, 2012, https://www.koreaherald.com/article/10353745.

8 *See, e.g.*, Bae Ji-sook, "Controversy Escalates over Plan to Pick Law School Graduates as Prosecutors," *The Korea Herald*, March 7, 2011, https://www.koreaherald.com/article/10336541; Anthony Lin, "Shaking Up the Old Order; Korea," *The Asian Lawyer*, June 1, 2011.

9 *See* description of "cram schools," *infra* note 25.

10 Jasper Kim, "Socrates v. Confucius: An Analysis of South Korea's Implementation of the American Law School Model," *Asian-Pacific Law & Policy Journal* 10, no. 2 (2009): 322, 326–7. In 2000, the total number of bar takers was 23,249, with 801 passing, indicating a 3 percent passage rate. *Ibid.* at 337.

11 *Ibid.* Until 1981, the national bar exam was designed primarily to recruit judges and prosecutors, with a low average passage rate of 1.9 percent between 1949 and 1980. *See* Yoon, *infra* note 12, at 38. In 1981, the quota of exam passage was raised from about 100 each year to 300. *Ibid.* at 37. Subsequent increases in the quota reached 1,000 in 2002, though with the increased number of applicants, the rate of passage remained just above 3 percent. *Ibid.* at 39–40.

12 *See* Dae-Kyu Yoon, *Law and Democracy in South Korea: Democratic Development since 1987* (Seoul: Kyungnam University Press, 2010), 137.

13 *See* Dae-Kyu Yoon, "The Paralysis of Legal Education in Korea," in *Legal Reform in Korea*, ed. Tom Ginsburg (London: Routledge, 2004), 36–46, 43.

14 *Ibid.* at 40.

15 *See ibid.* at 44.

16 *See* Matthew J. Wilson, "U.S. Legal Education Methods and Ideals: Application to the Japanese and Korean Systems," *Cardozo Journal of International and Comparative Law* 18 (2010): 295, 335.

17 *See* Nathan Schwartzman, "Female Lawyers Increasing in Korea," *Asian Correspondent*, January 24, 2008. The percentage of female bar passers rose from 10.8 percent in 1994 to 18.9 percent in 2000. Jae Won Kim, "The Ideal and the Reality of the Korean Legal Profession," *Asian-Pacific Law & Policy Journal* 2, no. 1 (2001): 45, 49–50. In 2010, the percentage of female bar passers reached a record high of 42 percent. Sagmin Lee, "Korea's Top Women's Law School Battles Reverse Discrimination Lawsuit," *Human Rights Monitor–Korea*, April 4, 2011.

18 Kim, *supra* note 17, at 47.

19 *See ibid.*

20 Yoon, *supra* note 12, at 135.

21 Most famously, former president Roh Tae Woo had no college education when he successfully passed the exam, and became a symbol of achieving the Korean Dream.

See Kyong-Whan Ahn, "Law Reform in Korea and the Agenda of 'Graduate Law School,'" *Wisconsin International Law Journal* 24, no. 1 (2006): 223, 227.

22 *See* Chang-Rok Kim, "The National Bar Examination in Korea," *Wisconsin International Law Journal* 24, no. 1 (2006): 243, 245.

23 *Ibid.*

24 *Ibid.* at 247. Between 1983 and 2005, the average age for exam passers was twenty-nine, indicating the majority of passers were not first-time takers. *Ibid.*

25 Wilson, *supra* note 16, at 337. Cram schools are a way of life in Korea. There are cram schools for all levels, even at the kindergarten level. *See* Ahn, *supra* note 21, at 225. Cram schools have spawned an industry that is based on the huge numbers of students studying for the national bar examination, including book stores, private libraries, and housing. *See* Dae-Kwon Choi, "Proposed Legal Education Reform in Korea: Toward a Professional Model," *Ritsumeikan Law Review* 18 (2001): 93, 98. These test prep "villages" are found near the country's top universities. *Ibid.* Cram school for the bar exam has been *de rigueur* for the majority of applicants for the bar due to the perception that university studies failed to prepare them adequately and the pressure created by the very quota for passage. *See* Mark E. Steiner, "Cram Schooled," *Wisconsin International Law Journal* 24 (2006): 377, 381. There are reportedly six major cram schools, each with between 30 *and* 40 teachers, that charge a monthly tuition rate of about 300,000 won, or about $270. *See* Kim, *supra* note 22, at 246. For those students who come from outside of Seoul and require housing and board, the monthly cost is about 900,000 won, or about $800. *See ibid.*

26 Wilson, *supra* note 16, at 337.

27 *Ibid.*

28 *Ibid.*

29 Yoon, *supra* note 12, at 135.

30 The exam has three components: first, multiple choice; second, essay; and third, interview. Kim, *supra* note 10, at 336. One must pass the first component to move on to the second, and then must pass the second component to move on to the third. *Ibid.* note 77. The multiple-choice component covers constitutional law, civil law, criminal law, one elective subject, and competency in English; the essay component tests the same subjects as covered by the multiple-choice component, plus commercial law, civil procedure, criminal law, and criminal procedure; the interview component includes the areas of ethics, specialized knowledge and ability to apply it, communication skills, manner and attitude, and creativity and perseverance. *See* Kim, *supra* note 22, at 244.

31 Yoon, *supra* note 13, at 40. The United States is also subject to the same critique, as noted in the Carnegie Report. *See* below "Opportunities to Integrate Key Skills and Values" section of this chapter.

32 *Ibid.*

33 *See* Setsuo Miyazawa, Kay-Wah Chan, and Ilhyung Lee, "The Reform of Legal Education in East Asia," *Annual Review of Law and Social Science* 4 (2008): 333, 352.

34 *See ibid.*

35 *See ibid.*

36 Ahn, *supra* note 21, at 240. This issue has been addressed in the law creating the new law school system through a provision requiring that 20 percent of the law school faculty have five or more years of practical experience. *See* GLSA, *infra* note 58, article 16(4).

37 *Ibid.*

38 Yoon, *supra* note 12, at 119.
39 *See ibid.* at 121.
40 *Ibid.* at 126.
41 *Ibid.* at 127. While the actual numbers of bar passers increased, the percentage of takers to passers remained low during this period at about 3 percent due to the related increase in the number of takers.
42 *See* Choi, *supra* note 25, at 190. A second attempt to establish graduate law schools, in 1998–1999, also failed. *Ibid.* at 191.
43 Yoon, *supra* note 12, at 128.
44 *Ibid.*
45 *See* Wilson, *supra* note 16, at 335. The need for a more globalized legal industry in Korea and the need for more access to legal services for Koreans were part of the basis for the proposal. *See ibid.*
46 Yoon, *supra* note 12, at 129–30. Another area of reform involved the creation of a jury system for a limited category of criminal cases. *See generally* Jae-Hyup Lee, "Getting Citizens Involved: Civil Participation in Judicial Decision-Making in Korea," *East Asian Law Review* 4, no. 2 (2009): 177, 188–90.
47 *See* Choi, *supra* note 25, at 109.
48 *See* Yoon, *supra* note 12.
49 *Ibid.* The majority of law professors in Korea are not licensed to practice law and are not among the bar passers. *See* Kim, *supra* note 10, at 341, note 93. For example, even at Korea's top university, Seoul National University, only about 41 percent of the faculty have passed the bar exam. *Ibid.*
50 *See* Miyazawa et al., *supra* note 33, at 353.
51 *See ibid.*
52 *Ibid.* The cost of three years at the new law schools is about 100 million Korean won ($87,800). *See* "S. Korea's First-Generation Law School Graduates Face Uncertain Future," *The Korea Herald*, December 9, 2011, https://www.koreaherald.com/article/10351336.
53 *See supra* note 25.
54 *Ibid.*
55 Yoon, *supra* note 12, at 139.
56 Choi, *supra* note 2, at 187.
57 Ginsburg, *supra* note 5, at 434–45.
58 "The Law on Establishing and Operating a Legal Professional Graduate School [Beophak Jeonmun Daehakwon Seolchi Unyeong-e Gwanhan Beopruyl]," Law No. 8544 (2007) amended as Law No. 8852 (2008) (S. Korea) [hereinafter GLSA].
59 Yoon, *supra* note 12, at 140.
60 *Ibid.*
61 *Ibid.*
62 Miyazawa et al., *supra* note 33, at 353.
63 GLSA, *supra* note 58, article 8. There are questions regarding the future of existing undergraduate law programs, from their role in law education overall, to the utility of a four-year undergraduate law program that does not qualify students to sit for the bar. *See* Ahn, *supra* note 21, at 238–9.
64 GLSA, *supra* note 58, article 26.
65 Kim, *supra* note 10, at 324.

66 Wilson, *supra* note 16, at 339.
67 *Ibid.* at 339–40.
68 *Ibid.* The first Lawyer Admission Test was administered in January of 2012, two years after the Justice Department administered a mock version of the new bar exam. *See* Young-Cheol K. Jeong, "Korean Legal Education for the Age of Professionalism: Suggestions for More Concerted Curricula," *East Asian Law Review* 5 (2010): 155, 191. It is anticipated that the old bar exam will be replaced by 2018, and the old system completely phased out by 2020. *See, e.g.*, Sarah Kim, "First Law School Grads Face Trial over Jobs," *Korea JoongAng Daily*, January 11, 2012, https://koreajoongangdaily.joins.com/2012/01/10/socialAffairs/First-law-school-grads-face-trial-over-jobs/2946913.html; "Law School Grads Face Tough Job Market," *The Korea Herald*, January 5, 2012. The new exam was administered over the course of four days.
69 Wilson, *supra* note 16, at 340.
70 Bar Examination Act [Byeonhosa Siheom-beop] (Law No. 9747, May 28, 2009), article 7(1).
71 Yoon, *supra* note 12, at 142. In raw numbers, this passage rate is expected to yield 1,500–2,000 students each year, starting in 2012. Wilson, *supra* note 14, at 340. Of the 1998 students that entered the new schools in 2009, 1,698 students took the new exam, the rest opting to take civil service exams or choosing to forego a legal career altogether. *See* Kim, "First Law School Grads Face Trial over Jobs." The 75 percent quota on passage of the new exam, while dramatically higher than the old state bar exam, has had a sobering effect on the prospect of obtaining legal jobs after graduation.
72 Si-soo Park, "Law School Students Threaten to Quit," *The Korea Times*, December 6, 2010, https://www.koreatimes.co.kr/southkorea/20101206/law-school-students-threaten-to-quit.
73 Peter A. Joy et al., "Building Clinical Legal Education Programs in a Country without a Tradition of Graduate Professional Legal Education: Japan as a Case Study," *Clinical Law Review* 13 (2006): 417, 457.
74 *Ibid.*
75 *See* Hyung Tae Kim, "Legal Market Liberalization in South Korea: Preparations for Change," *Pacific Rim Law & Policy Journal* 15, no. 1 (2006): 199, 229.
76 *Ibid.*
77 GLSA, *supra* note 58, article 2.
78 *See* Wilson, *supra* note 16, at 340.
79 *Ibid.*
80 *See* Kim, *supra* note 10, at 327.
81 *See ibid.* at 328.
82 *See* Jeong, *supra* note 68, at 177.
83 *Ibid.* at 178.
84 Miyazawa et al., *supra* note 33, at 352.
85 *Ibid.*
86 GLSA, *supra* note 58, article 16(4).
87 Miyazawa et al., *supra* note 33, at 341 (citing article 13 of the Enforcement Decree of the Act on the Establishment and Operation of Law School).
88 *Ibid.* at 341.
89 Jeong, *supra* note 68, at 176.

90 *See, e.g.*, Park, "Law School Students Threaten to Quit" (current law students rally in anticipation of Ministry of Justice's proposed quota on passage of new bar exam); Jeong-ju Na, "Law School Graduates Face Grim Reality," *The Korea Times*, August 1, 2011, https://www.koreatimes.co.kr/southkorea/20110801/law-school-graduates-face-grim-reality (the 2000 or so graduates from the new law schools entering the work force will face fierce competition for a limited number of jobs); "Law Loses Luster as New Attorneys Face Unemployment," *The Chosun Daily*, August 28, 2009, http://english.chosun.com/site/data/html_dir/2009/08/28/2009082800354.html (more JRTI graduates have had difficulty finding employment as of 2009; starting in 2012, about 2000 graduates from the new law schools will join 1000 JRTI graduates in vying for legal jobs); Si-soo Park, "Dispute Deepening over Recruitment of Prosecutors," *The Korea Times*, March 2, 2011, http://koreatimes.co.kr/www/news/include/print.asp?newsIdx=82368 (JRTI trainees protested against government plans to hire prosecutors from the top students at the new law schools by boycotting the opening ceremony of the JRTI).

91 Japan undertook a legal education reform based on the three-year graduate law school in 2004. *See* David S. Clark, "American Law Schools in the Age of Globalization: A Comparative Perspective," *Rutgers Law Review* 61 (2009): 1037, 1073–4. While Korea was the first to raise the idea to emulate the American-style system in 1995, the reform stalled because of political opposition there, and Japan was able to implement a similar reform first. Ginsburg, *supra* note 5, at 437. In Japan, there was a substantial gap between the number of law school graduates and those permitted to pass the national bar exam, and threatened to endanger many of the sixty-six new law schools. *Id.* Because Korea and Japan have had similar legal education systems, Korea can learn from the specific challenges Japan faced in its experience with legal education reform. *See* Wilson, *supra* note 16, at 341–2. Australia, Hong Kong, Taiwan, and the Philippines have also embarked on legal education reform toward an American-style system. *Ibid.* at 31 note 2.

92 Clark, *supra* note 91, at 1075.

93 *See* Sang Hyun Song, "Different Modes of Legal Education and Legal Thinking: Three Most Important Issues of Korea's Legal Educational System That Others Ought to Know" (paper presented at the International Association of Law Schools Conference "Learning from Each Other: Enriching the Law School Curriculum in an Interrelated World," 2007), at 141.

94 Korean lawmakers passed the Korean Foreign Legal Consultants Act, a bill authorizing the partial opening of domestic legal services to foreign lawyers working in Korea. Kyungho Choi, "Korean Foreign Legal Consultants Act: Legal Profession of American Lawyers in South Korea," *Asian-Pacific Law & Policy Journal* 11, no. 1 (2009): 100–2.

95 *See* Clark, *supra* note 91, at 1074.

96 *Ibid.* Prior to 2004, applicants chose one of several language tests, namely, English, French, German, Japanese, Chinese, and Spanish. *Ibid.*

97 *See* Nakin Sung and Won-Woo Lee, "Reform of Legal Education in the Age of Globalization," *Journal of Korean Law* 5, no. 2 (2005): 85, 88.

98 The first class of graduates from the new schools seems to be facing a job market that is unprepared to deal with the influx of a greater number of graduates. Both companies hiring in-house counsel and government departments need to develop legal positions and recruiting mechanisms to facilitate the hiring process. *See, e.g.*,

Si-soo Park, "Law School Students Sing Job Blues," *The Korea Times*, November 23, 2011, http://koreatimes.co.kr/www/news/include/print.asp?newsIdx=99420.

99 For example, at Seoul National University, the most competitive school in Korea whose graduates are prevalent among the bar passers, more than one third of the law faculty have an American J.D. or LLM. *See* Seoul National University (official website), https://en.snu.ac.kr/.

100 *See* Song, *supra* note 93, at 467.

101 *Ibid.*

102 *Ibid.*

103 *Ibid.*

104 *Ibid.* at 468.

105 *See ibid.* at 469.

106 Chan Jin Kim, "Korean Attitudes towards Law," *Pacific Rim Law & Policy Journal* 10, no. 1 (2000): 1, 10. However, rapid industrialization and economic development have sped up the democratization process by making the social structure more horizontal, rather than vertical, through expansion of the middle class. *Ibid.* at 20. As a result, the rule of law is becoming more integrated into daily life, and the gap between the values is narrowing. *Ibid.*

107 Wilson, *supra* note 16, at 344.

108 *See ibid.*

109 *See* Charles R. Irish, "Reflections of an Observer: The International Conference on Legal Education Reform," *Wisconsin International Law Journal* 24 (2006): 5, 8–9.

110 *See* Wilson, *supra* note 16, at 344–5.

111 *See, e.g.*, Kathryn M. Stanchi, "Step Away from the Case Book: A Call for Balance and Integration in Law School Pedagogy," *Harvard Civil Rights-Civil Liberties Law Review* 43 (2008): 611; Byron D. Cooper, "The Integration of Theory, Doctrine, and Practice in Legal Education," *Journal of the Association of Legal Writing Directors* 1 (2002): 50; Myron Moskovitz, "Beyond the Case Method: It's Time to Teach with Problems," *Journal of Legal Education* 42, no. 2 (1992): 241.

112 *See* Jeong, *supra* note 68, at 184.

113 *See ibid.* at 188.

114 *See ibid.* at 194.

115 It is important for the foreign legal educators teaching US methods and curricula to appreciate the existing cultural context, rather than assume that the US model must fit everywhere. *See* James E. Moliterno, "Exporting American Legal Education," *Journal of Legal Education* 58, no. 2 (2008): 274, 278.

116 *See* Jo-Ellen D. Lewis, "Developing and Implementing Effective Legal Writing Programs in Korean Law Schools," *Journal of Korean Law* 9, no. 1 (2009): 125 (Summarizes legal writing course development workshop conducted at Seoul National University).

117 *See infra*, notes 119 and 130.

118 American Bar Association, Section of Legal Education and Admissions to the Bar, *Legal Education and Professional Development—An Educational Continuum: Report of the Task Force on Law Schools and the Profession: Narrowing the Gap* (Chicago: American Bar Association, 1992), 138–40 [hereinafter "MacCrate Report"].

119 *See* Roy T. Stuckey, "Preparing Students to Practice Law: A Global Problem in Need of Global Solutions," *South Texas Law Review* 43 (2002): 649, 663–4.

120 *See* MacCrate Report, *supra* note 118, at 245.

121 *See supra*, notes 72–5.
122 *See* William M. Sullivan et al., *Educating Lawyers: Preparation for the Profession of Law* (Carnegie Foundation for the Advancement of Teaching; Jossey-Bass, 2007), 50–1 [hereinafter "Carnegie Report"].
123 Irish, *supra* note 109, at 8. Early introduction of skills is contrary to the pre-reform system in Korea, where undergraduate and cram school studies focused primarily on theory and practical skills were only introduced once a student gained entry into the JRTI.
124 *See ibid.* at 11.
125 *See* Jeong, *supra* note 68, at 183.
126 *Ibid.* at 188.
127 *See supra* note 58, article 3.
128 Wilson, *supra* note 16, at 348.
129 *See* Carnegie Report, *supra* note 122, at 50–1.
130 *See ibid.* at 187.
131 *See ibid.*
132 *See ibid.* at 188.
133 Wilson, *supra* note 16, at 352–3.
134 *See* Carnegie Report, *supra* note 122, at 164.
135 *Ibid.* Student feedback about the final exam model was that the nature of their studying was unrelated to their performance on the final exam. *Ibid.* Further, they reported that there was no opportunity to practice what will be tested, and they were not able to gauge how they were doing in the course without feedback. *Ibid.* at 165.
136 *Ibid.* at 173.
137 *Ibid.*
138 *See ibid.* at 355.
139 *See* Robert J. Rhee, "On Legal Education and Reform: One View Formed from Diverse Perspectives," *Maryland Law Review* 70 (2011): 310, 314.
140 *See* Stuckey, *supra* note 119, at 675.

Bibliography

Ahn, Kyong-Whan. "Law Reform in Korea and the Agenda of 'Graduate Law School.'" *Wisconsin International Law Journal* 24, no. 1 (2006): 223–42.

American Bar Association, Section of Legal Education and Admissions to the Bar. *Legal Education and Professional Development—An Educational Continuum: Report of the Task Force on Law Schools and the Profession: Narrowing the Gap*. Chicago: American Bar Association, 1992.

Bae, Ji-sook. "Controversy Escalates over Plan to Pick Law School Graduates as Prosecutors." *The Korea Herald*, March 7, 2011. https://www.koreaherald.com/article/10336541.

Choi, Dae-Kwon. "Proposed Legal Education Reform in Korea: Toward a Professional Model." *Ritsumeikan Law Review* 18 (2001): 93–112.

Choi, Kyungho. "Korean Foreign Legal Consultants Act: Legal Profession of American Lawyers in South Korea." *Asian-Pacific Law & Policy Journal* 11, no. 1 (2009): 100–13.

Clark, David S. "American Law Schools in the Age of Globalization: A Comparative Perspective." *Rutgers Law Review* 61 (2009): 1037–77.

Cooper, Byron D. "The Integration of Theory, Doctrine, and Practice in Legal Education." *Journal of the Association of Legal Writing Directors* 1 (2002): 50–64.
Ginsburg, Tom. "Transforming Legal Education in Japan and Korea." *Penn State International Law Review* 22, no. 3 (2004): 433–9.
Irish, Charles R. "Reflections of an Observer: The International Conference on Legal Education Reform." *Wisconsin International Law Journal* 24 (2006): 5–22.
Jeong, Young-Cheol K. "Korean Legal Education for the Age of Professionalism: Suggestions for More Concerted Curricula." *East Asian Law Review* 5 (2010): 155–96.
Joy, Peter A., Shigeo Miyagawa, Takao Suami, and Charles D. Weisselberg. "Building Clinical Legal Education Programs in a Country without a Tradition of Graduate Professional Legal Education: Japan as a Case Study." *Clinical Law Review* 13 (2006): 417–58.
Kim, Chan Jin. "Korean Attitudes towards Law." *Pacific Rim Law & Policy Journal* 10, no. 1 (2000): 1–46.
Kim, Chang-Rok. "The National Bar Examination in Korea." *Wisconsin International Law Journal* 24, no. 1 (2006): 243–60.
Kim, Hyung Tae. "Legal Market Liberalization in South Korea: Preparations for Change." *Pacific Rim Law & Policy Journal* 15, no. 1 (2006): 199–231.
Kim, Jae Won. "The Ideal and the Reality of the Korean Legal Profession." *Asian-Pacific Law & Policy Journal* 2, no. 1 (2001): 45–68.
Kim, Jasper. "Socrates v. Confucius: An Analysis of South Korea's Implementation of the American Law School Model." *Asian-Pacific Law & Policy Journal* 10, no. 2 (2009): 322–53.
Kim, Sarah. "First Law School Grads Face Trial over Jobs." *Korea JoongAng Daily*, January 11, 2012. https://koreajoongangdaily.joins.com/2012/01/10/socialAffairs/First-law-school-grads-face-trial-over-jobs/2946913.html.
Lee, Jae-Hyup. "Getting Citizens Involved: Civil Participation in Judicial Decision-Making in Korea." *East Asian Law Review* 4, no. 2 (2009): 177–207.
Lee, Jae-min. "Bleak Job Prospects for Law Grads." *The Korea Herald*, January 10, 2012. https://www.koreaherald.com/article/10353745.
Lee, Sagmin. "Korea's Top Women's Law School Battles Reverse Discrimination Lawsuit." *Human Rights Monitor–Korea*, April 4, 2011.
Lewis, Jo-Ellen D. "Developing and Implementing Effective Legal Writing Programs in Korean Law Schools." *Journal of Korean Law* 9, no. 1 (2009): 125–46.
Lin, Anthony. "Shaking Up the Old Order; Korea." *The Asian Lawyer*, June 1, 2011.
Miyazawa, Setsuo, Kay-Wah Chan, and Ilhyung Lee. "The Reform of Legal Education in East Asia." *Annual Review of Law and Social Science* 4, no. 1 (2008): 333–60.
Moliterno, James E. "Exporting American Legal Education." *Journal of Legal Education* 58, no. 2 (2008): 274–89.
Moskovitz, Myron. "Beyond the Case Method: It's Time to Teach with Problems." *Journal of Legal Education* 42, no. 2 (1992): 241–70.
Na, Jeong-ju. "Law School Graduates Face Grim Reality." *The Korea Times*, August 1, 2011. https://www.koreatimes.co.kr/southkorea/20110801/law-school-graduates-face-grim-reality.
Park, Se-Il. "The Value of American-Style Law Schools." *The Chosun Daily*, September 7, 2007. https://www.chosun.com/english/opinion-en/2007/07/09/Q5UT3WFD2QJPOPG5WUMY3MBZGI/.
Park, Si-soo. "Dispute Deepening over Recruitment of Prosecutors." *The Korea Times*, March 2, 2011. http://koreatimes.co.kr/www/news/include/print.asp?newsIdx=82368.

Park, Si-soo. "Law School Students Sing Job Blues." *The Korea Times*, November 23, 2011. http://koreatimes.co.kr/www/news/include/print.asp?newsIdx=99420.
Park, Si-soo. "Law School Students Threaten to Quit." *The Korea Times*, December 6, 2010. https://www.koreatimes.co.kr/southkorea/20101206/law-school-students-threaten-to-quit.
Rhee, Robert J. "On Legal Education and Reform: One View Formed from Diverse Perspectives." *Maryland Law Review* 70 (2011): 310–40.
Schwartzman, Nathan. "Female Lawyers Increasing in Korea." *Asian Correspondent*, January 24, 2008.
Song, Sang Hyun. "Different Modes of Legal Education and Legal Thinking: Three Most Important Issues of Korea's Legal Educational System That Others Ought to Know." Paper presented at the International Association of Law Schools Conference, "Learning from Each Other: Enriching the Law School Curriculum in an Interrelated World," 2007.
Stanchi, Kathryn M. "Step Away from the Case Book: A Call for Balance and Integration in Law School Pedagogy." *Harvard Civil Rights–Civil Liberties Law Review* 43 (2008): 611–14.
Steiner, Mark E. "Cram Schooled." *Wisconsin International Law Journal* 24 (2006): 377–95.
Stuckey, Roy T. "Preparing Students to Practice Law: A Global Problem in Need of Global Solutions." *South Texas Law Review* 43 (2002): 649–81.
Sullivan, William M. Anne Colby, Judith Welch Wegner, Lloyd Bond, and Lee S. Shulman. *Educating Lawyers: Preparation for the Profession of Law*. San Francisco: Jossey-Bass, 2007.
Sung, Nakin, and Won-Woo Lee. "Reform of Legal Education in the Age of Globalization." *Journal of Korean Law* 5, no. 2 (2005): 85–96.
The Chosun Daily. "Law Loses Luster as New Attorneys Face Unemployment." *The Chosun Daily*, August 28, 2009. http://english.chosun.com/site/data/html_dir/2009/08/28/2009082800354.html.
The Korea Herald. "Law School Grads Face Tough Job Market." *The Korea Herald*, January 5, 2012.
The Korea Herald. "S. Korea's First-Generation Law School Graduates Face Uncertain Future." *The Korea Herald*, December 9, 2011. https://www.koreaherald.com/article/10351336.
Wilson, Matthew J. "U.S. Legal Education Methods and Ideals: Application to the Japanese and Korean Systems." *Cardozo Journal of International and Comparative Law* 18 (2010): 295–342.
Yoon, Dae-Kyu. *Law and Democracy in South Korea: Democratic Development since 1987*. Seoul: Kyungnam University Press, 2010.
Yoon, Dae-Kyu. "The Paralysis of Legal Education in Korea." In *Legal Reform in Korea*, edited by Tom Ginsburg, 36–46. London: Routledge, 2004.
Yoon, Dae-Kyu, and Tom Ginsburg, eds. *Legal Reform in Korea*. London: Routledge, 2004.
Yun, Suh-young. "Law School Students Sing Job Blues." *The Korea Times*, November 23, 2011. http://koreatimes.co.kr/www/news/include/print.asp?newsIdx=99420.
Zamora, Stephen. "The Cultural Context of International Legal Cooperation." *Journal of Legal Education* 51, no. 3 (2001): 462–68.

This chapter was previously published under the same title in Brooklyn Journal of International Law 38, no. 1 (2012): 49–75.

3

The Influence of US Legal Education on South Korean Legal Education

Jaewan Moon

Introduction

Modern legal education system in South Korea was heavily influenced by Japan and Germany. Japan had adopted the German legal system during the Meiji Restoration and transplanted it to Korea during the Japanese colonial period.[1] Even after Korea's liberation from Japan in 1945, Japanese influence was still prevalent in the content and the structure of legal education.[2] With the emergence of the need for reform of legal education as a social issue in the 1990s, the influence of the US legal education as an aspirational model grew rapidly. Its influence reached a peak when the US-influenced law school system was established in March 2009. During the same time period, there were also active discussions on globalization of the legal market.[3] In Korea, there was also considerable interest in issues relating to the dominance of American[4] law firms in the global legal market and the education and training systems for American practitioners.

Before the Adoption of Law School

American Law School as an Ideal Legal Education Model

Many legal activists in Korea thought of the American law school model as an ideal system for Korean legal education. It seemed like a "magic wand" that could solve all problems in Korean jurisprudence and legal community. Every time the legal education reform was discussed, the adoption of the American law school model was regularly brought up as a possible alternative.

Prior to establishment of the current law school system and the bar exam, selection of legal professionals was accomplished through the National Judicial Exam (NJE). The Judicial Research and Training Institute (JRTI) was established in January 1971 under the supervision of the Judiciary to be responsible for the training of those who had passed the highly competitive NJE.[5] It required no formal legal education as prequalification to taking the exam, and the number of successful applicants was predetermined by the Ministry of Justice. Passing the exam was like a token guaranteeing future with wealth and honor, and the scores obtained in NJE were treated as if the applicant's legal ability had been officially recognized by the state.

Such limited number as well as prevalent Confucius belief which considered public service as prestigious[6] brought about situation where the passers of NJE were conferred relatively high rank within the government and were given salaries from the government while they participated in the training course. Those who passed NJE and attended JRTI seemed to have a common mindset that they were the privileged.

But as Korean economy developed and society became more diversified and globalized, JRTI's teachings, which mainly focused on litigation, revealed limitations in training lawyers' capability to deal with complicated legal disputes professionally and effectively. American law schools emerged as possible alternative to solve the issues that were identified in the legal education and training systems, and also as a path to improving the international competitiveness of Korean lawyers. In 1995, the Globalization Committee, established by President Kim Young-sam, proposed the adoption of the American law school model as a part of the judicial reform. After much debate, the American law school model was still not introduced, but the number of NJE passers increased from 300 to 1,000.

Internal and External Factors That Make the US Law Education Idea

In order to understand why the American law school is considered as an ideal model for Korea, one should look at the environment of law education up to such adoption. It was JRTI that has the responsibility to educate lawyers. College-level legal education was departed from educating lawyers. However, there was awareness in legal academia that it was not possible to nurture legal professionals suited for globalized and diversified society under such system.

Globalization is definitely one of the major factors that contributed to the increasing appreciation of the US legal education system. As the Korean economy increased in size, so did the demand for more developed legal services. Especially in the 2000s, as the issue of opening up the legal market to foreign law firms came to the forefront, the improvement of lawyers' global competitiveness was a new challenge that the Korean legal community faced. Large law firms attempted to tackle this issue and ran programs to prepare for globalization.[7] One of the ways was by sending their lawyers to American law schools to acquire LLM.s and allowing them to take practical training in American law firms for six months to a year.[8]

Adoption of Law Schools

Influence of the American Law School

Korean law school system in many aspects adopts that of the United States. Like the American law schools, it is three-year-long post-baccalaureate professional school, and like most states in America only the graduates of law schools are allowed to take the bar exam.[9] And like the United States, there is no requirement of practical training after passing the bar exam.[10] And akin to the American legal education system, the ratio of professors to students is low. Ethics and professional skill classes are included in law school curriculum.

Differences from American Law School

Though Korean law school is similar to the American law school in form, there are many differences in its content. One crucial difference lies in the relationship between the bar exam and legal education. Korea has a long history of selection of high-ranking public officials through examinations.[11] Same attitude applies to the bar exams. The passing of bar exam is considered an absolute measure of the quality of legal ability in Korea unlike the United States where it verifies only a qualification to act as a lawyer.

In Korea, the number of passers is determined each year by the minister of justice after hearing opinions from the Supreme Court, the Korean Bar Association, and the Korean Association of Law Schools.[12] This differs significantly from the United States. The Code of Recommended Standards of Bar Examiners,[13] clearly states that the purpose of the bar exam is "not to limit the number of lawyers admitted to practice." In this system, law school education is subverted by the bar exam. In turn, school education inevitably becomes centered on the subjects included in the bar exam.

Ten Years after the Adoption of Law School System

Education System

The year 2019 marked the tenth anniversary of the commencement of the law school format. Evaluations after ten years are generally positive. In the interim, there have been attempts to uproot the basic framework of law school system, but fortunately, the law school system has managed to remain intact as it had been established. Following are a few positions that support changes to the law school system.

First is the position supporting the retention of the judicial exam. NJE had existed until 2017. However, there have been continuing assertions that the system producing lawyers through NJE should be maintained. A constitutional complaint was filed asserting that abolition of the judicial exam was unconstitutional. The Constitutional Court decided on September 29, 2016, that the abolition of the judicial exam was not unconstitutional.[14]

Second is the position supporting enactment of the preliminary exam, which supported the idea of maintaining the framework of NJE under the law school system. The preliminary exam advocates asserts that the person who passed the preliminary exam be allowed a waiver to such requirement and be allowed to take the bar exam. The fact that Japan operates a preliminary exam system is a major basis supporting such argument. This issue is still unsettled.

Third is a continuing demand for online law schools. In the previous government, the ruling party promised to introduce an online law school as part of its 2020 general election campaign.[15] However, the promise was not fulfilled. The prospect of such a law school is not bright due to strong opposition from both the Korean Bar Association and the Korean Association of Law Schools.

Education Contents

Merits and Demerits of Law School Education

One of the positive developments as a result of establishment of law schools is that the original purpose of cultivating legal professionals through legal education has been realized to some extent.[16] Since graduating from an approved law school is a requirement that needs to be met by those taking the bar exam, law school education is linked to the selection of legal professionals. However, this gave rise to a new problem that made legal education overly linked and even subordinated to the bar exam. As the bar exam pass rate becomes lower year by year, given the cap existing for the number of applicants passing the bar, only lectures in subjects that help prepare for the bar exam are opened, and the other lectures are closed due to lack of student attendance. The bar exam pass rate had fallen from 87.15 percent in the first exam in 2012 to 49.35 percent in 2018 and is now just over 50 percent.[17]

It is difficult to say whether the law school system is successful in diversifying the content of legal education. The law school system was introduced with the idea of preparing for the globalization, but the current system, which focuses solely on passing the bar exam, has proven to be difficult to achieve.[18]

American Influence in Law School Education

There is little room for American legal education to influence substantive legal education in law schools. There are many assertions that law school education should focus on cultivating the ability to identify issues and solve problems as they do in the United States[19] rather than just delivering specific legal information but the reality faced by law schools does not allow such teachings. The law school classes are subordinate to the bar exam, and the bar exam is mostly structured to assess whether he/she knows the content of the specific cases.[20] A study showed that law school students need to memorize as many as 10,000 court cases to prepare the bar.[21]

On the other hand, practical education is influenced considerably by US legal education. Practical education in areas such as legal ethics, legal research, drafting legal documents, mock trials, and legal clinics is provided similar to the American law schools' courses. Now legal ethics is mandatory for all law schools, and applicants must pass a separate legal ethics exam in addition to the bar exam.[22]

Education Method

There are two main methods of teaching in law schools. One is the lecture format, and the other is the writing correction format that was typical in JRTI. Generally, the former is used for theoretical courses, and the latter is used for practice classes. The lecture type is a way for the professor to introduce the theory and the contents of recent cases. At the beginning, some law school professors tried the Socratic method of education as offered in the American law school. However, unlike the United States, in Korea, the Confucian culture which respects hierarchy inhibits the process and it is difficult for students to discuss on equal standing with the professor in the classroom.[23] Moreover, due to the pressure of the bar exam, the students require lectures to help them pass the exam.

Educators

The composition of full-time faculty members of law school has been influenced by the American model. In the past, there were about ten full-time professors on average in each university's college of law. Most of them earned doctorate degrees from the countries with continental law systems or domestic universities. There were few professors with practical experience.

The current law mandates employment of at least twenty full-time professors at each law school.[24] More than 20 percent of the faculty is required to be professors with at least five years of practical legal experience.[25] At the time of the introduction of the law school system, competition among universities for government accreditation was fierce, and all universities applying for law school accreditation had hired twenty or more professors. It is also noteworthy that the number of practitioners who enter the academic world has significantly increased. The recent recruitment pattern of law school professors shows preference for doctoral degree holders with practical experiences rather than doctoral degree holders without license to practice law.

Outlook

Education System

There are still many people who have nostalgia for the past, but the law school framework has been established firmly enough simply not to revert to the past. Discussions on improving the law school system will continue. The issues of raising the bar exam pass rate and amending the contents of the exam suitable for the twenty-first century will be continuously discussed. The mile marker in this discussion is the American bar exam. However, it should be kept in mind when pursuing this line of discussion that the average pass rate in the United States is currently little less than

62 percent, which is not that much higher than the current pass rate in Korea of 53 percent. The more important distinction is that the US bar exam is not intended purely to limit the number of practitioners to certain number. Although each state has different standards, generally a candidate can pass the bar if he/she meets a certain standard, not if his/her score is within a certain percentile. Of course, this doesn't address the larger issue that bar pass rates should not be used as the sole measure of the quality of a law school.

The average level of lawyers' salaries and social status has declined due to the surge in the number of lawyers since the establishment of the law school. This will inevitably lead to a revision of the law school system. Still, lots of students want to enter the law school. The number of applicants for legal aptitude test, which is necessary for law school admission, is 19,400 in 2024, which is the largest since 2008, the first year that had 9,690 applicants.

Education Contents

The argument that the legal education in the law school should be liberated from the bar exam is a strong one. Such separation is not likely to become reality. Because the traditional approach of measuring capability through the exam dominates the Korean legal profession, the bar exam is likely to take the form of an assessment of current legal knowledge as an indicator of success in the future. There is a social demand for creativity in solving new types of legal conflict, but it is unlikely that the law school education will change in response to this demand. What the legal circle demands of the law school is education faithful to the fundamentals of law. The impact of US legal education on Korea is very limited in the current situation where legal education is subject to the bar exam.

Education Methods

Unless the bar exam changes, it will be difficult to change the current education method. It is very unlikely that the Socratic method of American law school will become popular in Korea. Although there is still interest in legal clinic education, there is no possibility that it will become much more active unless the heavy burden of the bar exam is lightened.[26]

As legal education is an evolving subject that needs to meet societal changes, Korea like other countries will continue discussing how to improve its legal education. And most likely under the current climate efforts to restructure law schools modeling the US legal education system will still be most influential.

Notes

1 Neil Chisholm, "The Faces of Judicial Independence: Democratic versus Bureaucratic Accountability in Judicial Selection, Training, and Promotion in South Korea and Taiwan," *American Journal of Comparative Law* 62, no. 4 (2014): 893.

2 Jay Murphy, *Legal Education in a Developing Nation: The Korean Experience* (Seoul: Seoul National University Press & Oceana Publications, 1967), 65.

3 Korea opened up its legal service market in September 26, 2009. *See* Jaewan Moon, "Impact of Globalization on Legal Profession," *HUFS Global Law Review* 4, no. 2 (2012): 13–35.

4 The terms "American" and "United States" have been used interchangeably in this chapter.

5 NJE had existed from 1963 to 2017. The average pass rate during the entire period is 2.93 percent (20,609 passers out of 702,513 applicants). For more information on NJE before introduction of law school in Korea, *see* Chang Rok Kim, "The National Bar Examination in Korea," *Wisconsin International Law Journal* 24, no. 1 (2006): 243.

6 For Confucius culture in Korean education, *see* Jasper Kim, "Socrates v. Confucius: An Analysis of South Korea's Implementation of the American Law School Model," *Asian-Pacific Law & Policy Journal* 10, no. 2 (2009): 322, 347–9.

7 Neil Chisholm, "Legal Diffusion and the Legal Profession: An Analysis of the Processes of American Influence on South Korea's Lawyers," *Columbia Journal of Asian Law* 26, no. 2 (2013): 267.

8 Carole Silver, Jae-Hyup Lee, and Jeeyoon Park, "What Firms Want: Investigating Globalization's Influence on the Market for Lawyers in Korea," *Columbia Journal of Asian Law* 28, no. 1 (2014): 1.

9 American Bar Association, *ABA Standards and Rules of Procedure for Approval of Law Schools, 2019–2020* (American Bar Association, Section of Legal Education and Admissions to the Bar, 2019), Chapter 3 sets out clear perimeters of such matters as objective and curriculum of ABA requirements along with other matters.

10 It should be noted there has been greater emphasis placed practical training on law school in recent years such as some states requiring testing of practical skill as part of their bar exams.

11 The national civil service examination called "Gwageo" was established in 958 and maintained its position as the only entrance to high-ranking public officials during the Joseon dynasty.

12 National Bar Examination Act (Act No. 9747, May 28, 2009 Amended by Act No. 10923, July 25, 2011 Act No. 15154, December 12, 2017), Article 10 (1).

13 Code of Recommended Standard for Bar Examiner recommends to all the national governing bodies of the respective states the "bar exams should test the ability of the applicant to identify legal issues ... and to arrive a logical solution by application of legal principles, in a manner which demonstrates a thorough understanding of these principles," Judith A. Gundersen and Claire J. Guback, eds., *Comprehensive Guide to Bar Admission Requirements* (The National Conference of Bar Examiners and the American Bar Association Section of Legal Education and Admissions to the Bar, 2019), ix.

14 Constitutional Court of Korea, Judgment of September 29, 2016, 2012Hun-Ma1002, 28–2 KCCR 477.

15 Hye-seong An, "Minjudang, Bangtongdae Yagan Roseukul Doip Chongseon Gongyak Gesi [Democratic Party of Korea Made a Campaign Promise to Introduce Online and Night Law School]," *Beomnyuljeoneol* [The Law Journal], March 11, 2020.

16 Jae Hyup Lee, June Woonge Rhee, and Jung Hyun Hwang, "Roseukul Chulsin Beomnyulga, Geudeureun Nuguinga? [Law School Lawyers in Korea, Who Are They?]" *Seouldaehakgyo Beopak* [Seoul Law Journal] 56, no. 2 (2015): 406; Jaewan Moon, "Bubhak Gyoyukgwa Bubhakgeonmundaehakwon [Legal Education and

Law School]," in *Hankuk Bubhakgwa Bubhakgeonmundaehakwon* [Legal Education and Law School in Korea], ed. Yugicheon-gyosu-ginyeom-saeop-chulpan-jaedan (Gyeonggi: Bobmunsa, 2018), 80–9.

17 The pass rate in 2024 is 53.05 percent.

18 *See* Young-Cheol K. Jeong, "Korean Legal Education for the Age of Professionalism: Suggestions for More Concerted Curricula," *East Asia Law Review* 5 (2010): 155; Jaewan Moon, "How to Change Law School Education in an Age of Oversupply of Lawyers," *HUFS Global Law Review* 8, no. 1 (2016), 45–59.

19 Important point of note however is that on May 17, 2019 the Council of the ABA Section of Legal Education and Admission to the Bar approved of major change in the bar passage standard. The newly approved Standard 316 requires that 75 percent of the law school graduates who sit for the bar pass it within two years. The Council is recognized by the Department of Education as national accreditor of law school and has the final say on the accreditation of law schools. It will be interesting to see where this leads as this seems to be an attempt to link legal education to outcome-based performance scale of passing the bar. Council of the ABA Section of Legal Education and Admission to the Bar, *Standard 316* (Approved May 17, 2019).

20 According to a research paper published by seventeen professors of the Seoul National University Law School in May of 2018, the reason for not being able to meet the goals of law school system at the time of its introduction is mostly due to the excessively difficult and competitive bar exam.

21 Jae-Min Lee, "After 10 Years, Legal Education Reform at Its Crossroads," *The Korea Herald*, November 27, 2018.

22 Speaking accurately, the National Bar Examination consists of a written examination with multiple-choice questions, essays, and a separate Legal Ethics Examination. Republic of Korea, *National Bar Examination Act*, Article 8(1) and Article 10(1) (Acts No. 9747, 10923, 15154).

23 Kim, *supra* note 6, at 322, 347–9.

24 Republic of Korea, *Act on Establishment and Management of Professional Law Schools*, Articles 16(3).

25 *Ibid.* at Article 16(4).

26 It is noteworthy that the SNU law school, a leading law school in Korea, hired six clinical professors in various field in March 1, 2020. However, it is wait and see whether clinical education will expand to other law schools.

Bibliography

American Bar Association. *ABA Standards and Rules of Procedure for Approval of Law Schools, 2019–2020*. Chicago: American Bar Association, Section of Legal Education and Admissions to the Bar, 2019.

An, Hye-seong. "Minjudang, Bangtongdae Yagan Roseukul Doip Chongseon Gongyak Gesi [Democratic Party of Korea Made a Campaign Promise to Introduce Online and Night Law School]." *Beomnyuljeoneol* [The Law Journal], March 11, 2020. https://www.lec.co.kr/news/articleView.html?idxno=717384.

Chisholm, Neil. "The Faces of Judicial Independence: Democratic versus Bureaucratic Accountability in Judicial Selection, Training, and Promotion in South Korea and Taiwan." *American Journal of Comparative Law* 62, no. 4 (2014): 893–949.

Chisholm, Neil. "Legal Diffusion and the Legal Profession: An Analysis of the Processes of American Influence on South Korea's Lawyers." *Columbia Journal of Asian Law* 26, no. 2 (2013): 267–98.
Gundersen, Judith A., and Claire J. Guback, eds. *Comprehensive Guide to Bar Admission Requirements*. Chicago: The National Conference of Bar Examiners and the American Bar Association Section of Legal Education and Admissions to the Bar, 2019.
Jeong, Young-Cheol K. "Korean Legal Education for the Age of Professionalism: Suggestions for More Concerted Curricula." *East Asia Law Review* 5 (2010): 155–96.
Kim, Chang Rok. "The National Bar Examination in Korea." *Wisconsin International Law Journal* 24, no. 1 (2006): 243–60.
Kim, Jasper. "Socrates v. Confucius: An Analysis of South Korea's Implementation of the American Law School Model." *Asian-Pacific Law & Policy Journal* 10, no. 2 (2009): 322–53.
Lee, Jae Hyup, June Woong Rhee, and Jung Hyun Hwang. "Roseukul Chulsin Beomnyulga, Geudeureun Nuguinga? [Law School Lawyers in Korea, Who Are They?]" *Seouldaehakgyo Beopak* [Seoul Law Journal] 56, no. 2 (2015): 367–411.
Lee, Jae-Min. "After 10 Years, Legal Education Reform at Its Crossroads." *The Korea Herald*, November 27, 2018. https://www.koreaherald.com/article/1851194.
Moon, Jaewan. "Bubhak Gyoyukgwa Bubhakgeonmundaehakwon [Legal Education and Law School]." In *Hankuk Bubhakgwa Bubhakgeonmundaehakwon* [Legal Education and Law School in Korea], edited by Yugicheon-gyosu-ginyeom-saeop-chulpan-jaedan, Gyeonggi: Bobmunsa, 2018.
Moon, Jaewan. "How to Change Law School Education in an Age of Oversupply of Lawyers." *HUFS Global Law Review* 8, no. 1 (2016): 45–59.
Moon, Jaewan. "Impact of Globalization on Legal Profession." *HUFS Global Law Review* 4, no. 2 (2012), 13–35.
Murphy, Jay. *Legal Education in a Developing Nation: The Korean Experience*. Seoul: Seoul National University Press & Oceana Publications, 1967.
Ruehrwein, Erin. *ABA Standards and Rules of Procedure for Approval of Law Schools*, 2019–2020. Chicago: ABA Publishing, 2019.
Silver, Carole, Jae-Hyup Lee, and Jeeyoon Park. "What Firms Want: Investigating Globalization's Influence on the Market for Lawyers in Korea." *Columbia Journal of Asian Law* 28, no. 1 (2015): 1–40.

This chapter was previously published under the same title in Waseda Bulletin of Comparative Law 39 (2021): 13–22.

Part Two

Restructuring the Legal Profession

From State Monopoly to Market Competition

4

Legal Education Reform in Korea

Toward a More Diverse Profession?

Michelle Kwon

Understanding the Reasons for Legal Education Reform in Korea

In 1995, President Kim Young-sam led judicial reform in the name of globalization by focusing on legal education reform: the adoption of the American law school to help cultivate a new breed of global lawyers in South Korea ("Korea"). Demanding multilateral trade negotiations like the liberalization of the rice market during the World Trade Organization's Uruguay Round and complex terms of the 1997 International Monetary Fund $55 billion bailout challenged the Korean government officials to successfully negotiate on behalf of the Korean people. However, the legal profession and universities with LL.B. programs vehemently opposed reforms and effectively buried any changes in legal education. Domestically, "different kinds of ills and unethical practices related to the judiciary and legal profession, including the shortage of lawyers, excessive lawyers' fees, 'preferential treatment' (jeunkwanyewoo), and the unkind and arrogant, superior attitudes of lawyers in government and practice toward citizen-clients"[1] prompted judicial reform in Korea.

The Goshinangin Phenomenon

Prior to the establishment of the graduate law schools in Korea, the way to become a judge, prosecutor, or lawyer consisted of two steps: (1) passing all three stages of the judicial exam (sabeopgosi);[2] and (2) successfully completing a two-year, practical training program at the Judicial Research and Training Institute (JRTI) supervised by the Supreme Court. The Korean government strictly controlled the number of successful exam takers each year by quota. A compilation of Judicial Examination statistics from 1949 to 1980 shows that only 1,902 people (1.7 percent) of a total of 101,454 applicants were successful in passing the exam.[3] From 1981 to 2002, only 9,755 people out of a total number of 375,017 applicants successfully passed the judicial exam for an annual pass rate percentage of 2.65 percent.[4] Since there were no educational prerequisites, anyone could sit for the judicial exam and try to achieve the Korean Dream. While the chances of success were slim, many people saw studying for the judicial exam as a viable way to achieve social distinction with a prestigious career in Korean society.

The popularity of the judicial exam created a stagnation of human resources in Korean society, leading to the term "gosinangin,"[5] or people who exclusively study for state examinations,[6] including the judicial examination. By spending anywhere from seven to ten years on average to pass the judicial exam,[7] many exam hopefuls flocked to cram schools situated near Seoul National University's gosichon (cram school village), known for its high density of cram schools for the judicial exam. A study found that many gosinangin who successfully pass the judicial exam spent on average a total of 9.98 years (including the two-year JRTI training period after the bar exam) and 97,409,000 Korean won (about US$89,000) in pursuit of becoming a judge, prosecutor, or lawyer.[8]

However, what about the vast majority who were unsuccessful? While most applicants to the judicial exam were college graduates who majored in law, many college students put more priority on cram school courses that taught to the judicial exam than their studies at university. The average age of the majority of those who failed to pass the bar exam would have been older when entering the workforce, especially brutal for Korean males who are legally required to serve in the military for at least two years. Many who failed to pass the exam found it hard to compete for jobs with younger college graduates with better grades.[9]

Another serious problem concerned competition for college admissions. Many high school seniors enrolled in college entrance exam preparation courses at cram schools to get scores to get admissions to the college of law at university. If they failed, they might repeat the process until they got into a good school. Like the gosinangin, parents usually bore the cost of cram schools. The frenzy over college of law admissions created a bottleneck in college entrance competition.

Access to Legal Services

The paucity of lawyers in Korea restricted citizens' access to efficient and affordable legal assistance.[10] Even with an increase in the annual admissions quota of 300 lawyers in 1981 to 300 lawyers per year and in 2001 to 1,000 lawyers per year, Korea lagged considerably in comparison to other Organization for Economic Cooperation and Development (OECD) member countries. The thirty OECD member countries' average ratio of lawyers to members of the public was one lawyer to 1,399 people. However, Korea's average ratio of lawyers to members of the public in 2006 of one lawyer to 7,633 people ranked 30 out of the 30 OECD member countries.[11] The government-controlled quota on annual admissions of lawyers has had a direct effect on access to legal services and the cost of such services. Legal service fees in Korea at that time were six times higher on average compared to the United States.[12] Such a small lawyer community could not adequately and efficiently serve Korean society both domestically and internationally.

"Special Privileges": Jeungwanyoo[13] Practice

After former government officials (including judges and prosecutors) left office to go into private practice as attorneys, they would use their former connections from the judiciary and prosecutor's office to request favors from former colleagues to get favorable outcomes for their clients. Their shared experiences of challenges in successfully passing the difficult judicial exam and intensive, two-year training at the JRTI built a strong sense of camaraderie that essentially resulted in an elite caste of legal professionals. With each graduating JRTI class, this practice of granting privileges became custom among the legal establishment.

Even the best-skilled attorneys could not compete with those using special privileges. Attorneys with prior experience in the judiciary or prosecutor's office could demand expensive legal fees to take on a case. Clients, who could afford to, would pay exorbitant fees to guarantee success for their legal case. The shortage of lawyers and the fees they could command with preferential treatment among the legal establishment created popular distrust of the legal profession.[14] The lack of judicial impartiality endangered the ethical operation of the judicial system for Korean society.

Lack of Diversity and Specialization

The lack of diversity and specialization in the legal profession would also become a target of judicial reforms. Year after year, the majority of those who passed the judicial exam were college graduates who majored in law and were relatively young males—between 25 and 30 years old.[15] Many new lawyers lacked "general knowledge and awareness of social issues" due to intense studies for the judicial exam. Korean legal professionals were generalists well versed in Korean law, but unable to deal with international law matters that required foreign law fluency and specialization in trade and finance. Later on, the public criticized the legal profession's arrogant attitude and air of superiority in practice toward citizen-clients.[16] The future-impending liberalization of the legal services market in 2009 helped proponents of reform in Korea resuscitate the 1995 judicial reform movement long opposed by the legal profession.

Are Law Schools Failing in Korea?

As other Asian[17] and Latin American[18] countries have considered legal education reform based upon the American law school model, examining the reform efforts and experiences of other countries like Korea could prove beneficial. In *Failing Law Schools*, Professor Brian Z. Tamanaha argued that American law schools are in crisis as "[t]he most problematic combination is a law school with high average indebtedness among graduates, a low percentage of lawyer jobs, and a low salary on graduation."[19] For the Korean case, even if individuals can afford the opportunity cost of attending law school for three years, they have to pass the bar exam within five years of graduation. Even if they succeed in passing the bar exam, there is a division between the lawyers who passed the judicial exam ("JRTI lawyers") and those who passed the bar exam ("JD lawyers"). With the introduction of law schools in 2009 and the new bar exam in 2012, the judicial exam was phased out with the last exam in 2017. Despite the reforms, the JRTI lawyers have been able to command higher salaries than the JD lawyers because they are perceived to be more skilled and better trained after surviving such intense competition through the exam and training. In addition, there is often a preference for lawyers who graduated from law schools in Seoul, which makes it difficult for new lawyers from law schools outside of Seoul to compete with the former group.

This chapter first reviews the reasons for the legal education reform and then examines the legal education reforms and how they affected law school admissions, faculty, curricula, bar passage, and recruitment. Based on data respective to these areas, this chapter investigates how and to what extent the demographics have changed. By comparing the data from the judicial and bar exams, the pool of successful JD students has shown an increase in more women, non-law majors, who are older than recent college graduates, which may mean more work experience prior to attending law school. This chapter concludes that while the reforms have succeeded in bringing more diversity to the legal profession in terms of gender, age, and work/study background, those same reforms have replicated patterns of elitism within the Korean legal profession.

Faculty, Admissions, and Curricula in the New Graduate Law School

In 2003, judicial reforms revived under President Roh Moo-Hyun and the Judicial Reformation Committee culminating in the National Assembly passing the Law for the Establishment and Operation of Law Schools on July 3, 2007.[20] Out of a total ninety-one colleges of law nationwide, the Korean government granted permission to only twenty-five schools to establish graduate law schools. Twenty-five new law schools modeled upon the American law school system opened their doors in March 2009 to 2000 students nationwide.

A main problem with pre-reform legal education at the undergraduate level stemmed from the full-time faculty who had doctorates in law but no legal practice experience. The Law School Act requires that at least 20 percent of the full-time faculty at each law school be practitioners with a minimum of five years of work experience[21] and a limit of fifteen students per full-time professor.[22] So, law schools sought to recruit Korean law practitioners to teach law students "how to think like lawyers" in more practical legal skills courses traditionally taught at the JTRI,[23] in addition to establishing legal clinics. Law students are also required to complete two-week externships to introduce them to the practice of law. In addition, law schools are also encouraged to hire foreign-licensed lawyers to teach foreign and international law in foreign languages (mainly English). Moreover, each school began to offer more diverse concentrations to promote specialization within the law.

The Law School Act also requires a more diverse student body. Historically, an overwhelming majority of those who passed the judicial exam had majored in law as undergraduates. Now, law schools are highly encouraged to enroll "students with diverse knowledge and experiences."[24] That is, students with work experience or specializations who would eventually add more specialization to the legal profession. According to research conducted by People's Solidarity for Participatory Democracy, a nongovernmental organization, admissions data provided by all twenty-five law schools listed a wide variety of students with work experience: doctors, pharmacists, nurses, veterinarians, oriental medical doctors, reporters, teachers, public servants, military personnel, patent lawyers, laborers, financial services personnel (e.g., fund managers), certified public accounts, office workers, legal department personnel, and so on.[25]

According to Article 23 ("Selection of Students") of the Law School Act, each law school should select students by two methods: (1) general screening and (2) special screening.[26] Most students are selected by general screening to meet the total enrollment number as determined by the minister of education, science, and technology.[27] However, law schools are required to grant admissions with full scholarship (pending academic performance each semester) to applicants recognized by the government to have special circumstances (i.e., veterans, people with disabilities, social welfare recipients, etc.). A minimum of 5 percent of the total annual enrollment at each law school should be dedicated to the recruitment for special screening. In addition, at least one-third of each entering class should come from non-law major backgrounds.[28] From 2009, the Korean Association of Law Schools categorized non-major student enrollment into the following twelve types: (1) economics; (2) social sciences; (3) humanities; (4) engineering; (5) natural sciences; (6) education; (7) medicine; (8) the arts and athletics; (9) pharmacology; (10) agriculture; (11) theology; and (12) other. The highest enrollment of non-majors was in 2009 with 1,294 (64.76 percent) students and the lowest of 937 (44.64 percent) in 2013, and an annual average of 53.42 percent.[29] Since the total number of students of all twenty-five law schools is roughly 2,000 per year, the one-third requirement at a minimum is 660 students nationwide each year. As seen from the data above, the combined statistics of all twenty-five schools satisfy minimum enrollment of non-law majors.[30] To encourage fair competition among the schools located in Seoul versus those in the provinces (and to offer more equal opportunities for its law students/graduates), at least one-third of the student body each year had to have graduated from a different university.[31] However, law schools appear to still prefer granting admissions to graduates from universities in Seoul. For example, Seoul National University Law school, which the most successful passers per year under both the judicial and bar exams, admitted 141 students (90.38 percent) out of its 156 students from Korea's top three universities in 2020: 141 (66.03 percent) from Seoul National University, 22 (14.1 percent) from Yonsei University, and 16 (10.26 percent) Korea University.[32] In comparison, only six students (3.8 percent) of the admitted students came from provincial universities with the remaining nine students (5.77 percent) from universities in Seoul.[33]

To apply to law school, applicants must have a bachelor's degree, take the Legal Education Eligibility Test (LEET) exam, and submit English- or other foreign-language test scores. Previously, gosinangins who gave up trying to pass the judicial exam often encountered difficulties with their job searches after failing to pass the judicial exam because they had to compete with younger college graduates. Requiring a bachelor's degree for law school admissions helped to prevent any problems associated with the gosinangin's job search after failing to pass the judicial exam.[34] Even if a law school graduate fails to pass the bar exam, his or her ability to look for a job fares better than the gosinangin since law school admissions are highly competitive and require excellent grade point averages. By establishing law schools as a graduate program, the fierce competition among high school seniors applying for admissions to colleges of law has been diffused.

Problems arose out of the new curricula, the compressed content, and the teaching ability of the practitioner-professors. Essentially, the new curricula are the mandatory core courses on the bar exam, the legal skills courses taught at the JTRI, and other electives branded as a part of the specialization and internationalization of the new law school education. Time-wise, the new law school curricula squeeze roughly five and a half years (four years of undergraduate law studies and one and a half years of practical training JRTI classes) into three years.[35] Students who did not major in law are often overwhelmed at the fast pace professors teach core bar exam courses, usually with rigorous testing throughout the semester. The ambitious syllabi of such courses leave little room for implementation of the Socratic method. Another complaint from students is that while some practitioner-professors have practice experience, their ability to teach students and effectively transfer what they know as a lawyer varies considerably from one person to another. Some proponents of the old judicial exam have stated that the cram school instructors are much more skilled at preparing students for the bar exam.[36] As schools sought to satisfy the 20 percent requirement for practitioner-professors in order to get law school certification, how effectively a prospective candidate could teach might not have been as great a priority in hiring criteria.

Despite efforts in creating fair competition among the law schools and their respective students, the preference for top-tier law school graduates is reflected in the numbers of law school students fulfilling their externship at major law firms. From 2009 to 2011, twenty-three out of the twenty-five law schools reported a total of 1,543 law students who had participated in externships at major law firms: 525 (34 percent) Seoul National University law students, 257 (16 percent) Korea University law students, and 204 (13 percent) Yonsei University law students took 63 percent of the total positions available.[37] The externship can be argued to be a gateway to further job prospects. However, many law school students (especially from the provincial law schools) have had difficulty in securing externships when trying to compete with law students in Seoul, especially the top three universities mentioned above.

Licensure and Career Paths

Before the establishment of law schools in Korea, the only path to the legal profession had two hurdles to overcome: (1) the extremely hard-to-pass judicial exam; and (2) the two-year practical training at the also competitive JRTI. Immediately upon graduation from the JRTI, judges, prosecutors, and lawyers emerged. Now, law students need to first graduate from law school, pass the new bar exam, and then complete a six-month practical training requirement before they are authorized to practice law or open their own legal practice.[38] Special requirements for those who want to pursue legal careers as judges and prosecutors involve testing and/or applications with other prerequisites apart from the new bar exam.

The New Bar Exam

By making having a JD degree a prerequisite for sitting for the new lawyer exam,[39] it limits the number of applicants that can sit for the bar exam to those candidates for graduation from the pre-screened pool of 2,000 students from twenty-five law schools admitted each year. In addition, test takers are restricted in how many times they can sit for the bar exam. Unlike before the new law school system was introduced, applicants are only given five times in five years after law school graduation to pass the annual bar exam.[40] The reforms have arguably solved many problems associated with the gosinangin with such prerequisites and restrictions while also increasing the supply of lawyers entering the legal market with the target quota of 1,500 successful candidates per year. However, many people are now barred from sitting for the new bar exam: those who had low GPAs or a lack of experience or extracurriculars during college, high school graduates who did not go onto college, or students who attended less prestigious universities.[41] Undergraduates from the three elite SKY[42] schools have comprised 48.14 percent of law school students from 2009 to 2017, with students from Seoul National University making up an overwhelming 88.7 percent of SKY graduates in the Class of 2017 at Seoul Law Schools.[43] Arguably, the introduction of law schools has not alleviated the social problems of the "hampering of social productivity and distorting the distribution of human resources" that it aimed to solve.[44]

Even so, some students majoring in law as undergraduates argued before the Korean Constitutional Court that the abolition of the judicial exam violated their basic right to occupational freedom as protected under the Korean Constitution.[45] From 2006 to 2015, college students (including college dropouts) consistently came in second place after college graduates in sitting for the judicial exam even surpassing college graduates in 2012 with 49.8 percent participation in the exam.[46] The Korean Constitutional Court ruled in 2016 that the Addendum to the Bar Examination Act, which stipulates the abolition of the judicial exam in 2017, and that the five times in five years restriction for sitting for the bar exam was constitutional.[47]

Diversity in the New Bar Exam

One of the main goals of the legal education reforms was to cultivate a more diverse and specialized legal profession to better serve the public. The quintessential JRTI lawyer was highly likely to be a young male who had majored in law as an undergraduate at one of the top universities in Seoul. Every year, the Ministry of Justice publishes bar exam statistics regarding the successful bar exam applicants, including but not limited to gender, undergraduate major (law or non-law), age ranges, and school affiliation. To examine to what extent the reforms have been successful in diversifying the legal profession through the adoption of the graduate law school, various data published by the Ministry of Justice for both the judicial exam and bar exams have been compiled and analyzed to show what trends have occurred.

Gender

As seen in Table 4.1 below, more males than females passed the judicial exam on an average of 61.07 percent over this nine-year period from 2009 to 2017. However, during this same period, a downward trend closing the male lead can be observed, starting from 28.78 percent in 2009, and eventually falling to 9.1 percent in 2017. The table also shows the successful candidates for the judicial exam by gender and males consistently capturing the majority of the pool with the highest point in 2014 with 66.67 percent and the lowest point in 2017 with 54.55 percent. From the total number of successful candidates for this nine-year period, males made up for 61.49 percent with females with 37.81 percent marking a 37.11 percent lead for males over females on a cumulative basis.

From 2012 to 2020, males outnumbered females in passing the bar exam with a high of 59.39 percent in 2016 and a low of 54.98 percent in 2020, as seen in Table 4.2 below. However, unlike the judicial exam statistics above, a noticeable decrease in the male lead can be observed with a wider gap of 18.78 percent in 2016 and a smaller gap of 9.96 percent in 2020. Under the bar exam, the gap between bar passage has narrowed considerably.

Major: Law or Non-Law

Under the judicial exam, the majority of successful applicants had majored in law. From 2009 to 2017, law majors accounted for anywhere between 74.55 percent in 2017 to 87.58 percent in 2015 of those who had passed, as seen in Table 4.3 below. Majoring

Table 4.1 Judicial Exam Passage by Gender (2009–17)

	Male	Female	Male–Female	Total
51st (2009)	642 (64.39%)	355 (35.61%)	28.78%	997
52nd (2010)	476 (58.48%)	338 (41.52%)	16.93%	814
53rd (2011)	443 (62.66%)	264 (37.34%)	25.32%	707
54th (2012)	295 (58.30%)	211 (41.70%)	16.6%	506
55th (2013)	183 (59.80%)	123 (40.20%)	19.6%	306
56th (2014)	136 (66.67%)	68 (33.33%)	33.34%	204
57th (2015)	94 (61.44%)	59 (38.56%)	22.88%	153
58th (2016)	69 (63.30%)	40 (36.70%)	26.6%	109
59th (2017)	30 (54.55%)	25 (45.45%)	9.1%	55

Source: *Beommuyeongam* [Judicial Yearbook], 2009–17.

Table 4.2 Bar Exam Passage by Gender (2012–20)

	Male	Female	Male–Female	Total
1st (2012)	856 (58.09%)	595 (41.01%)	17.08%	1,451
2nd (2013)	848 (55.14%)	690 (44.86%)	10.28%	1,538
3rd (2014)	869 (56.06%)	681 (43.94%)	12.12%	1,550
4th (2015)	893 (57.06%)	672 (42.94%)	14.12%	1,565
5th (2016)	939 (59.39%)	642 (40.61%)	18.78%	1,581
6th (2017)	876 (54.75%)	724 (45.25%)	9.50%	1,600
7th (2018)	906 (56.66%)	693 (43.34%)	13.32%	1,599
8th (2019)	935 (55.29%)	756 (44.71%)	10.58%	1,691
9th (2020)	972 (54.98%)	796 (45.02%)	9.96%	1,768
Total	8,094 (56.43%)	6,249 (43.57%)	12.86%	14,343

Source: Compiled from The Annual Lawyer's Exam Statistics (2012–20), Ministry of Justice.

Table 4.3 Judicial Exam Passage by Major: Law v. Non-law (2009–17)

	Law	Non-law	Law–non-law	Total
51st (2009)	809 (81.14%)	188 (18.86%)	62.28%	997
52nd (2010)	686 (84.28%)	128 (15.72%)	68.56%	814
53rd (2011)	574 (81.19%)	133 (18.81%)	62.38%	707
54th (2012)	433 (85.57%)	73 (14.43%)	71.14%	506
55th (2013)	248 (81.05%)	58 (18.95%)	62.1%	306
56th (2014)	166 (81.37%)	38 (18.63%)	62.74%	204
57th (2015)	134 (87.58%)	19 (12.42%)	75.16%	153
58th (2016)	85 (77.98%)	24 (22.02%)	55.96%	109
59th (2017)	41 (74.55%)	14 (25.45%)	49.1%	55

Source: *Beommuyeongam* [Judicial Yearbook], 2009–17.

in law as an undergraduate appears to have greatly increased the likelihood of passing the judicial exam.

With the bar exam, however, the non-law majors can be seen to have outperformed the law majors five out of the past nine years, as shown in Table 4.4 below. Non-law majors started out strong in 2012 and 2013 by capturing 61.96 percent and 59.62 percent, respectively, of the successful applicant pool. Between 2014 and 2017, law majors took back the lead albeit less pronounced as seen in the judicial exam statistics above. Under the old system, successful non-law majors were an overwhelming minority. Now, non-law majors appear to be competing better against law majors on the bar exam and bringing more diverse educational backgrounds into their professional career as the reforms had intended.

Table 4.4 Bar Exam Passage by Major: Law v. Non-law (2012–20)

	Law	Non-law	Law–non-law	Total
1st (2012)	552 (38.04%)	899 (61.96%)	−23.92%	1,451
2nd (2013)	621 (40.38%)	917 (59.62%)	−19.24%	1,538
3rd (2014)	825 (53.23%)	725 (46.77%)	6.46%	1,550
4th (2015)	918 (58.66%)	647 (41.34%)	17.32%	1,565
5th (2016)	926 (58.57%)	655 (41.43%)	17.14%	1,581
6th (2017)	876 (54.75%)	724 (45.25%)	9.5%	1,600
7th (2018)	787 (49.22%)	812 (50.78%)	−1.56%	1,599
8th (2019)	698 (41.28%)	993 (58.72%)	−17.44%	1,691
9th (2020)	637 (36.03%)	1,131 (63.98%)	27.95%	1,768

Source: Compiled from the Annual Lawyer's Exam Statistics (2012–20), Ministry of Justice.

Age

Under the judicial exam, the majority of successful exam takers were twenty-five to twenty-nine years old from 2006 to 2015, with up to 53.53 percent in 2008 and 41.67 percent in 2014.[48] In the last two years that the judicial exam was offered, the thirty- to thirty-four-year-old group outperformed other age groups with 43.12 percent in 2016, and 47.27 percent in 2017. These statistics reinforce that the educational background of the most successful group with the judicial exam from 2006 to 2015 was college graduates. With the university degree requirement for law school admissions, bar exam applicants could arguably be older than the twenty-five to twenty-nine-year-old group from the judicial exam. From 2012 to 2020, males in the thirty- to thirty-four-year-old group surpassed other groups with the exception of females in the twenty- to twenty-nine-year-old group for 2016, 2017, and 2018 with 25.93 percent, 25.94 percent, and 23.51 percent, respectively.[49]

School Affiliation

Under the judicial exam, students from SKY universities were the most successful at passing the exam. Between 2006 and 2013, these three universities represented anywhere between 51.77 percent (2011) to 60.81 percent (2010) of successful test takers with Seoul National University dominating the group with 21.54 percent (2012) to 33.70 percent (2006). Likewise, as seen in Table 4.5 below, the SKY schools have been the most successful in producing new lawyers in Korea, which corresponds to their individual contributions of new lawyers admitted in the first ten years of the new bar exam. Notably, the only school outside of Seoul to get ranked in the top ten list is Yeongnam University with an overall pass rate of 90.72 percent for its law graduates. To some extent, these statistics help shed light on why attending law school in Seoul, especially at any of the SKY universities, is so competitive. Students admitted to these

Table 4.5 Ranking of Bar Passage by School (2012–21)

Rank	Law school (number of students admitted per year)	Total number of graduated students (2012–21)	Successful bar applicants (2012–21)	Percentage
1	Seoul National University (150)	1,448	1,371	94.68
2	Yonsei University (120)	1,141	1,083	94.65
3	Korea University (120)	1,156	1,080	93.69
4	Sungkyunkwan University (120)	1,148	1,056	91.99
5	Kyung Hee University (60)	572	524	91.61

Source: Compiled from the 10th Annual Lawyer's Exam Statistics (by School), Ministry of Justice.

law schools in Seoul have a better chance of passing the bar exam upon graduation and starting their career as a new lawyer.

By comparing the data from the judicial exam and the bar exam above, the pool of successful JD students has shown an increase in more women, non-law majors, who are older than recent college graduates, which may mean more work experience prior to attending law school. The one noticeable continuation from the judicial exam to the bar exam is the schools most successful in producing new lawyers. The SKY universities prove to noticeably outperform the other schools based on the cumulative data from the first ten years of bar exam performance.

The Six-Month Practical Training Requirement for New Lawyers

After passing the bar exam, all new lawyers are required to fulfill a practical training requirement before being admitted to the Korean bar. On May 17, 2011, an amendment to the Attorney-at-Law Act introduced a new practical training requirement on law school graduates who passed the bar. Article 31-2(1) of the Attorney-at-Law Act requires all law school graduates who have passed the lawyer exam to obtain practical training for at least six months prior to being admitted to the Korean Bar Association.[50] Furthermore, it restricts such graduates from representing clients before completing the six-month practical training requirement and also requires such graduates to train with more experienced lawyers (of at least five years) at law firms or partnerships. Any violation of the six-month practical training requirement is punishable by removal from the master roll of lawyers authorized to practice law for one year or a 10,000,000 Korean won fine.[51]

The purpose of this post-exam requirement is to prepare law school graduates with the practical skills to start entry-level work competently as a legal professional. Unlike their JRTI counterparts whose practical training was organized and administered by the JRTI (under the auspices of the Supreme Court) as an entire semester of structured practical training in the courts, prosecutor's office, or law firms, law school graduates are now solely responsible for finding and getting practical training before being able to register with the bar association and practice law. In 2012, when the first law school class graduated in Korea, only 600 of the 1,500 successful candidates on the bar exam had completed the practical training requirement because there were only 314 places designated for such training.[52] This left the other 286 individuals to find practical training on their own.

An alternative way to fulfill the practical training requirement is through the Korean Bar Association, which offers a six-month lecture course for 300,000 Korean won (about US$275).[53] Many law school graduates view this as a last resort since it usually means that they have not secured jobs. For those law school graduates who pass the bar exam and have jobs waiting for them after graduation, the practical training requirement commences upon employment. After six months, the restrictions to practice law or open up a practice are lifted for everyone who has completed the requirement.

Some view the six-month practical training requirement as discriminatory. JRTI graduates are recognized as lawyers able to practice upon graduation and can even perform certain legal services during their practical training at the courts, prosecutor's office, or law firms. In a recent case brought before the Constitutional Court of Korea, three law school graduates argued that their right to freedom of employment was infringed by the six-month practical training requirement and other restrictions on the practice of law during such training and 2011 amendments to the Attorney-at-Law Act.[54] However, the Constitutional Court found that such a requirement and accompanying restrictions were not unconstitutional since the requirement was necessary to ensure a skilled legal profession from the new law school system. More recently, problems with procuring adequate practical training opportunities for new law school graduates have emerged. Lack of quality training and proper treatment for new lawyer-trainees has prompted discussions among the legal profession, including the Korean Bar Association, lawmakers, and law schools. Some call for the abolition of the six-month requirement, while others propose for such training to be scheduled between the semesters during law school.[55]

Employment in the Legal Profession

The judicial exam and the JRTI training structure produced judges and prosecutors who wielded formidable bureaucratic authority and power. Lawyers were also members of this elite caste. The ills of the legal profession arose out of the way judges and prosecutors were selected from the graduating JRTI. Many of those selected who came into power based on merit saw themselves entitled to special privilege. Two ways judicial reform sought to solve these problems were through changing the way judges were appointed and closely monitoring caseloads of former judges and prosecutors going into private practice.

The Unification of the Legal Profession: The 2011 Amendment to the Court Organization Act

In 2011, the Court Organization Act was amended[56] to conform to a unified legal system to replace the way judges were appointed.[57] Gone are the days where top JRTI scores promised prestigious positions as judges. Problems arising from judges' lack of real-world experience outside of intensive legal studies alone led to judicial decisions and behavior lacking common sense.[58] For example, an unmarried female judge had disclosed to the press public details of private divorce proceedings she had decided on, which resulted in a loss of confidence in the judiciary.[59]

The amendment requires a minimum of ten years of professional legal experience as a prerequisite for eligibility for judgeships. Beginning with the appointment of judges from January 1, 2013, the amendment gradually increases the requirement for appointment of judges from three years until December 31, 2017; to five years until December 31, 2021; to seven years until December 31, 2025; and finally to the full ten years for those judges appointed after January 1, 2026.[60] A gradual increase in the work experience requirement began in 2014 with the forty-third JRTI graduating class and the third law school graduating classes, whose prospective applicants need to accrue at least three years of legal experience before applying for a judgeship. Since neither the remaining JRTI graduates nor law school graduates who successfully pass the bar are able to become judges immediately, the amendment effectively changed graduates' preferences for prospective employment from judge, prosecutor, and then attorney to prosecutor, attorney, and then judge.[61] As a result, law clerks who have excellent academic achievement and who have passed the difficult law clerk exam[62] are in a quandary because they need to look outside of the courts to fulfill the time requirement in order to apply for a judgeship later. Since law clerks hold two-year positions at courts, law firms do not see any benefit in training and hiring former law clerks who will only work for one year to return to the courts. Some law firms refuse to participate in what they refer to as a "revolving door" of employment since a number of clerks still go to law firms and then back to the courts.[63]

Employment for Law School Graduates

The first graduating law school class from all twenty-five schools in 2012 had an employment average of 60.7 percent,[64] 73 percent for the second graduating class in 2013,[65] and 92.6 percent for the third graduating class in 2014.[66] With the changes in the appointment of judges and the separate exams for prosecutors and law clerks, less than 10 percent of law graduates found jobs in the historical upper echelon of the legal profession in 2012 and 2013, as seen in Table 4.6 below. For those same years, just over 5 percent of graduates landed coveted jobs in the "Top 6" law firms with starting salaries of 150,000,000 Korean won.[67]

For over more than 85 percent of each graduating class in 2012 and 2013, starting salaries were a fraction of "Top 6" law firms. For example, a named partner in charge of hiring at a law office in Seoul acknowledged that JRTI graduates are seen as superior to

Table 4.6 Postgraduate Employment for First and Second Law School Graduates (2012 and 2013)

	First graduating class (2012)	**Second graduating class (2013)**
Prosecutor	42 (2.89%)	37 (2.51%)
Law clerk	100 (6.89%)	50 (3.39%)
Top 6 law firms*	75 (5.17%)	77 (5.21%)
Other (Medium-small law firm, business, government, etc.)	123 (85.04%)	1313 (88.9%)
Total number of graduates	1451	1477

* The top six law firms in Korea currently are considered to be: Kim & Chang; Shin & Kim; Bae, Kim, & Lee; Lee & Ko; Yulchon; and Yoon & Yang; Data based on all twenty-five law schools.Source: Dong-eun Kim and Hyeonjeong Lee, "Roseukul 2gi Byeonhosasihom Hapgyeokja 1477myeongui Jinro," *MK News*, May 6, 2013, https://www.mk.co.kr/news/society/5541623.

law school graduates: "All things equal between two such candidates, I could hire a law school graduate for two million Korean won per month, which is noticeably less than a graduate would be offered for the same position."[68] The more senior JRTI lawyers appear to place greater preconceived value on their JRTI juniors, which has created a systematic bias in the legal profession in Korea. Other sources report that law school graduates only receive 70 percent to 80 percent of what JRTI graduates are offered in salaries: 40 million Korean won for the law school graduate and 50 million Korean won for the JRTI graduate.[69] However, as the number of lawyers increase, lawyers' salaries seem to be decreasing. In 2002, starting salaries for lawyers were 80 million to 100 million Korean won a year; in 2008 or 2009, 50 million to 60 million Korean won; and in 2012, 30 million won per year—less than what a new hire at a large conglomerate would make straight out of college.[70] Similarly, a JD lawyer shared that different treatment has appeared in other ways before the judicial exam was abolished in 2017: While a JRTI graduate may get to have his or her own office, two law school graduates may have to share an office.[71]

The law schools located in Seoul, especially the SKY universities, have proven to be the most successful in not only bar passage, but also employment for their graduates. The employment data for new lawyers in 2017[72] showed that Seoul National University ranked first in overall employment with 123 out of 150 students employed after graduation. Law firms were the biggest employers listed, employing 583 new lawyers. Fifty-four students of the Seoul National University graduating students that year were hired by law firms, followed by Yonsei University with forty-eight students, and Korea University with forty-five students.

By looking at legal profession statistics for lawyers, prosecutors, and judges in Table 4.7 below, female representation overall in the legal profession has dramatically increased.

Table 4.7 Women Representation in the Legal Profession by Role (Male–Female Analysis)

		Total	Lawyer	Prosecutor	Judge
2006	Total	12,211	2,221	1,567	8,423
	Male	11,011	1,846	1,386	7,779
	Female	1,200	375	181	644
	Female percentage	9.8	16.9	11.6	7.6
2008	Total	14,228	2,378	1,671	10,165
	Male	12,457	1,879	1,411	9,154
	Female	1,771	499	260	1,011
	Female percentage	12.4	21.0	15.6	9.9
2010	Total	14,616	2,532	1,782	10,302
	Male	12,424	1,913	1,417	9,094
	Female	2,192	619	365	1,208
	Female percentage	15.0	24.4	20.5	11.7
2012	Total	17,116	2,738	1,865	12,513
	Male	13,948	2,005	1,425	10,518
	Female	3,168	733	440	1,995
	Female percentage	18.5	26.7	23.6	15.9
2014	Total	19.696	2,770	1,985	14,941
	Male	15,425	2,015	1,453	11,957
	Female	4,271	755	532	2,984
	Female Percentage	21.7	27.3	26.8	20.0
2015	Total	25,380	2,851	1,998	20,531
	Male	18,901	2,057	1,440	15,404
	Female	6,479	794	558	5,127
	Female percentage	25.5	27.8	27.9	25.0
2017	Total	25,255	20,182	2,076	2,997
	Male	18,651	15,065	1,468	2,118
	Female	6,604	5,117	608	879
	Female percentage	26.1	25.4	29.3	29.3

Source: Hanguk Yeoseong Jeongchaek Yeonguwon, "Yeoseong Beobjoin Hyeonhwang (Jigeopbyeol), 2006–2019," accessed July 18, 2025, at https://gsis.kwdi.re.kr/statHtml/statHtml.do?orgId=338&tblId=DT_1HB1109N.

Despite the predominantly male lead over females in the legal profession, the data clearly shows the gap is closing from 9.8 percent in 2006 to 26.1 percent in 2017. Before 2012, the majority of females can be seen in the lawyer category, then the prosecutor, and then the judge. However, the gap between the three groups starts to shrink until 2015, when female representation in prosecutors overtakes lawyers by 0.1 percent.

Then, in 2017, female representation in judges catches up with prosecutors with both resulting in 29.3 percent participation in each group.

Conclusion

The legal education reforms aimed at producing more diverse and qualified lawyers, while resolving long-standing issues of stagnation of human resources associated with the former judicial exam. From 2012 to 2021, 16,049 law students (or 76.86 percent of admitted students) have passed the bar exam. In 2019, the Korean Bar passed a milestone of 30,000 registered lawyers and continues to expand with approximately 1,600 students passing the bar each year.[73] Despite the resistance by the legal establishment in Korea to judicial reform, sweeping changes in legal education based on the American law school model have brought more diversity and promise of increased specialization in the legal profession in Korea. Law school regulations on admissions have had the effect of producing more women, non-law majors, and students with work experience and specialties to pursue legal studies, which has successfully produced a more diverse class of lawyers.

The findings show that the legal education reforms that established law schools and the bar exam have brought much more diversity into the legal profession in Korea in regard to gender, majors, and age. In terms of gender, males were more predominant in the judicial exam, which automatically meant more of presence in the JRTI and legal profession overall. Unlike the judicial exam where law majors comprised an overwhelming majority (75–88 percent) of exam passers, non-law majors have outnumbered law majors in bar exam passage with a lead of 64 percent in 2020, and an overall lead five out of the past nine years since the bar exam was first administered in 2012. Age-wise, the most successful age group was college graduates in the judicial exam. However, now with law school graduation as a requirement to sit for the bar exam, older test takers have led the pack of successful individuals. From 2012 to 2020, males in the thity- to thirty-five-year-old group surpassed other groups with the exception of females in the twenty-five- to twenty-nine-year-old group for the 2016 to 2018 exams. Lastly, the top-performing schools from the judicial exam era remain the same even after the legal reforms. School affiliation in the legal profession remains elitist. The SKY schools still take the top three positions for overall bar passage, followed by other law schools located in Seoul. Law schools from the provinces—especially those with smaller student enrollments—have found it hard to compete with the law schools in Seoul. Law schools have stratified the legal profession even more than before—JRTI lawyer v. JD lawyer—with SKY and in-Seoul law schools coming out on top.

One of the main complaints and criticisms about the new law schools in Korea, however, concerns the high price of tuition. In addition to four years of undergraduate tuition, students interested in pursuing careers in law are now required to pay anywhere from 10 million to 20 million Korean won per year in tuition alone, absent scholarships or grants.[74] A recent survey of law school graduates found that the average education loan amounted to 29,570,000 Korean won with an average repayment period of 4.14 years.[75] As discussed above, the increase of lawyers in the Korean bar has brought lawyers' salaries down a great deal due to competition with other law school graduates, but also JRTI graduates, who prospective employers arguably prefer. Critics of law schools in Korea have argued that the high costs only allow those with financial means to attend and make it more elite, which bars entrance for those with lesser means. Even after successful entry into the legal profession, JD lawyers are often perceived to be less skilled than the JRTI lawyers by employers and clients frequently resulting in different positions and salaries. With the increase in bar membership, intense competition for law firm jobs has forced new lawyers to seek employment in corporations, public institutions, and other nontraditional positions in government, business, and other organizations. Even within the JD lawyer cohort, those who graduated from law schools in Seoul, especially the SKY universities, have a better chance of landing a job at a coveted law firm job in Seoul.

While the regulation of law schools in Korea has undoubtedly produced more lawyers from diverse backgrounds into the legal profession, the reforms in legal education has made it more difficult to pursue a career in law because graduating from law school is a mandatory prerequisite to sitting for the bar exam, which has brought about litigation in the Constitutional Court from individuals claiming violation of their basic right to occupational freedom. Calls for more reforms to law schools, including the establishment of online and evening law schools to accommodate people with full-time jobs, have been proposed to create more opportunities to study to become a lawyer. In order for diversity in the legal profession in Korea to increase, more people from different types of backgrounds should be given the opportunity and assistance in attending law school. Further research and discussion between lawyers, law schools, and legislators need to take place to find ways to make law school more accessible to a wider range of people.

Notes

1 Dai-Kwon Choi, "Judicial Reform in Perspective with Particular Focus on Legal Education," in *Judicial System Transformation in the Globalizing World*, eds. Dai-Kwon Choi and Kahei Rokumoto (Seoul: Seoul National University Press, 2007), 304.

2 The judicial exam's focused on the selection and training future judges and prosecutors. *See* Dae-Kyu Yoon, *Law and Political Authority in South Korea* (Boulder: Westview Press and Kyungnam University Press, 1990), 112.

3 Dae-Kyu Yoon, "The Paralysis of Legal Education in Korea," in *Legal Reform in Korea*, ed. Tom Ginsburg (London: Routledge, 2004), 38.

4 *Ibid.* at 40.

5 "Gosi" means state examination and "nangin" means unemployed person.

6 In addition to the judicial exam, two other national exams for foreign affairs and civil service have come under reform. Se-jin Gwon, "Isyu: Oemugosi Pyejihago Silsihan 'Oegyogwanhuboja Seonbalsiheom' Ttukkeong Yeoreoboni," *Chosun Ilbo*, November 30, 2013, https://monthly.chosun.com/client/news/viw.asp?nNewsNumb=201312100018; Jin-young Lee, "Sabbeopgosi, Oemugosi Pyeji …

Ijeneun Haengjeonggosi," *EToday*, March 17, 2015, https://www.etoday.co.kr/news/view/1091992.

7 Chang-rok Kim, "Byeonhosasihom Yebisihom Doip, Sasi Jonchiui Budangseong," in *Beobhak Jeonmun Daehagwon Hyeonhan Gwanryeon Gongcheonghoe: Roseukul Chulbeom 6nyeonui Hyeonhwanggwa Gwaje*, ed. Hangug Eonron Jinheungjaedan (Seoul: Hangug Eonron Jinheungjaedan, 2014), 95–110.

8 *Ibid.*

9 Simon Spencer Reyner Lee, "Legal Education in Korea: New Law School Reforms," in *Legal Education in Asia: Globalization, Change, and Contexts*, eds. Stacey Steele and Kathryn Taylor (England: Routledge, 2010), 169–82.

10 "Business services: constraints on entry, form of practice, advertising and foreign participation have limited the size of this sector and should be relaxed. For example, the decision to cap total enrolment in law schools at 2 000, despite the fact that the number of lawyers per capita in Korea is only a quarter of the OECD average, restricts competition and keeps prices high" (OECD, "OECD Economic Surveys, Korea," accessed July 19, 2025, http://oecd.org/content/dam/oecd/en/publications/reports/2008/12/oecd-economic-surveys-korea-2008_g1gha18e/eco_surveys-kor-2008-en.pdf).

11 Lee, *supra* note 9, at 171.

12 *Ibid.*

13 "Jeungwanyewoo" literally means "granted privileges from prior post."

14 Choi, *supra* note 1, at 309.

15 Ministry of Justice, *Beommuyeongam* [Judicial Yearbook] (Ministry of Justice, Republic of Korea, 2004), 338. For example, out of the 1,009 people who passed the bar exam in 2004, 763 (75.6 percent) were men; 446 (44.20 percent) were between 25 and 30 years old; 549 (54.41 percent) were college graduates; and 748 (74.13 percent) had majored in law.

16 Choi, *supra* note 1, at 304.

17 Thomas Chih-hsiung Chen, "Legal Education Reform in Taiwan: Are Japan and Korea the Models?" *Journal of Legal Education* 62, no. 1 (2012): 32–65.

18 Juny Montoya, "The Current State of Legal Education Reform in Latin America: A Critical Approach," *Journal of Legal Education* 59, no. 4 (2009): 545–66.

19 Brian Z. Tamanaha, *Failing Law Schools* (Chicago: University of Chicago Press, 2012), 154.

20 Act on the Establishment and Management of Professional Law Schools, Act No. 8544 (passed July 27, 2007; enforced September 28, 2007).

21 *See ibid.* Article 16(4).

22 *See ibid.* Article 16(1).

23 For example, law schools offer civil practice attorney skills, criminal practice attorney skills, and prosecutor skills courses.

24 *See* Law School Act, *supra* note 20, Article 26(1).

25 Chamyeoyeondae, "[Toronhoe] Roseukul Doip 5nyeon Jeomgeomgwa Gaeseonbanghyang," accessed July 19, 2025, at https://www.peoplepower21.org/Judiciary/1037503.

26 *See* Law School Act, *supra* note 20, Article 23.

27 *See ibid.* Article 7.

28 *See ibid.* Article 26(2).

29 Chamyeoyeondae, *supra* note 25.
30 Whether or not each school has satisfied the requirement cannot be ascertained from the data provided by the Korean Association of Law Schools.
31 *See* Law School Act, *supra* note 20, Article 26(3).
32 Hye-seong An, "Olhaedo Seouldae Roseukul Sinipsaeng 'Yeorui Ahop SKY Chulsin," *Beomnyul Jeoneol* [The Law Journal], March 6, 2020, http://www.lec.co.kr/news/articleView.html?idxno=745936.
33 *Ibid.*
34 Kim, *supra* note 7, at 102. Statistics on the number of 16,500 successful judicial exam applicants from 1981 to 2010 show that 8,423 people were university graduates (51 percent); 3,517 people were enrolled in or had graduated from graduate school (21 percent); and only 29 people had community college or lower educational backgrounds (0.18 percent). President Roh Moo-Hyun (2003–8) was the only high school graduate to pass the seventeenth Judicial Exam in 1975.
35 The last semester of on-site practical training conducted at the courts, the prosecutor's office, or law firms for JRTI trainees has been excluded from the calculation above.
36 Beomnyul Jeoneol [The Law Journal], "Naneun Wae Heonbeopsowon Cheongguhaetna … Byeonhosasihom Eungsijagyeok Hwagdahael Iyuu," *Beomnyul Jeoneol* [The Law Journal], May 2, 2018, http://www.lec.co.kr/news/articlePrint.html?idxno=47492.
37 Hu-yeon Lee, "Roseukul Jaehaksaengui Bulpyeonhan Jinsil, Dong-Seoryeol-Gyeongjaeng … Yebi Beobjoinui 'Samjunggo,'" *Hankyung Gyeongje Maegajin*, August 13, 2012, https://magazine.hankyung.com/business/article/202102246441b.
38 Attorney-at-Law Act [Act No. 10627] (May 17, 2011), Articles 32-2(1) and 21-2(1).
39 National Bar Examination Act, Act No. 10923 (July 25, 2011) ("Bar Exam Act"), Article 5(1)(2).
40 *See ibid.* Article 7.
41 Seong-su Hong, "Hanguk Roseukul Ip'ak Jedoui Munjejeom: Gongjeongseonggwa Dayangseongeul Jungsimeuro," *Beobhak Nonchong* 23 no. 2 (2016): 105.
42 "SKY" refers to Seoul National University, Korea University, and Yonsei University. Collectively, SKY is regarded as the three most elite universities in Korea.
43 Eun-ji Yun, "2017 Seouldaeroseukul Hapgyeokja 'SKY Chulsin 88.7%' [88.7% of the Class of 2017 in Seoul Law Schools Are SKY Graduates]," *Veritas*, July 25, 2017, http://www.veritas-a.com/news/articleView.html?idxno=90503.
44 Won Soon Kim, "A Study of Occupational Freedom in the German and Korean Constitutions and Examination of the Constitutionality of the Korean Law School's Admission System," *KLRI Journal of Law and Legislation* 8, no. 2 (2018): 192.
45 Heonbeop Jaepanso, 2016Heonma267 (Byeonghap), September 29, 2016.
46 Ministry of Justice, *Beommuyeongam* [Judicial Yearbook] (Ministry of Justice, Republic of Korea, 2006–15).
47 *Ibid.*
48 Ministry of Justice, *Beommuyeongam* [Judicial Yearbook] (Ministry of Justice, Republic of Korea, 2006–17).
49 *Ibid.*
50 Attorney-at-Law Act, *supra* note 38, Article 32-2(1).
51 *See ibid.* Article 113.

52 Eun-jae Lee, "Roseukul Joreupsaeng Uimuyonsu 'Geudongan Hyetaegibeun Ropeom-i Damdanghaeya,'" *Legal Times*, March 7, 2012, https://legaltimes.co.kr/news/articleView.html?idxno=15102.
53 *See* Korean Bar Association website (in Korean): http://www.koreanbar.or.kr/training/train01_list.asp.
54 Heonbeop Jaepanso, 2012Heonma480 (October 24, 2013) (Byeonhosa Beop Je31jo-ui2 Je1hwa Wiheon Hwagin) [Hyeongongje 205ho].
55 Su-jin Choi, "Sinip Byeonhosa Silmususeup Jedo, Kkok Piryohanga?" *Beopjo Sinmun*, January 25, 2021, https://news.koreanbar.or.kr/news/articleView.html?idxno=22765.
56 Law No. 10861 (July 18, 2011), Amendment to Court Organization Act No. 12188 (January 7, 2014).
57 While this law only applies to the appointment of judges, some say that prosecutors should also be selected from an experienced pool of candidates. As of May 2015, the prosecutor's office selects both experienced candidates who were licensed under the JRTI system and new law school graduates. Law school students who are interested to apply to the prosecutor's office have to take certain practical training courses for prosecutors during law school, submit an application, pass a prosecutor's exam that tests criminal law and criminal procedure, and interview at the prosecutor's office upon passing the prosecutor's exam.
58 Yoon, *supra* note 3, at 114.
59 *Ibid.*
60 *See* Amendment to Court Organization Act, *supra* note 56, Article 42 ("Qualification for Appointment").
61 Sang-yeon Lee, "Sabbeopsihom Hapgyeoksaengdeul Geomsa Seonhodo 'Ssoeksssoek,'" *Beomnyul Jeoneol* [The Law Journal], October 17, 2014, http://www.lec.co.kr/news/articleView.html?idxno=34695.
62 A maximum of 200 law clerks are selected each year.
63 Seong-jin Lee, "Roseukul Chulshin Beobgwan 'Hoejeonmun Byeonron' Uihokkkaji," *Beomnyul Jeoneol* [The Law Journal], June 29, 2015, http://www.lec.co.kr/news/articleView.html?idxno=37188.
64 Sang-yeon Lee, "Roseukul 1gisaeng Pyeonggyun Chwieopnyul 62.4% … Ohaereun?" *Beomnyul Jeoneol* [The Law Journal], August 13, 2013, http://www.lec.co.kr/news/articleView.html?idxno=29177.
65 Chang-rok Kim, "Roseukul 2gi Joreupsaeng Chwieopnyul 73%," *Legal Times*, October 7, 2014, https://www.legaltimes.co.kr/news/articleView.html?idxno=23714.
66 Seong-jin Lee, "2014 Roseukul Chulshin Byeonhosa, Chwieopnyul 93%," *Beomnyul Jeoneol* [The Law Journal], February 27, 2015, http://www.lec.co.kr/news/articleView.html?idxno=35975.
67 Byeon-gil Kim, "Ilgam Mollin Daehyeong Ropeom Gwangjang Seongageup 10eokkkaji," *Hanguk Gyeongje*, December 19, 2011, http://www.hankyung.com/news/app/newsview.php?aid=2011121828821.
68 Uk Heo, "[Dallajin Byeonhosa Eopgye Pungsokdo] Jung-Sunansidae," *Asia Today*, November 12, 2014, http://www.asiatoday.co.kr/view.php?key=20141110010005872.
69 Hun Kang, "[Why] Roseukul Byeonhosa Gujik Jeonjaeng … 'Mugeumdo OK, Ildan Sseoboshijyo,'" *Chosun Ilbo*, June 23, 2012, https://www.chosun.com/site/data/html_dir/2012/06/22/2012062201278.html.
70 *Ibid.*

71 Heo, *supra* note 68.
72 Data collected and compiled from individual law school websites.
73 Sang-yeon Lee, "Byeonhosa Deungnok 3manmyeong Dolpa … 5nyeonsae 1manmyeong Neureo," *Beomnyul Jeoneol* [The Law Journal], December 18, 2019, http://www.lec.co.kr/news/articleView.html?idxno=715432.
74 Kim, *supra* note 7, at 124.
75 Jae Hyup Lee, June Woong Rhee, and Jung Hyun Hwang, "Roseukul Chulsin Beomnyulga, Geudeureun Nuguinga? [Law School Lawyers in Korea, Who Are They?]" *Seouldaehakgyo Beopak* [Seoul Law Journal] 56, no. 2 (2015): 367, 388.

Bibliography

An, Hye-seong. "Olhaedo Seouldae Roseukul Sinipsaeng Yeorui Ahop SKY Chulsin." *Beomnyul Jeoneol* [The Law Journal], March 6, 2020. http://www.lec.co.kr/news/articleView.html?idxno=745936.

Chamyeoyeondae. "[Toronhoe] Roseukul Doip 5nyeon Jeomgeomgwa Gaeseonbanghyang." Accessed July 19, 2025. https://www.peoplepower21.org/Judiciary/1037503.

Choi, Dai-Kwon. "Judicial Reform in Perspective with Particular Focus on Legal Education." In *Judicial System Transformation in the Globalizing World*, edited by Dai-Kwon Choi and Kahei Rokumoto, 287–318. Seoul: Seoul National University Press, 2007.

Choi, Su-jin. "Sinip Byeonhosa Silmususeup Jedo, Kkok Piryohanga?" *Beopjo Sinmun*, January 25, 2021. https://news.koreanbar.or.kr/news/articleView.html?idxno=22765.

Chen, Thomas Chih-hsiung. "Legal Education Reform in Taiwan: Are Japan and Korea the Models?" *Journal of Legal Education* 62, no. 1 (2012): 32–65.

Gwon, Se-jin. "Isyu: Oemugosi Pyejihago Silsihan 'Oegyogwanhuboja Seonbalsiheom' Ttukkeong Yeoreoboni." *Chosun Ilbo*, November 30, 2013. https://monthly.chosun.com/client/news/viw.asp?nNewsNumb=201312100018.

Hanguk Yeoseong Jeongchaek Yeonguwon. "Yeoseong Beobjoin Hyeonhwang (Jigeopbyeol), 2006–2019." Accessed July 18, 2025. https://gsis.kwdi.re.kr/statHtml/statHtml.do?orgId=338&tblId=DT_1HB1109N.

Heo, Uk. "[Dallajin Byeonhosa Eopgye Pungsokdo] Jung-Sunansidae." *Asia Today*, November 12, 2014. http://www.asiatoday.co.kr/view.php?key=20141110010005872.

Hong, Seong-su. "Hanguk Roseukul Ip'ak Jedoui Munjejeom: Gongjeongseonggwa Dayangseongeul Jungsimeuro [A Review of Korean Law School Concerning Fairness and Diversity in Admission]." *Beobhak Nonchong* 23, no. 2 (2016): 81–144.

Kang, Hun. "[Why] Roseukul Byeonhosa Gujik Jeonjaeng … 'Mugeumdo OK, Ildan Sseoboshijyo.'" *Chosun Ilbo*, June 23, 2012. https://www.chosun.com/site/data/html_dir/2012/06/22/2012062201278.html.

Kim, Byeon-gil. "Ilgam Mollin Daehyeong Ropeom Gwangjang Seongageup 10eokkkaji." *Hanguk Gyeongje*, December 19, 2011. http://www.hankyung.com/news/app/newsview.php?aid=2011121828821.

Kim, Chang-rok. "Byeonhosasihom Yebisihom Doip, Sasi Jonchiui Budangseong." In *Beobhak Jeonmun Daehagwon Hyeonhan Gwanryeon Gongcheonghoe: Roseukul Chulbeom 6nyeonui Hyeonhwanggwa Gwaje*, edited by Hangug Eonron Jinheungjaedan, 95–110. Seoul: Hangug Eonron Jinheungjaedan, 2014.

Kim, Chang-rok. "Roseukul 2gi Joreupsaeng Chwieopnyul 73%." *Legal Times*, October 7, 2014. https://www.legaltimes.co.kr/news/articleView.html?idxno=23714.

Kim, Dong-eun, and Hyeonjeong Lee. "Roseukul 2gi Byeonhosasihom Hapgyeokja 1477myeongui Jinro." *MK News*, May 6, 2013. https://www.mk.co.kr/news/society/5541623.

Kim, Won Soon. "A Study of Occupational Freedom in the German and Korean Constitutions and Examination of the Constiutionality of the Korean Law School's Admission System." *KLRI Journal of Law and Legislation* 8, no. 2 (2018): 163–205.

Lee, Eun-jae. "Roseukul Joreupsaeng Uimuyonsu 'Geudongan Hyetaegibeun Ropeom-i Damdanghaeya.'" *Legal Times*, March 7, 2012. https://legaltimes.co.kr/news/articleView.html?idxno=15102.

Lee, Hu-yeon. "Roseukul Jaehaksaengui Bulpyeonhan Jinsil, Dong-Seoryeol-Gyeongjaeng … Yebi Beobjoinui 'Samjunggo.'" *Hankyung Gyeongje Maegajin*, August 13, 2012. https://magazine.hankyung.com/business/article/202102246441b.

Lee, Jae Hyup, June Woong Rhee, and Jung Hyun Hwang. "Roseukul Chulsin Beomnyulga, Geudeureun Nuguinga? [Law School Lawyers in Korea, Who Are They?]" *Seouldaehakgyo Beopak* [Seoul Law Journal] 56, no. 2 (2015): 367–411.

Lee, Jin-young. "Sabbeopgosi, Oemugosi Pyeji … Ijeneun Haengjeonggosi." *EToday*, March 17, 2015. https://www.etoday.co.kr/news/view/1091992.

Lee, Sang-yeon. "Byeonhosa Deungnok 3manmyeong Dolpa … 5nyeonsae 1manmyeong Neureo." *Beomnyul Jeoneol* [The Law Journal], December 18, 2019. http://www.lec.co.kr/news/articleView.html?idxno=715432.

Lee, Sang-yeon. "Roseukul 1gisaeng Pyeonggyun Chwieopnyul 62.4% … Ohaereun?" *Beomnyul Jeoneol* [The Law Journal], August 13, 2013. http://www.lec.co.kr/news/articleView.html?idxno=29177.

Lee, Sang-yeon. "Sabbeopsihom Hapgyeoksaengdeul Geomsa Seonhodo 'Ssoeksssoek.'" *Beomnyul Jeoneol* [The Law Journal], October 17, 2014. http://www.lec.co.kr/news/articleView.html?idxno=34695.

Lee, Seong-jin. "2014 Roseukul Chulshin Byeonhosa, Chwieopnyul 93%." *Beomnyul Jeoneol* [The Law Journal], February 27, 2015. http://www.lec.co.kr/news/articleView.html?idxno=35975.

Lee, Seong-jin. "Roseukul Chulshin Beobgwan 'Hoejeonmun Byeonron' Uihokkkaji." *Beomnyul Jeoneol* [The Law Journal], June 29, 2015. http://www.lec.co.kr/news/articleView.html?idxno=37188.

Lee, Simon Spencer Reyner. "Legal Education in Korea: New Law School Reforms." In *Legal Education in Asia: Globalization, Change, and Contexts*, edited by Stacey Steele and Kathryn Taylor, 171–90. England: Routledge, 2010.

Ministry of Justice. *Beommuyeongam* [Judicial Yearbook]. Ministry of Justice, Republic of Korea, 2004 and 2006–17.

Montoya, Juny. "The Current State of Legal Education Reform in Latin America: A Critical Approach." *Journal of Legal Education* 59, no. 4 (2009): 545–66.

OECD. "OECD Economic Surveys, Korea." Accessed July 19, 2025. http://oecd.org/content/dam/oecd/en/publications/reports/2008/12/oecd-economic-surveys-korea-2008_g1gha18e/eco_surveys-kor-2008-en.pdf.

Tamanaha, Brian Z. *Failing Law Schools*. Chicago: University of Chicago Press, 2012.

Yoon, Dae-Kyu. *Law and Political Authority in South Korea*. Boulder: Westview Press and Kyungnam University Press, 1990.

Yoon, Dae-Kyu. "The Paralysis of Legal Education in Korea." In *Legal Reform in Korea*, edited by Tom Ginsburg, 36–46. London: Routledge, 2004.

Yun, Eun-ji. "2017 Seouldaeroseukul Hapgyeokja 'SKY Chulsin 88.7%' [88.7% of the Class of 2017 in Seoul Law Schools Are SKY Graduates]." *Veritas*, July 25, 2017. http://www.veritas-a.com/news/articleView.html?idxno=90503.

This chapter was previously published under the same title in Inha Law Review 24, no. 4 (2021): 349–387.

5

The Introduction of the Law School System and the Structure of the Legal Profession in Korea

Status and Prospects

Jae-Hyup Lee

Introduction

The number of legal professionals has rapidly grown in Korea.[1] After reaching 5,000 in 2001, the total number of registered lawyers surpassed 10,000 in just the next seven years; six years later, in 2014, the number had grown to more than 20,000. In addition, workplace environments, types of work, educational background of legal professionals, income level, and workplace size have also diversified.[2] More specifically, since 2012, the structure of the Korean legal profession has been transformed by the entry into the job market of legal professionals who, with the introduction of the law school system in 2009, went through an education and licensing process different from the previous national judicial examination system.

The law school system was introduced to contribute to the rule of law in Korea by educating and training "competent legal professionals" who could professionally and efficiently respond to the demand for legal services, which has been rapidly growing throughout the country, and react to changing international circumstances. To achieve the goal of this systemic reform, it is necessary to allow people with different socioeconomic backgrounds to enter the legal profession and pursue a variety of careers after completing their law school education and training. Because it has been five years since the first class of law school graduates was licensed as legal professionals, now is the time to examine empirically how this new cohort of professionals (the "Law School Graduates") is similar to and different from the generations of legal professionals who were qualified and licensed through the long-standing national judicial exam system, which included post-exam mandatory training at the Judicial Research and Training Institute (JRTI) (the "JRTI Trainees"). This comparative analysis is necessary to draw initial conclusions on whether the new system has been effective at advancing its goals.

In the United States, a systematic long-term study has been conducted on the American legal profession. The "After the JD" (AJD) project, jointly conducted by the National Association for Law Placement and the American Bar Foundation, tracked

5,000 legal professionals who graduated from law school in 2000.[3] That study analyzed from various angles the entry-level legal professionals' demographic composition, workplaces, work environments, incomes, satisfaction, turnover, the impact of gender and race and professional circumstances, and the role of law school experience; it then compared them after five and ten years to identify changes in the legal profession. The Japan Federation of Bar Associations has conducted a nationwide survey of its registered members every decade since 1980. Furthermore, Professor Setsuo Miyazawa and his research team conducted surveys in 2007, 2011, and 2014 and published their findings.[4]

This chapter presents the findings of a comprehensive study (the "Study") of the changes that have resulted from Korea's efforts to respond to its population's growing need for legal services, in particular the reform of legal education and attorney qualification and, relatedly, a new emphasis on diversified legal careers. The Study was conducted using the questionnaire method, informed by the AJD project in the United States and the survey studies in Japan. The Study focused on comparing the Law School Graduates with the JRTI Trainees by examining their socioeconomic backgrounds, career paths, work environments, and satisfaction, and then considering the implications of those comparative results for the ongoing efforts in Korea to accomplish the goals of legal profession reform.

Research Topics and Methods

Research Topics

The Study included four lines of research. The first line of research investigated the socioeconomic backgrounds of the Law School Graduates as compared with the JRTI Trainees who entered the legal profession. To measure socioeconomic background, the Study used variables such as parental socioeconomic status and parental educational level. Based on these variables, the Study examined whether parents of the Law School Graduates tend to have better jobs and/or higher levels of education than parents of the JRTI Trainees. Significantly, the Study also identifies whether there are legal professionals among their respective family members or relatives, and compares these two groups in that regard.

The second line of research considered diversity in the legal profession. More specifically, the Study examined whether the diversity of demographics and educational backgrounds identified in law school students results in diversity in occupations as the Law School Graduates enter the job market and pursue their legal careers. However, because most of the Law School Graduates are currently at an entry level, it is too early to observe many changes in jobs or to determine any trend in the occupational development of the Law School Graduates. In light of this, the Study analyzes the types of career paths that the Law School Graduates have taken so far, presents the framework for comparison based on this analysis, and discusses implications for future research.

The third line of research explored the work environment and job satisfaction of legal professionals. The Study included a multifaceted examination of annual salary, work environment, job satisfaction, and future prospects among and between the Law School Graduates and the JRTI Trainees.

The fourth and last line of research investigated what factors affect annual salaries and satisfaction in the legal profession. A previous study conducted in the United States reported that the gap between professionals in large law firms and those in other legal employment settings is widening, and that work environments continue to differ based on the race of legal professionals. In a similar way, the Study examines whether a high-ranking undergraduate school or a prestigious law school makes a difference in annual salary and job satisfaction in Korea, and whether this trend is more pronounced among the Law School Graduates than among their JRTI Trainee counterparts.

Research Methods

To identify whether the Law School Graduates are different from the JRTI Trainees in terms of background, viewpoint, and career orientation, the Study divided the legal professionals in Korea into three groups and applied a research method that established three samples representing each of these groups. The first group is Law School Graduates from the first to third classes of law school (those who entered law school from 2009 to 2011). The second group is JRTI Trainees who were trained in the JRTI in the same period as the Law School Graduates group attended law school (JRTI Trainees entering the JRTI from 2009 to 2012, or the fortieth to forty-third classes of the JRTI) (the "Peer JRTI Trainees"). The third group is JRTI Trainees who entered the JRTI before 2008 (the thirty-ninth and earlier classes of the JRTI) (the "Career JRTI Trainees"). The Study used these legal professional groups as populations for study and statistical analysis and used the *Database of Korean Legal Professionals* published by *The Law Times* as the sampling frame to take the three samples representing each of these three populations. In terms of region, the Study limited the subjects to legal professionals based in Seoul and the metropolitan areas of six other Korean cities.

The Study used systematic sampling, one of the random sampling methods. This method obtains the list of all those within a population who can be sampled from the sampling frame and selects the subjects at intervals that are calculated by dividing the population size by the desired sample size. With a target response rate of 20 percent, researchers initially made telephone requests to 5,026 legal professionals to complete a survey questionnaire; the number who completed the response in the initial samples (including recontact) was 719, while the number who completed the response after contact was 539, a response rate of 10.8 percent. The response rate by group was 20.7 percent for the Law School Graduates, 15.4 percent for the Peer JRTI Trainees, and 4.2 percent for the Career JRTI Trainees. To meet the target sample size, the researchers contacted the next target respondents in the sampling frame. As a result, the survey was completed for a total of 1,020 respondents: 308 in the target (Law School Graduates) group, 300 in the comparison (Peer JRTI Trainees) group, and 412 in the evaluation (Career JRTI Trainees) group.

The survey method used both oral interviews and written questionnaires. After requesting an interview by phone, researchers conducted in-person interviews with those legal professionals who said they would respond to the survey through meetings in their offices. For those who said they could not participate in person, a link was sent by e-mail to an online version of the questionnaire. Data were collected as described above. The research was conducted for two months beginning in August 2014, and the survey was conducted by Ipsos Korea, a research firm.

The questionnaire consisted of approximately thirty pages of structured questions. It contained questions common to all three groups, as well as questions unique to each group. All the groups were asked about their current workplace, job duties, and employment status. Respondents were also asked about their views and beliefs as legal professionals and their socioeconomic backgrounds.

Characteristics of the Respondents

Professional characteristics are shown in Table 5.1. In all three groups of legal professionals, lawyers in various forms of private practice (including at firms and in-house) accounted for the highest percentage (96.8 percent) of the final samples. The fact that the percentages of prosecutors (0.6 percent) and judges (2.6 percent) in the samples are very low indicates that their response rate was very low. Notably, no one in the Law School Graduates group had been yet appointed as a judge, and the one prosecutor respondent in that group was a law clerk.

Of the 1,020 respondents, 88 percent worked in Seoul, which was higher than the percentage of the population (i.e., the sampling frame) in Seoul (80.5 percent). While there was no significant difference between the proportion of the population and the sample of Law School Graduates based in Seoul, it was found that the Peer JRTI Trainees and Career JRTI Trainees based in Seoul responded relatively more than those based in other regions.

In terms of characteristics of the respondents based on career type (Table 5.2), the male respondents in the Career JRTI Trainees group accounted for 81.6 percent, which was relatively higher than in the Law School Graduates group and the Peer JRTI Trainees group. The average age was 42.8 in the Career JRTI Trainees group, followed by an average age of thirty-four for both the Peer JRTI Trainees group (34.1) and the Law School Graduates group (33.9). In regard to current workplace, about 60 percent of the respondents worked at Korean law firms, while the percentage of solo practitioners was higher in the Career JRTI Trainees group (12.1 percent) and the percentage of those working for companies and financial institutions was higher in the Law School Graduates group (19.2 percent).

Many of the respondents worked at large law firms, including Kim & Chang; Bae, Kim & Lee; Shin & Kim; Yulchon; Lee & Ko; and Yoon & Yang. The five largest law firms employed 17.9 percent of the respondents. In addition to those working at large law firms, most of the other respondents worked at small and medium law firms, listed companies, and solo practitioner law offices, while the response rate of those working in public institutions (local government, state-run companies, etc.) was relatively high. This distribution of occupations in the samples appears to generally represent the current landscape of the Korean law market.

Sampling frame		Law School Graduates		Peer JRTI Trainees		Career JRTI Trainees		Total	
		Sample	Sampling frame	Sample	Sampling frame	Sample	Sampling frame	Sample	Sampling frame
Total 9.1%		1,262	308	1,744	300	10,937	412	13,943	1,020
		30.2%	12.5%	29.4%	78.4%	40.4%			
Occupa-tion	1. Prosecutor	28	1	63	2	927	3	1,018	6
		2.2%	0.3%	3.6%	0.7%	8.5%	0.7%	7.3%	0.6%
	2. Judge	8	3	180	10	1,559	14	1,747	27
		0.6%	1.0%	10.3%	3.3%	14.3%	3.4%	12.5%	2.6%
	3. Lawyer (private practice)	1183	304	1489	288	8326	395	10,998	987
		93.7%	98.7%	85.4%	96.0%	76.1%	95.9%	78.9%	96.8%
	4. Others	43	-	12	-	125	-	180	-
		3.4%	0.0%	0.7%	0.0%	1.1%	0.0%	1.3%	0.0%
Region	1. Seoul	923	265	1,470	271	8664	362	11,057	898
		87.3%	86.0%	84.3%	90.3%	79.2%	87.9%	80.5%	88.0%
	2. Busan	37	13	69	5	590	17	696	35
		3.5%	4.2%	4.0%	1.7%	5.4%	4.1%	5.1%	3.4%
	3. Daegu	18	6	48	5	437	9	503	20
		1.7%	1.9%	2.8%	1.7%	4.0%	2.2%	3.7%	2.0%
	4. Incheon	18	7	55	8	435	7	508	22
		1.7%	2.3%	3.2%	2.7%	4.0%	1.7%	3.7%	2.2%
	5. Gwangju	28	10	43	5	312	7	383	22
		2.7%	3.2%	2.5%	1.7%	2.9%	1.7%	2.8%	2.2%
	6. Daejeon	23	5	33	5	337	4	393	14
		2.2%	1.6%	1.9%	1.7%	3.1%	1.0%	2.9%	1.4%
	7. Ulsan	10	2	26	1	162	6	198	9
		1.0%	0.6%	1.5%	0.3%	1.5%	1.5%	1.4%	0.9%
	8. Unidentified	205	-	-	-	-	-	205	-

Table 5.2 Respondents' Characteristics by Career Type

(%) 308 Law School Graduates		**Career type**		
		300 Peer JRTI Trainees	**412 Career JRTI Trainees**	
Gender	Male	59.7	54.0	81.6
	Female	40.3	46.0	18.4
Age	20s	9.1	7.3	-
	30~34	52.6	57.0	13.1
	35~39	29.9	27.7	27.9
	40~44	8.1	6.7	25.5
	45~49	0.3	1.0	14.1
	50 or older	-	0.3	19.4
	Average	33.9	34.1	42.8
Workplace (current)	Solo practitioner	10.1	8.3	12.1
	Korean law firm	60.4	59.0	61.7
	Court or prosecutor's office	1.0	3.7	4.1
	State-run company or public institution	5.2	4.0	4.6
	Company or financial institution	19.2	18.0	13.8
	Others	4.2	7.0	3.6

The Law School Graduates group represented a broad cross section of the current law school landscape, with at least three graduates of twenty-four out of the twenty-five law schools in Korea responding. Of the respondents in the Law School Graduates group, 62 percent were based in Seoul, with 38 percent working in other cities. The law schools with the highest numbers of respondents were, in the following order and with the following percentages of the total respondents: Seoul National University (17.21 percent), Sungkyunkwan University (7.47 percent), Ewha Womans University (7.14 percent), Kyungpook National University (5.84 percent), Chonnam National University (5.84 percent), Korea University (5.52 percent), Yonsei University (5.52 percent), and Pusan National University (5.52 percent).

Results

Socioeconomic Backgrounds of Legal Professionals

Parental Occupation and Educational Level

Table 5.3 shows the educational attainment levels of legal professionals' parents. As presented in Table 5.3, the JRTI Trainees group is subdivided into the Peer JRTI

Table 5.3 Educational Attainment of Legal Professionals' Parents

	Fater					Mother				
	Law school	**40th–43rd**	**34th–43rd**	**Prior to 34th**	**Total**	**Law school**	**40th–43rd**	**34th–43rd**	**Prior to 34th**	**Total**
Elementary school graduate or less	2%	7.1%	10.2%	18.4%	8.2%	4.6%	7.7%	15.0%	36.0%	13.4%
Middle school graduate	3%	4.4%	6.6%	14.9%	6.3%	7.6%	12.1%	12.3%	13.7%	11.1%
High school graduate	24%	23.1%	25.2%	22.4%	23.8%	32.8%	34.3%	31.3%	29.7%	32.4%
Two-year college graduate	3.6%	2.4%	1.3%	2.3%	2.5%	3%	3%	2.6%	2.3%	2.8%
Four-year university graduate	39.8%	39.1%	36.7%	31.6%	37.5%	41.1%	35.4%	33.0%	16.6%	33.3%
Master's degree	15.5%	14.6%	12.4%	6.3%	12.9%	8.9%	5.4%	4.4%	1.7%	5.6%
PhD degree	12.2%	9.2%	7.5%	4.0%	8.8%	2%	2%	1.3%	0.0%	1.5%
The number of the respondents (excluding no responses)	304	294	226	174	998	302	297	227	175	1,001

Trainees group, the JRTI Trainees from the thirty-fourth through the forty-third JRTI classes, and the JRTI Trainees from classes before the thirty-fourth class. The occupation and education level of an individual's parents at the time the individual graduates from high school serve as good indicators of the individual's socioeconomic background. In the aggregate, almost 50 percent of the parents of the respondents were college graduates or graduate degree holders (59.2 percent of the fathers and 40.4 percent of the mothers). The percentage of parents who had graduate degrees was also significant (21.9 percent of the fathers and 7.1 percent of the mothers). These numbers appeared very high when compared with the average educational level of the age groups to which these parents belonged, based on estimates of the parents' ages. In general, legal professionals tended to come from families where the parents are highly educated, a trend that is becoming more visible and pronounced over time.

Even after parents' educational level was divided into three subgroups (high school graduate or lower, college graduate, and master's degree or higher), no significant difference was found in fathers' educational level between the Law School Graduates group and the Peer JRTI Trainees group ($\chi 2=2.53$, df=2, $p=0.28$). The percentage of mothers who had obtained a bachelor's degree or higher by the time that respondents in the Law School Graduates group had finished high school (52 percent), when compared with the mothers of the respondents in the Peer JRTI Trainees group (42.8 percent), was close to a statistically significant difference ($\chi 2=5.72$, df=2, $p=0.057$).

In terms of the parents' occupation at the time that the subjects graduated from high school, only a few differences existed between the Law School Graduates group and the Peer JRTI Trainees group. The percentage of parents in the Law School Graduates group in occupations with ten or more subordinates (45.8 percent) ($\chi 2=4.11$, df=1, $p<0.05$) or in management or executive positions (24.7 percent) ($\chi 2=9.61$, df=1, $p<0.01$) was significantly higher than that of parents of the Peer JRTI Trainees group. However, there was no difference between the two groups in the percentage of parents working for companies with fifty or more employees, or in the percentage of parents who were self-employed or working as professionals. By contrast, there was a large difference in the occupations of parents of those in the JRTI Trainees group from and since the thirty-fourth class of the JRTI (1,000 of whom passed the national judicial exam) and those before the thirty-fourth class. The parents of JRTI trainees in the thirty-fourth class and later were more prominently represented than the parents of JRTI Trainees before the thirty-fourth class in all the employment settings that the survey separately tracked, including companies with fifty or more employees, management or executive member positions, and professional positions (Table 5.4). This distinction demonstrated that the parental socioeconomic backgrounds of young legal professionals were, on average, higher than those of older legal professionals.

Taken as a whole, parents of legal professionals were relatively highly educated and had stable jobs, and in this regard, there was little difference between the Law School Graduates group and the Peer JRTI Trainees group. A significant generational difference, however, was identified between younger legal professionals and older legal professionals. Parents of the former were, on average, more educated and had more stable jobs than those of the latter. This difference in parental socioeconomic

Table 5.4 Parents' Occupations by Legal Professional Group

	Law school	40th–43rd	34th–43rd	Before 34th	Total	
					%	n
Company with 50 employees or more	39.6%	40.0%	37.0%	26.9%	36.9%	376
10 subordinates or more	45.8%	37.7%	33.5%	27.5%	37.4%	381
Self-employed	39.0%	33.0%	34.8%	29.7%	34.5%	353
Management or executive member	24.7%	14.7%	14.8%	9.9%	16.9%	172
Professional such as doctor and lawyer	18.5%	16.7%	13.5%	7.7%	14.9%	152

Note: This table shows the percentage of occupations of one parent at the time the subjects graduated from high school, and therefore, some numbers in the columns could overlap.

background could reflect intergenerational changes in Korea, as Korea has grown rapidly for the past half-century and its people have achieved greatly enhanced average educational levels and living standards. Parents of legal professionals are a typical example of this growth and change in socioeconomic background. The contrast is illustrated by the clear difference between the classes of the JRTI before the thirty-fourth class and the other legal professionals included in the Study. By subdividing the JRTI Trainees according to particular ranges of JRTI Trainee classes (before the thirty-fourth, thirty-fourth class and later [thirty-fourth to forty-third], and since the fortieth class [fortieth to forty-third]), the trend toward higher education level and higher professional status of parents reaches levels that approach, and in some respects match, the levels of the Law School Graduates group.

Presence of Legal Professionals in the Family

Table 5.5 shows the data for the presence of other legal professionals in the family. Among all the respondents, those who had a parent who practiced law represented 3.4 percent of the group, and those whose nuclear family member (parent, spouse, brother, or sister) practiced law represented 8.9 percent. In addition, 30.3 percent of respondents had an extended family member or relative who was a legal professional. When each of the three groups was examined as to whether any parent ($\chi2=2.65$, df=2, p=0.26), nuclear family member ($\chi2=1.63$, df=2, p=0.44), or extended family member or relative ($\chi2=4.70$, df=2, p=0.10) was a legal professional, however, no significant difference was found. By contrast, when the Career JRTI Trainees group was divided into those before and after the thirty-fourth JRTI class, there was a stark difference: The

Table 5.5 Presence of Legal Professionals in the Family

	Law school	40th–43rd	34th–43rd	Before 34th	Total	
					%	n
At least one parent is a legal professional	3.6%	4.7%	3.0%	1.6%	3.4%	35
At least one nuclear family member is a legal professional	8.4%	10.7%	8.7%	7.1%	8.9%	91
At least one extended family member or relative is a legal professional	26.3%	29.7%	33.0%	17.8%	30.3%	309

results of career legal professionals of the thirty-fourth and later classes were similar to those of Law School Graduates and the fortieth to forty-third classes of the JRTI. Accordingly, it appears that the tendency of a law family to generate legal professionals has solidified in recent years, regardless of whether the new professional is a Law School Graduate or a Peer JRTI Trainee.

When the results above are considered together, it is difficult to argue that the introduction of the law school system allows only people from wealthy or legal professional families to enter law school. Few differences in socioeconomic background existed between the Law School Graduates group and the Peer JRTI Trainees group. Whether from law school or the JRTI, however, the current generation of legal professionals shows a parental socioeconomic level that is significantly higher than that of the Career JRTI Trainees group. More important, before and after the thirty-fourth class of the JRTI (i.e., the point at which the number of those passing the exam increased to 1,000), differences in parental socioeconomic background increased. The phenomenon of legal professionals with parents of a higher level of income and education, or as it is commonly understood, of a higher socioeconomic background, is consistent with the broader pattern by which the Korean population has become more highly educated and prosperous over the past fifty years. Notably, this trend is pronounced among the parents of respondents of both the Law School Graduates group and the Peer JRTI Trainees group.

Distribution and Diversity of Legal Occupations

Distribution of Legal Occupations

Regarding the current workplaces of legal professionals in the Study (Table 5.6), about 60 percent of the respondents said they worked in Korean law firms (large firms, 19.9 percent; medium firms, 19.4 percent; and small firms, 21.2 percent), followed by private-sector companies (16.7 percent), solo practices (10.4 percent), and public institutions (8.6 percent).

Table 5.6 Distribution of Legal Professions by Gender

	Solo practitioner	Law firm (small)	Law firm (medium)	Law firm (large)	Public institution	Private-sector company	Others	Total
Female	7.1%	22.8%	16.3%	16.9%	11.8%	19.2%	5.9%	338
Male	12.0%	20.4%	21.0%	21.4%	7.0%	15.4%	2.8%	682

The workplace distribution of men and women differed ($\chi 2$ =24.61, df=6, p<0.001). Among the respondents, relatively more women held positions at small law firms (22.8 percent) and private-sector companies (19.2 percent), while relatively more men were employed at medium and large law firms (42.4 percent).

A comparison of the three education and training groups (Law School Graduates, Peer JRTI Trainees, and Career JRTI Trainees) (Table 5.7) reveals statistically significant differences in their workplace distributions ($\chi 2$ =62.05, df=12, p<0.001). In short, the percentage of the Law School Graduates group and the Peer JRTI Trainees group working at small law firms and private-sector companies was higher than that of the Career JRTI Trainees group, while those in the Career JRTI Trainees group were more likely to work at large law firms than their younger counterparts. The fact that both the Law School Graduates group and the Peer JRTI Trainees group are employed relatively more in private-sector companies implies that a considerable number of entry-level positions in recent years have been in non-law firm settings.

Differences between the Law School Graduates group and the Peer JRTI Trainees group are on the edge of statistical significance ($\chi 2$ =12.51, df=6, p=0.051). Differences between the two groups are found in the percentages of those working for small law firms and large law firms. Peer JRTI Trainees were more likely to begin their careers in large law firms. By contrast, Law School Graduates joining a firm were more likely than Peer JRTI Trainees to begin their careers at small law firms or as solo practitioners; the percentage of the Law School Graduates group going into public institutions or other jobs was lower than that of the Peer JRTI Trainees group.

Given these findings, the question of whether Law School Graduates are pursuing a greater variety of jobs than Peer JRTI Trainees cannot be conclusively answered. This is because Law School Graduates, like Peer JRTI Trainees, are still at an entry level, having begun work only a few years ago. It will be possible to draw a meaningful conclusion about the diversity of occupations pursued by Law School Graduates only if career paths are tracked and statistically analyzed for a longer period.

Job Choice Factors and Desired Turnover

Respondents, grouped according to whether they worked in the private sector or the public sector, were asked whether particular factors affected their job choice (Table 5.8). Between these two groups, significant differences were identified in "expectations for mid- and long-term income" (t=-2.64, df= 37.42, p<0.05), "interest in a particular law-

Table 5.7 Distribution of Legal Professions by Legal Professional Group

	Solo practitioner	Law firm (small)	Law firm (medium)	Law firm (large)	Public institution	Private-sector company	Others	Total
Law School Graduates	10.1%	31.2%	17.9%	11.4%	7.1%	19.2%	3.2%	308
Peer JRTI Trainees	8.3%	22.0%	19.0%	18.0%	9.3%	18.0%	5.3%	300
Career JRTI Trainees	12.1%	13.1%	20.9%	27.7%	9.2%	13.8%	3.2%	412
Total (N=1020)	10.4%	21.2%	19.4%	19.9%	8.6%	16.7%	3.8%	1,020

related field" ($t=2.32$, $df=40.46$, $p<0.05$), "expectations for balance between work and personal life" ($t=2.03$, $df=38.44$, $p<0.05$), "opportunity to make social contributions" ($t=2.73$, $df=37.70$, $p<0.01$), "fame in the sector" ($t=2.70$, $df=40.88$, $p<0.01$), and "opportunity for a career path in the future" ($t=3.09$, $df= 46.18$, $p<0.01$).

In total, 45.1 percent of respondents stated a desire to change jobs, with the percentage varying depending on workplace ($\chi2=77.08$, $df=6$, $p<0.001$). The percentage of solo practitioners (17.9 percent) and those working at large law firms (31.5 percent) who desired to change jobs was relatively low compared with that of those working in public institutions (60.0 percent) or others (66.7 percent).

When turnover desire was examined by group (Law School Graduates, Peer JRTI Trainees, and Career JRTI Trainees), younger legal professionals (Law School Graduates, 52.3 percent; Peer JRTI Trainees, 51.3 percent) were more likely to desire a change of job than older legal professionals in the Career JRTI Trainees group (35.2 percent) ($\chi2=27.44$, $df=2$, $p<0.001$).

Table 5.8 Job Choice Factors by Sector

	Law school total	Private sector (n=276)	Public sector (n=32)
Expectations for mid- and long-term income	4.52	4.60	3.81
Interest in a particular law-related field	4.67	4.60	5.25
Annual salary enough to pay off student loans	2.83	2.88	2.41
Whether student loan repayment support or a student loan repayment program is provided	1.63	1.59	1.94
Opportunity to develop professional knowledge	5.02	4.97	5.38
Expectations for balance between work and personal life	4.60	4.53	5.19
Opportunity to make social contributions	3.91	3.82	4.69
Fame in the field	4.46	4.38	5.13
Opportunity for a career path in the future	4.85	4.78	5.47
Others	3.68	3.68	3.69

Career Path

To examine whether the introduction of the law school system has increased the diversity of legal occupations at the entry level, it is necessary to consider how legal professionals in the past chose and changed careers. The issue of career path is inherently a dynamic analysis, so rather than conduct a cross-sectional study of career choices at a specific point, the analysis must examine the changes and dynamics of the legal profession and track particular career trajectories. To do this, the Study recorded how often those in the Career JRTI Trainees group changed their workplaces and what kind of career paths they took. The reason the Study only considered the career paths of the Career JRTI Trainees group was that those in the Law School Graduates group and the Peer JRTI Trainees group were, in most cases, still in their first legal professional job, and so no depth of analysis could be provided by considering their work histories.

The average length of the post-JRTI career of the respondents in the Career JRTI Trainees group was 11.63 years, and it was most often the case that they reported changing their workplace once (40.8 percent). Of the others, 25.2 percent stated they changed their workplace twice, while 13.4 percent indicated three times. The remaining 15.1 percent said they had not left for another job and instead continued at their first workplace. It was most often the case that their first jobs were in Korean law firms (49.0 percent), followed by the judicial branch (10.2 percent), solo practice (9.5 percent), public institutions (8.7 percent), and prosecutor's offices (6.6 percent). The average number of years of service at the first job for legal professionals who had changed jobs at least once was five. The average number of years at the first job was relatively longer among female legal professionals, those at Korean law firms, those with an annual salary of less than 60 million Korean won, or about $53,500, and those with an annual salary of 200 million Korean won, equivalent to around $178,400 or more. Furthermore, when asked why they left their first job, 16.0 percent answered "to change their career," followed by 14.6 percent who responded that they "felt there was a limited possibility for career development."

Table 5.9 examines career paths, comparing the current workplace with the first workplace. Several types of career paths are revealed. Of the legal professionals who started as solo practitioners, 46.2 percent still worked as solo practitioners, 28.2 percent worked at small law firms, and 12.8 percent worked at medium law firms. The highest percentage of the legal professionals who had their first job at Korean law firms worked at large law firms (30.2 percent), followed by medium law firms (27.2 percent) and small law firms (14.4 percent), demonstrating that most legal professionals who began their career at law firms continued to work at law firms. Also, most of those who began their careers in the judicial branch currently work in large law firms (35.7 percent) or medium law firms (26.2 percent), and a few moved on to practice law as solo practitioners (4.8 percent). Meanwhile, the highest percentage of those whose first jobs were in prosecutor's offices currently worked as solo practitioners (33.3 percent), followed by large law firms (25.9 percent) and medium law firms (14.8 percent). In addition, of those with a first job in a private-sector company, most transitioned to

Table 5.9 Career Paths

First/current	Solo practitioner	Law firm (small)	Law firm (medium)	Law firm (large)	Public institution	Private-sector company	Others	Total
Solo practitioner	46.2%	28.2%	12.8%	5.1%	2.6%	0.0%	5.1%	9.5%
Korean law firm	7.4%	14.4%	27.2%	30.2%	3.5%	13.9%	3.5%	49.0%
Judicial branch	4.8%	11.9%	26.2%	35.7%	21.4%	0.0%	0.0%	10.2%
Prosecutor's office	33.3%	3.7%	14.8%	25.9%	11.1%	7.4%	3.7%	6.6%
Public institution (excluding judge and prosecutor)	8.3%	2.8%	13.9%	27.8%	30.6%	8.3%	8.3%	8.7%
Private-sector company	0.0%	5.3%	0.0%	5.3%	5.3%	84.2%	0.0%	4.6%
Court-appointed defense attorney	0.0%	50.0%	0.0%	0.0%	50.0%	0.0%	0.0%	0.5%
Nonprofit organization	0.0%	100.0%	0.0%	0.0%	0.0%	0.0%	0.0%	0.2%
Educational institution	100.0%	0.0%	0.0%	0.0%	0.0%	0.0%	0.0%	0.2%
Financial institution	0.0%	0.0%	0.0%	0.0%	0.0%	100.0%	0.0%	1.9%
Others	5.7%	11.4%	17.1%	51.4%	14.3%	0.0%	0.0%	8.5%
Total	50	54	86	114	38	57	13	412

positions as in-house lawyers in other companies (84.2 percent), and in no case was such an individual shifted to work as a solo practitioner.

In summary, the following career paths for Career JRTI Trainees can be observed with some frequency: (1) solo practitioner → solo practitioner, (2) law firm → law firm, (3) court → law firm, (4) prosecutor's office → solo practitioner, and (5) in-house lawyer → in-house lawyer. It would be meaningful to examine whether the common career paths will remain the same or differ in the future as Law School Graduates continue their careers. Furthermore, once foreign law firms are allowed to employ Korean lawyers, the existing career landscape will change, and therefore, the types of career paths could be different from those of the previous generation of legal professionals. In the future, a follow-up study should track and analyze career trajectories in the changing landscape of Korean legal practice.

Work Environments of Legal Professionals

Annual Salary

The average annual salary of the legal professionals who responded to the survey was 154.5 million Korean won, or about $137,700, while the median was 82.5 million Korean won, or about $73,600. Because the annual salary is distributed unevenly and the standard deviation is high, it is more meaningful to compare the median than the average. Compared by type of workplace (Table 5.10), the median annual salary is far higher for large law firms (157.5 million Korean won, or about $140,500) than for any other group. Those working at large law firms earned two and a half times more than those working at public institutions or as solo practitioners (both at 60 million Korean won, or about $53,500), who had the lowest median annual salaries. The annual salary level for legal professionals employed at large law firms is among the highest of all occupations in Korea.

Table 5.10 Annual Salary by Type of Workplace in [Millions of] Korean Won

	Average annual salary	**Standard deviation**	**Median**	**Bottom 25%**	**Top 25%**
Solo practitioner	83.94	83.48	60.00	40.00	100.00
Law firm (small)	72.12	28.36	65.00	60.00	80.00
Law firm (medium)	115.10	81.08	99.00	80.00	120.00
Law firm (large)	181.68	84.15	157.50	137.88	200.00
Public institution	69.04	24.82	60.00	55.00	80.00
Private-sector company	89.34	36.73	80.00	65.00	100.50
Others	89.11	67.75	80.00	60.00	95.00
Total	105.45	73.57	82.50	60.00	130.00

Differences in annual salary among the three legal professional groups (Table 5.11) were statistically significant (F=105.7, df=2, p<0.001). The explanation for the fact that the Law School Graduates group had a lower median annual salary than the Peer JRTI Trainees group, at least in part, is a structural delay before Law School Graduates can commence legal practice: They are required to complete six months of practical training after they pass the bar exam. Subtracting these six months would affect the estimation of the annual salary. In addition, the data also reflect the fact that more respondents in the Peer JRTI Trainees group were employed at large law firms than those in the Law School Graduates group, as described in Table 5.7.

Table 5.12 compares salaries by gender and legal professional group. Neither the Law School Graduates group nor the Peer JRTI Trainees group had a significant pay gap based on gender. By contrast, the Career JRTI Trainees group showed a significant difference between the genders. Males accounted for 81.6 percent of the Career JRTI Trainees group, while females accounted for 18.4 percent. The average length of law career for males and females was 12.76 years and 6.57 years, respectively. The gender distribution in the Career JRTI Trainees group differed little from that for all the legal professionals (see Table 5.6). Relatively more female legal professionals worked at public institutions (14.5 percent) and private-sector companies (21.1 percent).

Table 5.11 Annual Salary by Legal Professional Group in [Millions of] Korean Won

	Average annual salary	Median	Bottom 25%	Top 25%
Law School Graduates	72.51	60.00	57.25	80.00
Peer JRTI Trainees	87.99	80.00	60.00	100.00
Career JRTI Trainees	144.81	115.00	94.00	175.00

Table 5.12 Annual Salary by Gender and Legal Professional Group in [Millions of] Korean Won

	Female				Male			
	Average annual salary	Median	Bottom 25%	Top 25%	Average annual salary	Median	Bottom 25%	Top 25%
Law School Graduates	72.54	60.0	53.0	80.0	72.50	60.0	60.0	80.0
Peer JRTI Trainees	87.31	80.0	60.0	98.0	88.59	80.0	65.0	100.0
Career JRTI Trainees	110.73	100.0	84.0	133.75	152.21	120.0	95.0	180.0

Working Hours

Table 5.13 shows data on working hours. It was found that the average number of working hours per week of the respondents was slightly above fifty. Time worked in the office accounted for 42.2 out of those 50 hours per week; and outside the office, 7.0 hours. Overtime amounted to 9.6 hours per week outside regular working hours. On the other hand, it was found that respondents, on average, spent 3.7 hours per week on professional networking outside their working hours.

The average number of working hours among different workplaces showed significant differences ($F=13.41$, $df=6$, $p<0.001$). More specifically, large and medium law firms had a statistically significant greater length of working hours than solo practices, small law firms, private-sector companies, and others. However, no statistically significant difference was found among the other workplaces.

The percentage of those working 60 hours or more per week was higher in medium and large law firms than in other institutions ($x2=75.28$, $df=6$, $p<0.001$). Approximately 27.4 percent of respondents reported that they worked 60 hours or more per week, and the highest percentage of those was in large law firms (41.9 percent). Meanwhile, the percentages of those working 60 hours or more per week in private-sector companies (10 percent) and solo practice (17.9 percent) were relatively lower. However, it should be noted that 26 percent of respondents working in public institutions reported that they worked 60 hours or longer per week; thus, it appears that legal professionals work many hours not only in the private sector, but also in the public sector.

Table 5.13 Weekly Working Hours by Workplace Type

	Average	**Standard deviation**	**Median**	**Bottom 25%**	**Top 25%**	**The percentage of those working for 60 hours or more**
Solo practitioner	45.75	12.85	48	40.00	50	17.9
Law firm (small)	49.58	12.5	50	45.00	60	25.9
Law firm (medium)	54.67	13.93	50	48.25	60	38.9
Law firm (large)	55.53	15.00	55	49.50	60	41.9
Public institution	50.47	14.48	50	42.75	60	26.1
Private-sector company	46.83	10.78	48	44.25	50	10.0
Others	46.24	8.60	45	44.00	50	5.1
Total	50.84	13.68	50	45.00	60	27.4

Many legal professionals focused on work in a specialized field. The questionnaire asked whether they considered themselves specialists in their fields, and whether 50 percent of the work they performed was in their own field. Among those who focused more than half of their work on a particular field but nonetheless did not think of themselves as specialists were solo practitioners (22.6 percent), those in small law firms (35.2 percent), and those in public institutions (42.0 percent). By contrast, the percentage of legal professionals at large law firms who focused on a specific field in their actual work was high, and so was the percentage of those at large law firms who considered themselves specialists (70.4 percent).

Pro Bono Service

Under Article 27 of the Attorney-at-Law Act, lawyers are required to complete a minimum number of hours of pro bono service per year. In principle, the requirement is 30 hours, but local bar associations are allowed to reduce the requirement to 20 hours. *Lawyers' White Paper 2010* gave the average number of pro bono hours actually worked as 29.84. In the Study, hours of pro bono service varied depending on the workplace. The average showed significant differences among respondent groups ($F=8.82$, $d=6$, $p<0.001$). Solo practitioners performed 38.95 hours of pro bono service, followed by 26.01 hours for those working in large law firms.

Job Satisfaction

When the importance of the factors that respondents considered in choosing their current workplace was considered (Table 5.14), the average on a seven-point scale showed work environment and colleagues as highest (5.05), followed by corporate reputation (4.62) and annual salary (4.60). All three groups responded that they accorded the most weight to work environment and colleagues in choosing current workplace. In addition, all three groups gave the least consideration to providing convenience for family.

The items that showed statistically significant differences among the three groups included working hours, shared values, job stability, geographical location, training and education opportunity, and providing convenience for family. The Law School Graduates group considered working hours more than other groups did in choosing their workplace ($F=5.27$, $df=2$, $p<0.01$). As to whether their company shared the legal professional's values ("shared values"), the Peer JRTI Trainees group considered this less than the other two groups did ($F=5.57$, $df=2$, $p<0.01$). Job stability was also evaluated differently, and the Career JRTI Trainees group considered job stability more than the other two groups did ($F=7.26$, $df=2$, $p<0.001$). As to the workplace's geographic location, the Peer JRTI Trainees group considered it more important than the Career JRTI Trainees did ($F=3.54$, $df=2$, $p<0.05$). Training and education opportunity was also considered differently ($F=9.59$, $df=2$, $p<0.001$). The Law School Graduates group considered training and education opportunity more than the other two groups did. Career JRTI Trainees considered providing convenience for family less

Table 5.14 Job Satisfaction Factors by Legal Professional Group

	Total	Law School Graduates	Peer JRTI Trainees	Career JRTI Trainees
Annual salary	4.60	4.50	4.62	4.67
Employee benefits	3.88	3.91	4.00	3.77
Work environment /colleagues	5.05	5.14	5.02	5.01
Working hours	4.31	4.54	4.32	4.13
Opportunity for social contribution	3.25	3.29	3.25	3.22
Possibility of promotion	3.26	3.26	3.25	3.27
Shared values	4.40	4.58	4.14	4.45
Job stability	4.48	4.38	4.27	4.70
Geographic location	4.15	4.25	4.29	3.98
Corporate scale	4.33	4.28	4.49	4.25
Reputations	4.62	4.60	4.57	4.67
Training and education opportunity	4.30	4.65	4.28	4.06
Providing convenience for family	3.14	3.34	3.31	2.86

than the other groups did ($F=8.09$, $df=2$, $p<0.001$). No significant difference was found in the other items among the three groups.

Overall, legal professionals' job satisfaction with their current workplaces was high: 67 percent were "generally" or "very" satisfied. The average satisfaction on a five-point scale showed similarly high levels of satisfaction for the Law School Graduates group (3.64), the Peer JRTI Trainees group (3.65), and the Career JRTI Trainees group (3.76). Differences among the groups were not statistically significant. Based on gender, however, females' job satisfaction (3.60) was lower to a statistically significant extent than that of males (3.73) ($t=-2.44$, $df=643.981$, $p<0.05$).

In terms of satisfaction depending on the workplace (Table 5.15), large law firms and public institutions showed relatively higher levels of satisfaction. However, differences among large and small law firms, public institutions and small law firms, and private-sector companies and large law firms were statistically significant ($F=4.91$, $df=6$, $p<0.001$), while differences among other workplaces were not significant.

The overall level of satisfaction (Table 5.16) was high in large law firms, but differences were apparent in specific areas. Large law firms scored high in satisfaction with work or occupational competency factors such as annual salary, employee benefits, work environment, and corporate reputation. Meanwhile, private-sector companies and public institutions scored high in satisfaction with personal life, considering such factors as working hours, balance between work and personal life, and providing convenience for family (including newborn care).

After performing a principal component analysis using the fifteen detailed items above, the Study was able to derive three principal components of legal professionals'

Table 5.15 Workplace Satisfaction by Workplace Type

	Average	Standard deviation	Median	Bottom 25%	Top 25%
Solo practitioner	3.75	0.79	4	3	4
Law firm (small)	3.49	0.89	4	3	4
Law firm (medium)	3.67	0.79	4	3	4
Law firm (large)	3.89	0.76	4	4	4
Public institution	3.81	0.72	4	3	4
Private-sector company	3.64	0.80	4	3	4
Others	3.67	0.77	4	3	4
Total	3.69	0.81	4	3	4

Table 5.16 Overall Level of Job Satisfaction by Factor

	Average	Standard deviation
Annual salary	4.15	1.52
Employee benefits	3.73	1.58
Work environment, colleagues	4.91	1.44
Working hours, amount of work	4.35	1.60
Opportunity for social contributions including pro bono service	3.58	1.58
Possibility of promotion	3.61	1.55
Shared values	4.25	1.56
Job stability	4.31	1.55
Corporate reputations	4.59	1.52
Education and training opportunity (including personal mentoring)	4.14	1.67
Performance evaluation method	3.68	1.50
Balance between work and personal life	4.21	1.70
Autonomy in performing work	4.93	1.52
Opportunity to develop expertise	4.73	1.60
Providing convenience for family (including newborn care)	3.42	1.72

job satisfaction. They are: (1) work environment and values; (2) the amount of work and personal life; and (3) monetary compensation. As a statistical matter, these three principal components explained about 62 percent of the total variance.

Component (2), the amount of work and personal life, encompasses satisfaction variables such as working hours and the amount of work, balance between work and personal life, and providing convenience for family including newborn care. Component (3), monetary compensation, includes satisfaction variables such as annual salary and employee benefits. Component (1), work environment and values, had the most explanatory power, and it represents all the other variables.

The Study examined differences in these three satisfaction components depending on workplace (Table 5.17) and gender (Table 5.18). Different workplaces showed differences in all three components: work environment and values ($F=11.4$, $df=6$, $p<0.001$), the amount of work and personal life ($F=33.54$, $df=6$, $p<0.001$), and monetary compensation ($F=28.01$, $df=6$, $p<0.001$). For work environment and values, those in large law firms showed a higher level of satisfaction than those in other workplaces. Those in public institutions also showed a high level of satisfaction with work environment and values, which was higher to a statistically significant level than that of solo practitioners or those in small law firms.

As to the amount of work and personal life, those in large law firms showed the lowest level of satisfaction, while those in public institutions and private-sector companies showed the highest levels. Legal professionals at large law firms showed the highest level of satisfaction with monetary compensation, followed by those in private-sector companies. Legal professionals who were solo practitioners, those in small law firms, and those in public institutions showed lower levels of satisfaction with monetary compensation.

Table 5.17 Differences in the Three Principal Job-Satisfaction Components by Workplace

	Work environment and values	Amount of work and personal life	Compensation
Solo practitioner	-0.29	0.16	-0.36
Law firm (small)	-0.25	-0.04	-0.37
Law firm (medium)	-0.09	-0.28	-0.05
Law firm (large)	0.39	-0.55	0.64
Public institution	0.24	0.48	-0.35
Private-sector company	0.08	0.61	0.18
Others	-0.29	0.36	-0.07

Table 5.18 Differences in the Three Principal Job-Satisfaction Components by Gender

	Work environment and values	Amount of work and personal life	Compensation
Male	0.05	0.04	-0.02
Female	-0.11	-0.02	0.01

Gender differences were observed only in work environment and values. Males showed a higher level of satisfaction with work environment and values than females ($t=-2.41$, $df=653.84$, $p<0.05$). The other components did not show statistically significant differences.

Prospects for the Future

Differences in respondents' perceived future prospects are charted in Table 5.19.

While there was no difference observed between the Law School Graduates group and the Peer JRTI Trainees group about their prospects for the future, Career JRTI Trainees had a more negative outlook than the other two groups ($F=15.34$, $df=2$, $p<0.001$). On the other hand, no statistically significant difference in perceived prospects for the future was observed among different workplaces.

One of the most important factors to consider in predicting future prospects is the opening of the Korean legal services market, because competition is expected to become more fierce as the market opens. The Study investigated attitudes toward the opening of the legal services market (Table 5.20), whether positive (supportive) or

Table 5.19 Differences in Perceived Future Prospects by Legal Professional Group

	Average	Standard deviation	Median
Law School Graduates	3.04	0.66	3.00
Peer JRTI Trainees	2.94	0.64	3.00
Career JRTI Trainees	2.75	0.80	3.00
Total	2.89	0.73	3.00

Table 5.20 Attitude toward Opening of the Legal Services Market by Legal Professional Group

	Total (n=1020)	Law School Graduates (n=308)	Peer JRTI Trainees (n=300)	Career JRTI Trainees (n=412)
The current phase-by-phase opening of the law market will be sufficient.*	4.37	4.26	3.96	4.76
Foreign lawyers should be allowed to directly hire Korean lawyers and perform work.	3.37	3.81	3.23	3.15
Foreign lawyers should also be allowed to perform work related to Korean law in particular fields such as the financial sector.	2.72	3.19	2.51	2.53
I want to work at a foreign law firm.	3.63	4.01	3.70	3.29

	Total (n=1020)	Law School Graduates (n=308)	Peer JRTI Trainees (n=300)	Career JRTI Trainees (n=412)
Even if I work under foreign lawyers, I should be able to perform work related to Korean law independently.	4.38	4.60	4.40	4.20
Control and supervision should be implemented more thoroughly so that foreign lawyers cannot perform work related to Korean law.*	4.62	4.32	4.58	4.89
It is necessary to treat and manage foreign lawyers as members of the Korean Bar Association.	2.65	2.82	2.46	2.66
The combined score for the opening of the legal services market (combining the items above).	3.35	3.69	3.26	3.17

Note: A higher score in the items marked with * indicates respondents' negative attitude toward the opening of the legal services market.

negative (opposed), and measured the average level of support for the statements on a seven-point scale. The respondents gave 4.38 points on average to the statement, "Even if I work under foreign lawyers, I should be able to perform work related to Korean law independently." This statement garnered the most supportive responses on average. For the next statement, "I want to work at a foreign law firm," the respondents gave relatively supportive responses (3.63 points). Following that was "Foreign lawyers should be allowed to directly hire Korean lawyers to perform work," which scored 3.37 points, tending toward a less supportive view of the opening of the legal market. The statements "It is necessary to treat and manage foreign lawyers as members of the Korean Bar Association" and "Foreign lawyers should also be allowed to perform work related to Korean law in particular fields such as the financial sector" scored 2.65 points and 2.72 points, respectively, and showed relatively opposed responses. Two statements that suggested less agreement with the opening of the legal services market, namely, "The current phase-by-phase opening of the law market will be sufficient" and "Control and supervision should be implemented more thoroughly so that foreign lawyers cannot perform work related to Korean law" scored 4.37 and 4.62 points, respectively. The respondents who agreed with these two items scored above the median (4 points), indicating that respondents did not greatly support the opening of the legal services market.

Among the three groups, the level of support for the opening of the legal services market varied, from highest to lowest, as follows: the Law School Graduates group, the Peer JRTI Trainees group, and the Career JRTI Trainees group. More important, the Law School Graduates group (3.69 points) showed a combined score for support for the opening of the legal services market that was higher, at a statistically significant level, than the scores for the Peer JRTI Trainees group (3.26) and the Career JRTI Trainees group (3.17) ($F=16.34$, $df=2$, $p<0.001$).

Factors in Legal Professionals' Annual Salary and Satisfaction

Annual Salary

The Study performed a regression analysis, with the annual salary of legal professionals as a dependent variable, to identify what types of variables affected the income of legal professionals (Table 5.21). Because annual salary, a dependent variable, shows great deviations overall, and it is likely that its extreme values could distort the average, the Study used the common logarithm for analysis. Accordingly, the analysis provides more meaningful results by comparing the effect sizes among explanatory variables by using the "standardized regression coefficient" among other presented regression coefficients.

The most important variable in determining annual salary was workplace. After adjusting for the variables of gender and career, it was found that those in law firms, private-sector companies, and others had a higher level of annual salary than solo practitioners.

The parental background variable did not show a statistically significant effect in most cases. The respondent's annual salary was found to be higher when a parent worked in a company with fifty employees or more, but it is difficult to infer a causal relationship from this result. Because the significance of this variable was not consistent across the three groups, it is highly likely that this variable has an "interaction effect" that is highlighted only in a particular group.

Interestingly, those who identified themselves as specialists had a higher annual salary than those who did not. This result suggests that legal specialization may result in higher annual salaries.

Alma mater also made a difference in annual salary. Overall, the legal professionals who graduated from Seoul National University, Yonsei University, and Korea University, which are generally regarded as the most prestigious universities in Korea, received higher annual salaries than those who did not. This effect was not found in analyses of each of the groups. For the Law School Graduates group, the law school they attended had a statistically significant effect on salary and was more important than the undergraduate school. Graduation from those three universities did not show a statistically significant effect among the two other groups. It would be inappropriate to conclude that graduation from one of those three universities assures a legal professional of a high annual salary, though the particular value of a prestigious law degree for Law School Graduates may indicate that these factors are significant for entry-level positions.

In the Career JRTI Trainees group, only workplace, career, and specialization were statistically significant variables in relation to income level. Unlike young legal professionals, no significance was found in this group for undergraduate school, undergraduate grade point average (GPA), or parental background. While young legal professionals aiming to get their first job with a high annual salary benefit from a prestigious law school degree or an impressive law school or undergraduate GPA, the effect of these factors may fade as their career continues. In other words, over the course of a legal career, professional reputation may become the most important factor

Table 5.21 Regression Analysis: Annual Salary and Satisfaction

	Regression coefficient	Standardized regression coefficient		t value	p value
Constant	1.43***	0.00***		10.51	0.00
Gender (male)	0.02	0.04		1.48	0.14
Career	0.01***	0.40***		15.92	0.00
Law firm (small)	0.06**	0.10**		2.60	0.01
Law firm (medium)	0.18***	0.32***		8.21	0.00
Law firm (large)	0.38***	0.63***		15.96	0.00
Public institution	0.01	0.01		0.32	0.75
Private-sector company	0.15***	0.24***		6.41	0.00
Others	0.12***	0.10***		3.81	0.00
Specialist	0.05***	0.10***		4.43	0.00
Working hours	0.00	0.05		1.95	0.05
Paternal educational level	0.00	0.02		0.61	0.54
Maternal educational level	0.00	0.00		−0.09	0.93
Parental legal professionals	0.00	0.00		−0.01	0.99
Company with 50 employees or more	0.03*	0.07*		2.40	0.02
10 subordinates or more	−0.03	−0.05		−1.79	0.07
Self-employed	0.00	−0.01		−0.22	0.83
Management or executive member	−0.01	−0.01		−0.41	0.68
Professional	−0.03	−0.04		−1.55	0.12
Undergraduate from Seoul National University, Yonsei University, and Korea University	0.02*	0.05*		2.02	0.04
Undergraduate GPA	0.00	0.04		1.52	0.13
F	58.89***	df	847	R2	0.58

*p<0.05, ** p<0.01, *** p<0.001

in determining salary level, ultimately displacing the role of alma mater and GPA in setting the market value for a legal professional's services.

Job Satisfaction

A regression analysis was also conducted to identify the factors affecting job satisfaction (Table 5.22). The analysis was performed with the results of a five-point satisfaction scale, with current workplace as a dependent variable. As in the explanatory model used for annual salary, the Study used demographics, working hours, workplace, specialization, parental background, undergraduate school, and GPA as explanatory variables. In addition, annual salary and hours of pro bono service, which are expected to have a close correlation with job satisfaction, were included in the model.

The results of this regression analysis show that the factor with the largest effect on job satisfaction was annual salary. When other conditions remain the same, an increase of 1 point in annual salary leads to an increase of 0.65 points in job satisfaction, the largest change in job satisfaction of all the explanatory variables.

Workplace also had a significant effect. Compared with legal professionals in public institutions, those in small and medium law firms and those in private-sector companies showed a lower level of satisfaction. In an earlier simple comparison of job satisfaction averages, the satisfaction level of those in large law firms was found to be higher than that of legal professionals in public institutions. However, when adjusting for the effect of other variables (in other words, when the annual salary and other conditions remained the same), working in public institutions had a higher level of satisfaction.

Of the demographic factors, males had a higher level of job satisfaction than females, and older respondents tended to have a lower level of satisfaction. Among other parental background variables, the only variable that correlated to job satisfaction was whether a respondent had a parent who was a legal professional; in that case, respondents with such a parent had a higher level of job satisfaction than those for whom neither parent was a legal professional. This result invites the conjecture that satisfaction in the former case was higher because those respondents were accustomed to the work environment and lifestyle of legal professionals and were able to make educated choices to enter the legal profession.

The hours of pro bono service produced an interesting result: Longer hours of pro bono service correlated with higher job satisfaction. It may be the case that the experience of contributing to society through the provision of legal services to disadvantaged individuals, or with a public interest objective, leads to higher job satisfaction.

Table 5.22 Regression Analysis: Factors Affecting Job Satisfaction

	Regression coefficient	Standardized regression coefficient	t value	p value
Constant	1.86*	0.00*	2.38	0.02
Gender (male)	0.14*	0.08*	2.18	0.03
Age	-0.01*	-0.09*	-1.98	0.05
Annual salary	0.65***	0.19***	3.89	0.00
Working hours	0.00	-0.07	-1.95	0.05
Solo practitioner	0.00	0.00	-0.02	0.98
Law firm (small)	-0.27*	-0.14*	-2.52	0.01
Law firm(medium)	-0.27*	-0.14*	-2.44	0.01
Law firm (large)	-0.24	-0.12	-1.87	0.06
Private-sector company	-0.26*	-0.12*	-2.31	0.02
Others	-0.13	-0.03	-0.84	0.40
Specialist	0.10	0.06	1.81	0.07
Hours of pro bono service	0.00**	0.11**	3.07	0.00
Paternal educational level	0.01	0.03	0.55	0.59
Maternal educational level	0.02	0.03	0.61	0.54
Parental legal professionals	0.41*	0.09*	2.53	0.01
Company with 50 employees or more	0.13	0.08	1.90	0.06
10 subordinates or more	-0.12	-0.07	-1.63	0.10
Self-employed	-0.02	-0.01	-0.39	0.69
Management or executive member	0.13	0.06	1.67	0.10
Professional	-0.11	-0.05	-1.18	0.24
Undergraduate from Seoul National University, Yonsei University, and Korea University	0.08	0.05	1.34	0.18
Undergraduate GPA	0.01	0.05	1.41	0.16
F	4.024***	df 838	R2	0.10

*p < 0.05, ** p < 0.01, *** p < 0.001

Conclusions and Implications

A number of major conclusions and implications can be drawn from the Study. First, the Study's examination of socioeconomic and family background revealed differences that were primarily generational. A comparison of parental occupation and educational level of Law School Graduates and Peer JRTI Trainees revealed only slight differences (mothers of Law School Graduates were on average more educated, and their fathers were more likely to hold a manager-level position), and there were no significant and systematic differences in socioeconomic background. Instead, differences were identified among different generations. In other words, the socioeconomic background levels of Law School Graduates and Peer JRTI Trainees were systematically higher than those of Career JRTI Trainees. This generation gap was also observed in the likelihood of having a legal professional among parents or family members. There was no difference between Law School Graduates and Peer JRTI Trainees in the percentage of family members or extended family relatives who were legal professionals. Rather, the differences were generational: As compared with Career JRTI Trainees, younger legal professionals tended to have more legal professionals among their family members.

Second, it was found that the demographic or educational diversity of Law School Graduates had not yet led to diversity in legal occupations, at least at an entry level. As demonstrated by the Study's findings, young legal professionals overwhelmingly worked at law firms, and many more worked in the private sector than in the public sector. The number of those pursuing fields other than Korea's conventional legal occupations (judge, prosecutor, and lawyer in private practice) was also limited. It is not certain whether this distribution in legal occupations is attributable to individual choice or to structural restraints in the market for legal talent. In addition, most Law School Graduates are still at the entry level; thus, it is difficult to generalize and draw definitive conclusions, as it is too early to track and observe changes in their jobs and a longer trajectory in their legal careers.

The comparison of types of career paths of Career JRTI Trainees indicated that it is possible that future legal professionals will take different career paths from those of earlier generations. Already, Law School Graduates showed differences from the Career JRTI Trainees when it came to job choice preferences and their views on the opening of the Korean legal market. In a system in which the traditional barriers among judges, prosecutors, and lawyers in the judicial system are effectively eliminated, most young legal professionals would prefer to start their careers as lawyers in private practice. When the law market in Korea is entirely opened in the future, such practice could include employment at a foreign law firm. In the future, it should be possible to identify the dynamic changes (and, potentially, increases in diversity) within the Korean legal profession as the market opens and as Law School Graduates progress further into their careers.

Third, there were multifaceted findings related to legal professionals' work environments and job satisfaction. Generally, all three groups provided positive self-evaluations of their own workplaces, and their views of their prospects for the future were relatively favorable as well. Interestingly, annual salary, an external measure of the socioeconomic success, did not always correspond to internal self-satisfaction. While the Law School Graduates group had a lower average annual salary than the Peer JRTI Trainees group, there was no difference in job satisfaction. As suggested by the results, job satisfaction was affected by many factors, such as work environment and values, the amount of work and personal life, and monetary compensation; the level of satisfaction varied among respondents depending on how each legal professional prioritized those factors.

Fourth, workplace was found to be the most important variable influencing annual salary and job satisfaction. Differences in parental socioeconomic background did not affect annual salary, a result found in all three groups (Law School Graduates, Peer JRTI Trainees, and Career JRTI Trainees). In the Law School Graduates group, however, graduation from a prestigious law school and a high law school GPA affected annual salary. In comparison, undergraduate GPA affected annual salary in the Peer JRTI Trainees group. In contrast, the undergraduate school and GPA of Career JRTI Trainees did not affect their annual salary. This implies that while educational institutions and performance variables may be important in securing a first job at a workplace with a high salary, their effect diminishes as legal professionals accumulate more experience in law and compete successfully in the legal market.

In general, job satisfaction was highly correlated with annual salary; yet, when controlling for other variables, legal professionals in public institutions showed a higher level of satisfaction. This demonstrates that values other than annual salary are important in the life of legal professionals, and that satisfaction may differ depending on the degree of self-actualization. In addition, longer hours of pro bono service resulted in a higher level of satisfaction. Therefore, the Study indicates that, throughout successive generations of legal professionals, the occupation carries a sense of social responsibility to serve the public interest.

Notes

1 This chapter is an edited translation of the following articles originally published in the Korean language: Jae Hyup Lee, June Woong Rhee, and Hyunjung Hwang, “Roseukul Chulsin Beomnyulga, Geudeureun Nuguinga? [Law School Lawyers in Korea, Who Are They?]” *Seouldaehakgyo Beopak* [Seoul Law Journal] 56, no. 2 (2015): 367–411; Jae Hyup Lee, June Woong Rhee, and Hyunjung Hwang, “Beomnyulgaui Eommuhwangyeong, Manjokdo, Geurigo Jigyeokdayangseonge Gwanhan Tamsaekjeok Gochal: Beopakjeonmundaehagwon Doibe Ttareun Byeonhwareul Jungsimeuro [An Exploratory Study of Work Environment, Satisfaction, and the Diversity of Employment in the Korean Legal Profession],” *Seouldaehakgyo Beopak* [Seoul Law Journal] 56, no. 4 (2015): 185–221.

2 In this chapter, I use “legal professionals” to refer to qualified and licensed attorneys in Korea who hold law-related positions, including: attorneys in private practice; public prosecutors; judges; in-house counsel; and public interest attorneys.

3 Ronit Dinovitzer, *After the JD: First Results of a National Study of Legal Careers* (Overland Park: NALP Foundation for Law Career Research and Education, 2004).

The second and the third results of AJD study were published in 2009 and 2014, respectively.

4 Setsuo Miyazawa et al., "Stratification or Diversification: 2011 Survey of Young Lawyers in Japan," in *East Asia's Renewed Respect for the Rule of Law in the 21st Century: The Future of Legal and Judicial Landscapes in East Asia*, eds. Setsuo Miyazawa et al. (Leiden: Brill, 2015), 31–46.

Bibliography

Dinovitzer, Ronit. *After the JD: First Results of a National Study of Legal Careers*. Overland Park: NALP Foundation for Law Career Research and Education, 2004.

Lee, Jae Hyup, June Woong Rhee, and Hyunjung Hwang. "Beomnyulgaui Eommuhwangyeong, Manjokdo, Geurigo Jigyeokdayangseonge Gwanhan Tamsaekjeok Gochal: Beopakjeonmundaehagwon Doibe Ttareun Byeonhwareul Jungsimeuro [An Exploratory Study of Work Environment, Satisfaction, and the Diversity of Employment in the Korean Legal Profession]." *Seouldaehakgyo Beopak [Seoul Law Journal]* 56, no. 4 (2015): 185–221.

Lee, Jae Hyup, June Woong Rhee, and Jung Hyun Hwang. "Roseukul Chulsin Beomnyulga, Geudeureun Nuguinga? [Law School Lawyers in Korea, Who Are They?]" *Seouldaehakgyo Beopak* [Seoul Law Journal] 56, no. 2 (2015): 367–411.

Miyazawa, Setsuo, Atsushi Bushimata, Keiichi Ageishi, Akira Fujimoto, Rikiya Kuboyama, and Kyoko Ishida. "Stratification or Diversification: 2011 Survey of Young Lawyers in Japan." In *East Asia's Renewed Respect for the Rule of Law in the 21st Century: The Future of Legal and Judicial Landscapes in East Asia*, edited by Setsuo Miyazawa et al., 31–46. Leiden: Brill, 2015.

This chapter was previously published under the same title in Journal of Legal Education 68, no. 2 (2019): 460–490.

Part Three

Democracy and the Jury

Citizen Participation as Legal Reform

6

The South Korean Style of Jury System as a Kind of Legal Transplant

Comparative Analysis with an Anglo-American Jury

John Sanghyun Lee

Introduction: Legal Transplant

The jury trial, known as an Anglo-American institution, has been operating in South Korea since 2008 after several years-long consideration.[1,2] This was the first time Korea adopted and implemented civil participation into the decision process of a criminal trial throughout its modern judicial history. Although the National Parliament of the Republic of Korea, or South Korea, discussed the jury trial in 1948 when it enacted the first Constitution of the Republic of Korea, it decided that the jury trial would not be appropriate as a constitutional provision. After that, until 2008, professional judges had managed and decided all trials in courts.[3] Meanwhile, English law, as the origin of jury trial, reduced the coverage of the jury trial in its criminal procedure after English law took away the jury trial from its civil procedure.[4] The declining English jury was considered to be due to excessive costs and capricious acquittals by "juries made up of the unemployed, lower working classes and housewives."[5] The American legal system, although its actual usage of jury trial has decreased to a low level, around 1.3 percent of all whole criminal cases since the 1960s,[6] has remained a loyal ally to the jury trial in a democratic judicial system, overcoming severe challenges from those with dubious perceptions about the efficiency and effectiveness of jury trials.[7] From the latter part of the first decade of the twenty-first century, the jury trial has been under pioneer operation with careful research in some East Asian countries, such as Japan and South Korea.[8]

Now, with a five-year-long experience of jury trials, very new to Koreans, it turned out to be less used than expected despite the large amount of time, effort, and money invested to settle the new institution within the Korean judicial system. Nevertheless, Korean people and practitioners as well as scholars and civil-rights movement activists have positively accepted jury trial as a way for the public to join formal adjudication as well as a symbol for improving public trust toward the judicial system.[9] Serious discussions have been in progress regarding a way to rigorously activate the institution so as to attain its original goal of promoting public trust in judicial decisions.

Although it is a hasty conclusion that the adoption of the institution was a successful legal transplant for judicial democratization rather than a policy merely from legal populism, the growth and expansion of its supporter groups is quite inspiring to its original advocates.[10] This chapter first compares the American jury trial to the Korean one from the perspectives of history and institution. Then, it examines operational issues of the Korean jury trial on the basis of data and statistics. Then, this chapter throws out a suggestion to improve jury trials in Korea. Finally, it makes suggestions and conclusions for the successful settlement of the institution.

Comparison of Anglo-American Jury to Korean Jury System

Anglo-American Jury Trial

Historical Origin: Europe

The origin of the jury trial in criminal procedure dates back to ancient Greece in the sixth century BC,[11] when the jury had the power to both find a person guilty/not guilty and annul the law. During the medieval era, while such countries as France, Germany, and Italy, which adopted feudal systems, used trial by jury,[12] Anglo-Saxons rarely did[13] until the inquest of Frankish kings functioned as a historical prototype jury in England around the ninth century. Norman dukes, after their inheritance to English kingship, operated trial by jury, consisting of credible men from the dispute-arising area who were summoned to resolve the dispute among royal people.[14]

The modern-type jury trial came out of jury trials of some parts of England in the mid-twelfth century when usually six or twelve male representatives of local government and villages near a dispute, found a verdict on the basis, mostly, of their prior knowledge.[15] Criminal jury trials in England had two main institutional backbones during the twelfth to thirteenth century: Henry II's Assize of Clarendon in 1166 and the signing of Magna Carta by John I in 1215. Both events are acknowledged as the origins of the modern jury.[16] While the Assize of Clarendon contributed to a cooperative relationship between royal judges and local representatives, the signing of the Charter brought forward the concept of the right to a jury trial in England.[17] After the civil war in the late twelfth century, a criminal jury trial in England, as a substitute for the undermined system of ordeals, had been developed up until the late fourteenth century, through dividing the functions of sheriffs, juries, and royal justices.[18] A sheriff in charge of a case brought arguments and evidence to a trial. Juries passed their unanimous verdict through assessing witness testimony at a trial, and a royal justice supervised the trial by answering questions as to laws.[19]

In the eighteenth century, the British Parliament passed the Bill for Better Regulation of Juries, which prescribed that all people liable for jury service were to be posted on the list in each parish and that a jury panel would be selected by lot from the lists. The measure was aimed at improving the impartiality of jury selection and reinforcing the authority of the jury trial.[20]

Defendant's Right under American Constitutional Amendment

Jury trial, as stipulated in the Magna Carta in the early thirteenth century, was stipulated as a constitutional right of a defendant under Article 3 Section 2 of the US Constitution, more than five centuries later, in the late eighteenth century.[21] Jury trial very similar to the English jury system[22] had applied to America during the colonization era. After the independence of the United States, the United States adopted a right to jury trial as one of fundamental rights of Americans, particularly for defendants in criminal trials. The right to a public trial by an impartial jury was recognized as a fundamental right of the accused in all federal criminal prosecutions in the Sixth Amendment of the Bill of Rights. The right to a jury trial in federal criminal procedures under the Sixth Amendment was expanded to state-level criminal procedures through the Due Process clause under the Fourteenth Amendment.[23]

Coverage of Jury Trial and Power of Jury Decision

American trial by jury deals with felonies and a prosecutor's ability to appeal a not-guilty verdict is limited. Jury trial under the Sixth Amendment is provided for serious criminal cases. Those serious offenses include crimes in which the legal penalty is indeterminate but not less than a six-month imprisonment is imposed. Jurors have the power to decide facts, not legal issues, of a case. If a jury decides that a defendant is not guilty in the light of facts, a judge cannot impose a penalty on the defendant, nor can a prosecutor appeal a jury's not-guilty verdict.

Unanimity Requirement

In American criminal procedure, it has been accepted that a jury verdict in "federal criminal procedure" requires a unanimous decision among all jurors. However, the issue of unanimity for reaching jury verdicts in state criminal procedures caused heated discussion, particularly, within the US Supreme Court.[24] A majority of justices accepted less-than-unanimity for a jury verdict in state-level criminal procedure while they required unanimity for the verdict in federal criminal procedure.[25] As a result, each state has enjoyed autonomy regarding the quorum for a jury verdict. Meanwhile, the English abolished the unanimity rule and allowed returning a conviction based on a vote of "ten out of twelve" if jurors had deliberation for more than two hours, a shift partly due to growing disapproval for reaching a verdict among democratic juries.[26]

Transplanting Jury Trials in Korean Legal System

Legal Soils and Social Climate in Korea

South Korea has operated bench trials presided over by professional judges since the establishment of its modern judiciary system.[27] Even before the division of Korea into South and North, South Korea had never experienced any system of civil participation in adjudication. During the era of ancient, medieval, and modern monarchies, a single local magistrate dispatched by a king had dominated criminal trials as a sole judge under the "traditional" Asian bureaucratic system.[28] Judicial and administrative powers were held by a single local magistrate working as the highest-level official in a local county who passed the civil service examinations among nobles in the medieval classified society. Since the qualification to take the exam had been limited to the nobles, the so-called *yang-bahn*, and self-interests of the ruling class, or the *yang-bahn*, had shown no favor to let the common people join local leadership, the idea of the public participation in adjudication remained unfamiliar to Korean people.[29] As Confucianism, as the main ideology of the Chosun dynasty (lasting from 1392 to 1897) focusing on building virtues of local judges, covered the main subjects for the civil service examination, such judicial system had been maintained with a belief in local judges' integrity and ability.

After the coercive annexation of Chosun dynasty to Japan, the "Law Concerning Japanese Laws applicable in Chosun," promulgated in 1911, had worked as a legal ground to apply Japanese laws directly to Korea with the aim of transplanting a Japanese legal system without any autonomous spirits of modernization or independence from Korean people.[30] Authoritative construction and implementation of Japanese criminal procedure during the colonization period—from 1910 to 1945—had never included jury trials although Japan had experienced the special bureaucratic jury in the 1870s[31] and adopted the Jury Act in 1923. Japanese Jury Act of 1923, operating trial by jury consisting of twelve lay Japanese males, resembled Anglo-American jury trials, but narrowed down its coverage to the criminal cases with capital punishment and life imprisonment as penalties, thereby playing its limited role in criminal practices of mainland Japan.[32] The Japanese Jury Act founding jury's participation in judicial hearings, failing to overcome its hurdles in collecting potential jurors due to male conscriptions during the Second World War and being suspended in 1943, had never been applied to the Korean Peninsula during the entire colonization era.[33]

After establishment of the independent Republic of Korea, or South Korea, in 1948 and adoption of the Court Organization Act in 1949, Korea operated tribunals consisting of professional judges. Professional judges were appointed among the most competitive candidates who passed a qualification examination, notorious for its tough competition,[34] and graduated from the National Judicial Research Institute. Such merit-based and highly competitive examinations supported the people's respect for judicial decisions within Korean society. However, public respect for the judiciary, although elite, has been undermined due to growing and widespread spirits of democracy, arguably implicit collusion among legal professionals,[35] and the controversial custom that a lawyer in a case who used to be the former predecessor of a judge in charge of the case would be granted arguably *honorable treatment* by the judge.[36] Authoritarian manners or harsh words from presiding judges toward defendants or witnesses used to cause public blame.[37] Meanwhile, relatively lenient penalties for business tycoons and major politicians aggravated the suspicion of the public about transparency and fairness of a judicial decision-making process.[38]

Sprouting Jury Trials in South Korean Legal System

Public distrust in the fairness of the judiciary worked as pressure on judicial reform by both politicians and the judicial body. As a reformative judicial institution, civil participation into the judicial decision-making mechanism had been strongly suggested by some groups of law professors in 1990s. Since then, much research on jury trials has been done by the academic community and governmental and judicial committees.[39] The new Korean jury trial as one part of a major political reform agenda toward the establishment of a democratic and competitive judiciary was adopted in 2007 as a hybrid institution between an Anglo-American jury trial and a German lay judge.[40] Japan's, Taiwan's, and China's judicial reformative efforts to adopt civil participation into the judiciary also influenced Koreans' efforts to launch its unique jury system.[41]

Unlike an American-style jury trial, Korean jury trials have been functioning as opinion-providers to the bench, both on guilty/not-guilty verdict and sentencing. The Korean bench can dismiss a defendant's petition for a jury trial and decide with its discretionary power whether it will proceed as a jury or bench trial. When the Civil Participation in Criminal Trial Act (CPCTA) of 2007 was enacted[42] which adopted a jury system in enumerated criminal cases, it was announced that, after temporary operation from 2008 to 2012, a final form of Korean jury trial would be decided.[43] After the five-year-long temporary performance, the "Committee on Civil Participation in the Judiciary (CCPJ)," affiliated with the Supreme Court of Korea, recommended some revisions to the CPCTA of 2007, such as de facto binding power on both verdict and sentencing, a three-quarters quota for verdicts, and prosecutorial authority to request a jury trial.[44]

The CPCTA of 2007 reflected a so-called "defendant's right"-based approach. According to Article 8, a jury trial in a criminal procedure can be initiated from nothing but a defendant's petition for a jury trial, subject to the power to dismiss by a panel of judges in charge of the case.[45] Such an initiative for a defendant's right to trial by jury had been acknowledged by the Supreme Court of Korea.[46] On the other hand, Article 12 Paragraph 3 stipulates that jurors can express their opinions on conviction whether a defendant is guilty or not, application of law, and sentencing. Contrary to the wide coverage of a jury opinion, a jury's verdict has no binding but only recommendatory power on adjudication. On the other hand, the decision requires a unanimous verdict after the first discussion, but if jurors do not reach a unanimous verdict, a presiding judge may offer his/her opinion to the whole jury. Then, the jurors can vote on the issue under discussion, and the majority provides its verdict to the bench.[47]

Debate on Pruning of Korean Jury Trials: 2013 Revisions Proposed by CCPJ and MOJ

The 2013 revision bill of the CPCTA proposed by the CCPJ[48] is considered to place its focus on the so-called "public-participation" perspective, rather than the "defendant's right to a jury" approach. The CCPJ, consisting of six legal professionals, two law professors, and four learned men/women, shifted its approach from the perspective of defendant's rights to public-participation to allow more jury trials to take place. According to the 2013 revision bill, the authority to place a petition for jury trial is endowed upon a prosecutor, the bench, and the defendant. The bench has its own discretion to decide whether it starts a jury trial. If the 2013 bill passes the National Parliament of Korea, a criminal defendant should face a jury trial pursuant to the decision of the bench although he/she wants a trial by a panel of three professional judges. Such an imposition-styled jury trial, initiated by a prosecutor or bench, can conflict with "right of a defendant to have a trial by a judge pursuant to constitution and law," guaranteed by the Korean Constitution (Article 27, Section 1).

Regarding the binding power of a jury's decisions, a bench should respect both a jury's verdict on a case and the opinion on sentencing after the jury's deliverance unless it is violation of law, case law, or unfair.[49] A jury's opinion is considered to have de facto binding power. Its decision requires a stricter standard, a quorum of three-quarters of all jurors, in harmony with the increase in its power.[50] If a verdict does not reach three-quarters of the jurors' votes, then, the bench can only refer to the decision, with no duty to respect it.[51]

On the other hand, the Ministry of Justice (MOJ) suggested another revision bill (Table 6.1). The MOJ bill is currently under deliberation and discussion by the National Parliament of Korea, along with the bill of the CCPJ. The MOJ bill excludes from the coverage of CPCTA cases under bench trial pursuant to other laws, such as those violating the Public Election Act.[52] The cause of the revision is for adjudicating in a neutral way an election law violation case susceptible to political opinions of local people. It also provides the prosecution with power to bring a motion to dismiss a petition from a defendant to have a jury trial.[53] The Supreme Court of Korea expressed

Table 6.1 Comparison of Revisions Bills of CCPJ and MOJ

	Revision Bill of CCPJ	**Revision Bill of MOJ**
Cases qualified for jury trial	Felony criminal cases* adjudicated by three-judge panel (Art. 5 sec.1 no.1)	Felony criminal cases <u>except those by panel pursuant to other laws</u> (Art.5 sec.1 no.1)
Start of jury trial	1) Petition from defendant and prosecutor followed by judicial decision 2) bench's initiative power (Art. 5 sec. 2 & 3)	- Petition from both prosecutor & defendant followed by bench's decision (Art.5 sec.2 & 3) - No power of bench to initiate jury trial
Prosecutor's motion to dismiss defendant's petition	N/A	Panel can refuse to start jury trial in light of a prosecutor's motion (Art. 9, sec. 1)

Note: These are criminal cases upon which death penalty, life-imprisonment, or minimum one-year-imprisonment can be imposed with some exceptions. Court Organization Act of Korea article 32, section 1, no.3 and CPCTA article 5 (1).

its negative opinion regarding the MOJ bill, because it does not reflect the final draft/conclusions from the CCPJ, an ad hoc organization working on the issues, affiliated with the Court.

Comparative Analysis of American and Korean Jury Trials

Since Korea adopted and has operated a civil legal system, the role of a judge in Korean criminal procedure has reflected that of active fact-finder in an inquisitorial system rather than that of referee in the adversarial system in common law countries.[54] For example, a defendant should be examined by a prosecutor and a defense counsel after witness testimony, and a presiding judge may, if deemed necessary, examine the defendant.[55] Sudden change of judges' role in Korean criminal procedure mainly due to newly established jury trial might generate much confusion to judges as well as other practitioners. As Table 6.2 below indicates, the Korean jury system has characteristics different from the American jury trial.

The 2013 revision bill of CPCTA did not adopt the defendant's right-based approach. Distinguished from the US Constitution, Article 27 section 1 of Korean Constitution stipulates no right to jury trial provision but a "fundamental right to trial by a judge qualified by Constitution and acts." The Constitutional Court of Korea interpreted "a judge qualified by Constitution and acts" as "a professional judge," not a juror.[56] The binding power of a jury verdict and sentencing opinion could conflict with this article. Without a constitutional revision to stipulate the right to a jury trial, which does not seem likely in the near future, the binding power of the jury verdict as in America is hard to incorporate into CPCTA. The 2013 revisions, along with the traditional functionality of a judge as the main fact-finder, reflect more a civil-participation approach than a right-based approach.

The civil-participation approach appears to be in the same line as the Japanese institution called the Saiban-Inn, where six lay persons participated on the bench along with three professional judges. Under the Japanese institution, the total nine members, consisting of three professional judges and six laymen, discussed issues and decided guilt and sentences with the same voting power. Whenever the case fulfilled the conditions of the Saiban-Inn Law, lay judges were selected. The institution was not based on the right-based approach taken by the American criminal justice system. Similarly, the jury system of South Korea, although modeled in the form of an American criminal jury originally, has taken the characteristics of a civil-participation approach in which the jury can be made up regardless of a defendant's overt refusal. It is noteworthy that Korean criminal procedure, along with Japanese criminal procedure, has its root in and has operated under an inquisitorial system, as in civil law countries.

Korean jury trials from 2008 to 2011 issued more not-guilty verdicts than bench trials, producing results similar to American jury trials. During the same period, the acquittal rate of participatory trials, 8.4 percent, turned out to be almost 2.5 times higher than that of ordinary bench trials, 3.3 percent in Korea.[57] Among more criminal cases in the same period, juries' opinions on sentences, although a judge may participate

Table 6.2 Comparison between Anglo-American and Korean Jury

American jury	Korean jury
(a) Civil and criminal procedure	Civil participation in criminal procedure only
(b) Defendant's right to jury trial	A bench and a prosecutor, along with the defendant, can place a petition for jury trial←
(c) Fact-finding	Fact-finding & sentencing
(d) Binding power (not-guilty verdict not appealable)	De facto binding power derived from bench's duty to respect verdict and sentence (appealable)←
(e) Unanimity (federal) vs. non-unanimity (state)	Unanimity for the first discussion, majority (three quarters quorum requirement) for the second discussion←

Note: Changes in the 2013 Revision are marked with arrows.

in its discussion on sentencing, were lenient compared with bench sentences, as Table 6.3 shows.

Similarly, some research on American juries with power of a final verdict on guilty/not-guilty demonstrated that "not-guilty" verdicts in jury trials were more common than in bench trials.[58] Particularly, Kalven and Zeisel, both law professors, who asked trial judges how they would have decided each case where they and the jury participated, produced the result that not-guilty verdicts of the jury were six times more than those of the judges. Of 3,576 criminal cases with judges who filled a questionnaire during the deliberation of jury, decisions of both judges and jury were the same in 78 percent.[59] In 19 percent of the trials where the jury delivered "not guilty" verdict, the judge offered a guilty opinion. In 3 percent of the trials where the judge answered "not guilty," the jury issued a guilty verdict.[60] American judges have explained the "favorable" decision of jurors toward a defendant with the higher standard of proof, "beyond a reasonable doubt," for lay people, versus a judge's prejudice from information about prior criminal records or other charges dropped for lack of evidence, and sympathy with the defendant.[61]

Overall, the rate of agreement between judges and juries reached 80–90 percent of all cases in both countries. The reason for the higher rate of agreement in Korea seems to be that Korean judges, with the power of final decision, showed their respect for the jury verdicts after the verdicts were delivered. Additionally, a jury was more likely to be lenient toward a defendant than judges in both countries. American judges' explanations might apply to the high acquittal rate of jury trials in both countries.

Operating Jury Trials in South Korea

Low Rate of Usage

The usage of the jury trial had remained less than 0.3 percent of all criminal cases in 2008, 2009, and around 2 percent of all criminal cases qualified for jury trials,

Table 6.3 Comparison between Jury Opinions on Sentencing and Judges' Sentences

Jury opinion on sentencing and judges' sentences	Cases (%)
Discrepancy between judges' sentences & juries' opinions was no greater than 1 year	450 cases (92.6%)
Judges' sentence was harsher than jury's opinion by more than 1 year	23 cases (4.7%)
Jury's recommendation was harsher than judges' sentence by more than 1 year	13 cases (2.7%)
Total	486 cases (100%)

Note: Total 486 jury trials with convictions from January 1, 2008, to December 31, 2011.

Source: The table was made with data from Sang Hoon Han and Kwangbai Park. "Citizen Participation in Criminal Trials of Korea: A Statistical Portrait of the First Four Years." *Yonsei Law Journal* 3, no. 1 (2012): 61–3; Court/Committee of Civil Participation in the Judiciary (CCPJ), *2013 Hearing Kits for Determining Final Form of Participatory Trial* (Seoul: CCPJ, 2013), 64.

demonstrating the low popularity of this newly launched democratic institution. A major reason for the low usage was arguably due to the public's unawareness of the new institution and defendant's concerns about strict sentences from jury verdicts.[62] However, although the year of 2010, with growing propaganda from the Supreme Court, indicated a slight increase in usage, it still has remained around the level of 0.3 percent among total criminal cases indicted to district-level courts in Korea. The increase in 2012 and 2013 came after the 2012 revisions of the CPCTA, which expanded the coverage of jury trials to whole bench trials at district-level courts. Currently, a defendant whose case is qualified for a trial by three-judge panel can file a petition for jury trial. Table 6.4 reports the numbers regarding defendants' petitions for jury trials.

With the numbers increasing annually, more than 30 percent of petitions had been withdrawn for various reasons. According to research, the main reason for withdrawals was that defendants were concerned about judges' or prosecutors' tendencies to avoid jury trials, which would take much effort and time. The defendants forsook their petitions so that they might not rub judges/prosecutors the wrong way.[63]

Moreover, the number of judicial dismissals of the petitions increased from 2008 to 2012. In 2008, the judicial body dismissed 61 petitions (26.2 percent) of all 233 petitions for jury trials of defendants, very close to the number of jury trials, 64 (27.5 percent). The percentage of cases of judicial dismissal decreased to 63 of 489 petitions (12.9 percent) in 2011 when a total of 253 jury trials (51.7 percent) took place. However, the percentage started to go up, to 17.8 percent in 2014. The average rate of judicial dismissal or exclusion is around 17.3 percent; however, the high rate of judicial dismissal in the initial period, particularly from 2008 to 2009, demonstrated judges' hesitation to have jury trials.

Article 9 under the 2013 revision bill of CPCTA stipulates that judges may dismiss petitions for jury trials for four reasons: (1) worry about safety of jurors or fairness of trial, (2) other co-criminal's refusal, (3) sex crime victim's request, and (4) the improperness of a case for a jury trial.[64] The last reason was criticized

Table 6.4 Usage of Jury Trial in South Korea

Year	2008	2009	2010	2011	2012	2013	2014 Jan.–Jun.	Sub-total (average percent)
Defendant's petition	233 (0.10)	336 (0.14)	437 (0.19)	489 (0.20)	737 (0.29)	739 (0.31)	269 (0.24)	3240 (0.21)
Jury trial	64 (0.03) [27.5]	95 (0.04) [28.3]	162 (0.07) [37.1]	253 (0.10) [51.7]	274 (0.11) [37.2]	345 (0.15) [46.7]	131 (0.12) [48.7]	1324 (0.09) [40.9]
Withdrawal	90	138	176	178	273	319	90	1264
Dismissal	61 [26.2]	75 [22.3]	75 [17.2]	63 [12.9]	124 [16.8]	116 [15.7]	48 [17.8]	562 [17.3]
Pending	18	46	70	65	131	233	104	667
Total criminal cases indicted to district-level courts	231,508	242,266	225,739	243,178	257,732	235,743	109,956	1,546,122

Note: (% of total indicted criminal cases at district-level courts); [% out of annual petitions]

Source: Constitutional Court of Korea. "Jurisdiction-Statistics." Accessed July 20, 2025. https://english.ccourt.go.kr/site/eng/jurisdiction/caseLoadStatic.do.

for leaving much room for judges' arbitrary dismissals.[65] Such judicial exclusion of a defendant's request for a jury trial can be a great hurdle to launching a project of civil participation in adjudication, particularly in the pioneering stage. Safety and protection of a sex-crime victim(s) and other co-criminal's refusal may be persuasive reasons for such exclusions; however, improperness of a case for a jury trial is a less persuasive reason than the cause of expanding the experiences of lay people's participation.

Respect of Judiciary Body for Lay People's Decisions

In most cases, judges expressed their respectful attitudes toward jury opinions. In around 90 percent of all criminal cases with jury participation, judicial decisions have not deviated from the juries' decisions.[66] In 92.6 percent of all conviction cases, the sentences of judges were very similar to those of jurors' opinions. The differences between judges' and juries' sentences were no larger than one year in 92.6 percent.[67] Underlying such similarity, the Supreme Court of Korea held that, unless there is clear and persuasive evidence, an appellate tribunal should not repeal a jury's opinion that coincided with the first-level court judge's decision, thereby placing hurdles for a higher-level court to overturn a jury decision at a low-level court.[68] The series of decisions of the Supreme Court are considered to contribute to establishing the sound legal foundation of a jury verdict, which strictly has only advisory effect pursuant to statutory law.[69]

Exposure of the Public to Jury Experiences: The So-Called Shadow Jury

Since 2010, the Korean judicial body has operated a so-called "shadow jury" so as to let more people become exposed to jury deliberations. As current jury trials are limited in numbers, jury selection has been a restrictive process on a random-selection basis, not a voluntary one; people aspiring to be jurors have the limited chances to participate in criminal trials as mock jurors. Around five to ten applicants gather to watch a jury trial and function as mock jurors. The jurors who watched the jury trial in the audience can freely discuss a verdict and reach opinions on facts, laws, and sentences under instructions from a judge especially dispatched for guiding the shadow jurors' deliberations. The mock verdict, however, is never delivered to the bench, any judge, or any real juror in the actual case. The purpose of the mock jury is to widen the experiences similar to real jurors to any volunteer with no effect on the trial. Seoul District Court operated it through inviting a group of lay people who wanted to be a shadow jury. The institution has become widespread beyond the Seoul District. Currently, overall, courts operating jury trials gather shadow jurors in parallel through online and offline promotions.[70]

Analysis and Improvement of Korean Jury System

Operating Multi-Initiative Jury Trial Conflicts with Defendant's Right under Korean Constitution

Although the initiation of jury trial depends on a defendant's petition under the current legislation, or CPCTA of 2007, the 2013 revision bill of CPCTA allows a prosecutor to lay a petition for a jury trial and provides the bench with discretion to have jury trial on its initiative. Thus, when the new bill is passed, it will be up to the bench rather than to defendant's petition, to decide whether it finally goes to a jury trial.

A shift toward the diversified initiative approach to a jury trial[71] has its foundation in reasons such as the very low percentage of using jury trials under the current situation, and the need to expand civil participation in judicial decisions. It has been argued that, to stimulate jury trials in Korea, the current approach of being optional to the defendant should be changed to such a mandatory approach that the defendant cannot refuse a jury trial imposed by the bench, or a judicially imposed approach.[72] A so-called hybrid or diversified approach is an effective way to overcome the problem of low usage pursuant to widening the range of crimes qualified for jury trials, and to reduce the public's mistrust regarding judicial collusion on criminal cases involving politicians or tycoons. Along with the low usage, the need to expand civil participation in adjudication has gained more ground than the perspective of the civil right of a defendant for a jury trial.

However, the attitude of the 2013 revision bill might cause conflicts against the unwillingness of a defendant who does not want a jury trial.[73] Article 27 of the Constitution of Korea clearly supports the civil right to have a trial by "a judge entitled by the Constitution and the Act." The decision of the Constitutional Court of Korea construed the meaning of right to have trial by a judge under article 27 section 1 as "a professional judge."

> Article 27 section 1 secures the right to have a trial by a judge who was appointed through qualification and process stipulated by Constitution and laws and to whom independence from any influence of office and a person was guaranteed by the Constitution and laws. ... Therefore, since the right to have a trial by a judge entitled by the Constitution and the Act includes trial by a professional judge as a main element, *the right to have civil-participatory trial does not fall under the realm of protection of right to have trial secured by article 27 section 1 of Constitution*, held the Constitutional Court of Korea in 2009.[74]

As a result, the "defendant's right-based approach" under CPCTA of 2007 is more harmonized with Article 27 of the Constitution of Korea than the mandatory approach. The defendant's right to choose a bench trial or a jury trial should be respected by the bench. The jury trial has overcome many hurdles and survived in the United States despite its diminishing trend in other countries adopting the Anglo-American judicial system. It is noteworthy that America, with a defendant's right to a jury trial under a constitutional bill of rights, is the rare country where the jury trial has been working effectively.

Judicial Exclusion Should Be Reserved for Extreme Cases

The CPCTA has the following four reasons for a bench to dismiss petitions from defendants: risks to the safety and fairness of a jury, co-criminals' refusals, a sex crime victim's request and protection, and other reasons for improperness. Statistics indicate that most dismissals have come from defendants' intention to withdraw, not arguments between parties or sex crime victims' requests.

Judges need to create a comfortable atmosphere for a defendant to make a petition and/or withdrawal of a jury trial in a more intelligent and voluntary way because the petition is related to withdrawal of a constitutional right to have a trial by a "professional judge" under Article 27. In a case where there is any argument or legal issue to be argued between a defendant and prosecutor, a petition from a defendant to have a jury trial should be respected as much as possible. Complicated issues need to be coordinated and prepared sincerely for a jury trial when there is a request from a defendant. Unless there is extreme unfairness or abuse of the petition by the defendant, most defendants'

Table 6.5 Reasons and Numbers of Judicial Dismissals from 2008 to 2011

Reasons of judicial dismissal		Number of dismissals
Risks of safety of jurors & fairness of trial		1
Co-criminals' refusals		41
Other reasons		232
Defendant's side	Change of Mind (withdrawal)	85
	Incompetence, Disease (Illness)	21
	Expectation of additional indictments or prolonged detention against defendants	13
	Other reasons	8
Witness side	Protection of sex-crime victim, crime against family members	36
	Other reasons	21
Characteristics of case	No argument between parties, cases with little consequence	49
	Complicated issues or many witnesses	21
	Withdrawal of indictment	9
	Inadequacy of jury trial	18
Total		274

Source: Sang Hoon Han and Kwangbai Park. "Citizen Participation in Criminal Trials of Korea: A Statistical Portrait of the First Four Years." *Yonsei Law Journal* 3, no. 1 (2012): 62–4, Table 4 (Statistics of Supreme Court of Korea).

petitions for a jury trial need to be acknowledged. The statistics for the four years, as Table 6.5 indicates, show too many judicial interventions into defendants' petitions for jury trials, thereby underlining the need for a lesser degree of dismissal.

Jury Trials Should Be Widened to Other Trials besides Criminal Procedure

The very low percentage of using jury trial has been an issue under debate. Groups in favor of widening jury trials, including civil rights organizations and the judiciary body, argue that, to encourage the widespread democratic institution of jury trials, there need special considerations to overcome the low popularity. On the other hand, prosecutors, a professional group mostly objecting to the widening, appear to hesitate to expand jury trials institutionally because the rate of not-guilty verdicts in jury trial was shown to be three times higher than that in bench trials.[75] It is the purpose of the diversified approach or the mandatory approach for Korean jury trials, different from the Anglo-American one, that jury trials will be more used and embedded more deeply in Korean criminal procedure.

Meanwhile, the Chief Justice of Korea, Seung-Tae Yang, who expressed his positive opinion on jury trials, is said to have ordered intra-mural discussions on the issue of the expansion of jury trials into civil trials.[76] Ulsan District Court recently had experiences of operating jury trials in civil trials, and announced that there would be more test-operations for pioneering models of juries in civil procedure.[77] To settle jury trials in the Korean legal system, it is a better strategy to expand jury participation to civil, juvenile, and family law cases rather than to adopt the mandatory approach in conflicts with defendant's right to choose the form of a criminal trial.

The Level of Power of a Jury Decision

The CPCTA of 2007 does not provide binding power to jury decision regarding facts or sentencing. If a judge wants to impose a decision or sentence different from the jury's one, he/she used to explain the reason why the judicial decision differs from the jury's and stipulate it to holding. Current statistics indicate that around 90 percent of jury decisions are respected by judicial decisions.[78]

Meanwhile, the 2013 revision of CPCTA adopted a provision on a bench's duty to respect a jury opinion unless a case falls on the four reasons to disregard the opinion. In addition, unlike the constitution in any other country, Article 27 of the Constitution of Korea secures right to trial by a professional judge. So, the initiatives to operate jury trials, with binding power and no appeal, can cause constitutional problems, infringing on people's right to have a bench trial, as guaranteed by Article 27. If the Constitutional Court of Korea holds unconstitutional any provision of the 2013 revision of CPCTA, it may prevent the young buds of jury trials from sprouting all over the Korean judicial system.

When it is time for revising the Korean Constitution, a multi-initiative approach can be considered. However, it is premature to enforce a multi-initiative approach in

CPCTA under the context of the current Constitution. To evade constitutional controversies, the approach based on a defendant's right to jury trial should be the model for jury trials in Korea. Then, it is worthy of consideration that the jury's decision has binding power.

Conclusions

Rooting a jury trial in Korea has been considered an essential step toward a trustworthy and democratic judiciary system. Although cases adopting jury trials have occupied less than 0.3 percent of all first-level criminal trials, the percentage has been increasing and recent criminal trials which got much media attention, such as captain and crew's abandonment/murder charge of Sewol ferry sinking case, proceeded by jury trials.[79] Facing the time when jury trial is about to outgrow its infant stage, the Committee on Civil Participation in the Judiciary under the Supreme Court of Korea has reviewed the implementation of the CPCTA of 2007 and proposed the 2013 revision bill of the CPCTA to the National Parliament. To address cares from practitioners who hesitate to widen the institution, the revision acknowledges four situations for the bench to refuse as well as a duty to respect a jury's verdict. However, such refusal should be reserved for limited cases with extreme unreasonableness.

The Korean Constitutional Code, Article 27, stipulates no right to a jury trial of a defendant but the right to trial by a judge, particularly a professional judge pursuant to the Constitutional Court. The 2013 revision places its weight on so-called the multi-initiative approach rather than the fundamental-right-based approach. The multi-initiative approach might popularize the young institution to a slight, if any, extent. However, a jury trial against a unwillingness results in the infringement of the constitutional right to have trial by a *professional* judge. The compulsory imposition of a jury trial under the revision should be reconsidered unless Korean Constitution is subject to its ninth revision. Rather, judicial respect for a defendant's right to decide a type of criminal trial can increase the number of jury trials. Diverse reasons for withdrawal and dismissal of defendants' petitions under the uncontrolled discretion of the bench should be carefully examined and strictly scrutinized. It will be a better strategy to expand the coverage of jury trial from criminal trials to civil, juvenile, and family law trials.

The US jury trial, derived from the English jury, demonstrates that successful implementation of a foreign legal institution needs careful research, institutional support, and a reform process. Practical and professional training for judges and prosecutors and continuous and sufficient research for embedding jury trials in the adjudicatory procedure help to reduce hesitating practitioners' concerns, thereby contributing to expanding jury trials to other cases besides criminal trials. Building step-by-step institutional and legal foundations, including statutory laws and judicial rulings appropriate to the Korean judicial system, will play a valuable role in successfully implementing Korea-styled jury trials.

Notes

1 This chapter was initially presented at the East Asian Law and Society (EALS) Conference in 2011, and was revised reflecting discussions and further research on the 2013 revision bill of Civil Participation in Criminal Trial Act. Soongsil University College of Law. I appreciate for the efforts of Mr. Chung Ho Lee who gathered documents for this research.

2 There was no official comment from the Korean government until the Judicial Reform Promotion Committee as the Presidential Committee addressed the issue of civil participation into Korean judiciary in 1999. The Judicial Reform Committee in 2004 recommended the jury trial as judicial system reflecting the people's participation.

3 Sang Hyun Song, ed., *Introduction to the Law and Legal System of Korea* (Seoul: Kyung Mun Sa, 1983), 269–70 (in juvenile cases judges consider the opinions of psychiatrists, psychologists, social workers, and educators); Sang Woo Chae, *A Study on People's Participation in Criminal Procedure*, Master's thesis, Kun San National University Graduate School, 2009, 26–8 (except military tribunal where military officers participated).

4 England abolished the grand jury in 1975, and virtually got rid of the jury trial from civil procedure. Certain crimes (e.g., grand theft, assault, and battery) were also considered ineligible for jury trial in 1988. The Defamation Act of 1996 permitted non-jury criminal trials to be used in libel cases. Recently, the first non-jury criminal trial was held in more than 400 years in England. Jennifer Walker Elrod, "Is the Jury Still Out?: A Case for the Continued Viability of the American Jury," *Texas Tech Law Review* 44 (2012): 303, 306–7: Ryan Y. Park, "The Globalizing Jury Trial: Lessons and Insights from Korea," *American Journal of Comparative Law* 58 (2010): 525, 537.

5 Richard Vogler, *A World View of Criminal Justice* (Farnham: Ashgate Publishing, 2006), 212.

6 United Kingdom has the similar 1–2 percent usage of total criminal cases. Park, *supra* note 4, at 538–9.

7 *See* Elrod, *supra* note 4, at 303, 306–7. The United States has worked on reform of jury trial since the mid-1960s, which included such diverse issues as enactment of the Jury Selection and Service Act of 1968, for selecting jurors fairly, reflecting a cross section of a community, and *Batson v. Kentucky*, 476 U.S. 79 (1986) for limiting peremptory challenge based on race. Sangjoon Kim, *Research on American Jury Trial* (Seoul: Ewha Women's University Press, 2003), 45–61.

8 Hiroyuki Kuzuno, "Japanese Lay Judge Trial and Juvenile Cases," paper presented at the Asian Criminological Society Third Annual Conference, 2009, 260. Japan adopted a new lay judge system, so-called Saiban-Inn, in 2009 under which six lay people along with three professional judges were supposed to decide facts and a sentence in a criminal trial.

9 In Sup Han and Sang Hoon Han, *Civil Judicial Participation* (Gyeonggido: Kyungin Publishing, 2010), 40–442; Court/Committee of Civil Participation in the Judiciary (CCPJ), *2013 Hearing Kits for Determining Final Form of Participatory Trial* (Seoul: CCPJ, 2013), 8–170 (2008 survey showed around 70 percent of Korean people think positively about the effect of jury trial).

10 In the mid-1990s, there were a few law professors, rare pioneers who rigorously argued civil participation into the judiciary decision-making procedure of Korea, including Prof. Hong Kyu Park. Han and Han, *supra* note 9, at, 42–3.

11 The origin of juries in Athens coincided with the founding of Athenian democracy in B.C. 590. As many as 500 citizens, males with age over 30 selected by lot among volunteers, participated in the criminal trial against Socrates. A majority vote through secret ballot was necessary for conviction; in Socrates's case, he was found guilty by a 280:220 vote. University of Missouri–Kansas City, "Criminal Procedure in Ancient Greece and the Trial of Socrates," accessed July 2025, https://www.famous-trials.com/socrates.

12 Ralph V. Turner, "The Origins of the Medieval English Jury: Frankish, English, or Scandinavian?" *Journal of British Studies* 7, no. 2 (1968): 1–2.

13 William Forsyth, *History of Trial by Jury* (London: John W. Parker and Son, 1852), 55–8, 83. According to Mr. Forsyth, some authors misconceived compurgators as the jury.

14 Megan Healy McClung, "A Brief History of the Jury," *CBA Record* 19, no. 3 (March 2005): 36. But, for the different analysis, refer to Forsyth, *History of Trial by Jury*, 99–100 (Mr. Forsyth argued dispute-resolution by nobles during the Norman-conquest era such as one between Gundulf the bishop of Rochester and Pichot the sheriff did not have a characteristic of a jury trial, which was an inquest by twelve men summoned to determine a fact).

15 Refer to "Jury," Encyclopedia Britannica, accessed July 20, 2025, https://www.britannica.com/topic/jury.

16 Jury trial during the era envisaged community presentment, the antecedent of the grand jury, which continued to be conducted with traditional methods without any serious role in actual trials. Vogler, *supra* note 5, at, 199–201.

17 Clause 39 of the Magna Carta states that no free man shall be taken or imprisoned or disseised or outlawed or exiled or in any way ruined, nor will we go or send against him, except by the lawful judgment of his peers or by the law of the land. Vogler, *supra* note 5, at, 200.

18 The pope withdrew his support for ordeals, and the existing jury became an inevitable replacement for ordeals in English criminal procedure. *See* Vogler, *supra* note 5, at 201.

19 For further information regarding development of the English jury system, refer to McClung, "A Brief History of the Jury" (Jurors at the times used to hear hearsay of their local community). In the twelfth century, jurors as a source of evidence were summoned under individual questioning by a judge who could adopt one opinion against another's. However, by the late fourteenth century, royal judges divested themselves of power to evaluate evidence, perhaps due to manpower shortages among the canon-lawyers and the late development of the university in England, and/or political instability. *See* Vogler, *supra* note 5, at 201.

20 *See* McClung, *supra* note 14.

21 "The Trial of all Crimes, except in cases of impeachment, shall be by jury, and such trial shall be held in the state where the said crimes shall have been committed." The US Constitution, Article 3, Section 2, paragraph 3.

22 For subtle differences from the English jury, refer to Deborah A. Ramirez, "The Mixed Jury and the Ancient Custom of Trial by Jury De Medietate Linguae: A History and a Proposal for Change," *Boston University Law Review* 74, no. 4 (1994): 777 (composition of jury was different in terms of foreigners' participation due to distinguishing the interpretation of "aliens").

23 *Duncan v. Louisiana*, 391 U.S. 145 (1968). Even though the Seventh Amendment secured the right to civil jury trial in cases where the value of the object of the matter was greater than twenty dollars, the right to a civil jury trial has not been expanded to the state level by case law. In practice, most states have preserved the right to jury trial in civil cases for the same conditions the Seventh Amendment acknowledges.

24 Four of nine justices were pro unanimous verdict but four justices were against it. The other one, Justice Powell, argued a criminal jury trial required unanimity in the federal courts under the Sixth Amendment, but not in the state courts. Since the decision of the Supreme Court of America requires five votes, Justice Powell's opinion became the Court's decision. Russell Weaver, Leslie Abramson, John Burkoff, and Catherine Hancock, *Principles of Criminal Procedure* (St. Paul: West Academic Publishing, 2007), 26–7 (citing *Johnson v. Louisiana*, 406 U.S. 395–6 (1972)).

25 Apodaca v. Oregon, 406 U.S. 404 (1972); *Johnson v. Louisiana*, 406 U.S. 356 (1972).

26 Vogler, *supra* note 5, at 212–13.

27 Kyong Whan Ahn and In Sup Han, *Jury and Civil Participation in the Judiciary* (Seoul: Jipmoon, 2005), 48.

28 In ancient times, before the second century AD, it was argued that there were trials by village folks; however, as the ancient kingdom grew powerful, trials by an administrative officer from a royal regime replaced trials by folks. During the Goryeo (918–1392) and Chosun dynasties (1392 to 1897), an administrative officer in charge of a local county played the role of judge. The judicial system and penal code under the dynasties were deeply influenced by the Chinese system. Jae-Sang Lee, *Criminal Procedure*, 2nd ed. (Seoul: Pakyongsa, 2008), 14–15.

29 Jong Bok Kim, "Korean Civil Service System," in *Introduction to the Law and Legal System of Korea*, ed. Sang Hyun Song (Seoul: Kyung Mun Sa, 1983), 239–41.

30 Song, ed., *supra* note 3, at 258 (Japan took all the powers from Korea and authorized the government general to establish and abolish courts, appoint and reprimand judges and determine jurisdiction of courts and to administer the judiciary).

31 Anna Dobrovolskaia, "Japan's Past Experiences with the Institution of Jury Service," *Asian-Pacific Law & Policy Journal* 12, no. 1 (2010): 7–11 (The *sanza* panel, made up of not lay people but eleven to twelve government officials who had been appointed by the Counselors of State decided the guilt of the accused. Before Meiji reform, the representative Japanese institutional modernization movement, so-called sanza panel functioned at the he Makimura trial in 1873 and the Hirosawa Assassination case in 1877).

32 Dobrovolskaia, *supra* note 31, at 12–14 (The 1929 revision of the Jury Act limited its coverage by excluding criminal cases violating the Peace Preservation Act which penalized political criminals including communists and Korean independence activists).

33 Dobrovolskaia, *supra* note 31, at 15–17.

34 Kiljun Park, "Problems Concerning the Reform of Legal Education in Korea," *Korean Journal of Comparative Law* 6 (1978): 56–91 (Table 7 shows that the range of bar-exam passing rate is 0.20 to 2.29 percent from 1963 to 1975). The examination was called the National Judicial Exam (NJE) from 1963.

35 There were bribery cases where some lawyers were indicted after offering some rewards to local judges and prosecutors. Ji-sook Bae, "Korean Judge Suspected of Taking Lawyer Bribes," *Korea Herald*, December 29, 2012, https://m.koreaherald.com/article/10352913; Sang Hoon Han and Kwangbai Park, "Citizen Participation

in Criminal Trials of Korea: A Statistical Portrait of the First Four Years," *Yonsei Law Journal* 3, no. 1 (2012): 54–7.

36 Min-uck Chung, "PM Nominee Resigns," *The Korea Times*, May 28, 2014, https://www.koreatimes.co.kr/southkorea/20140528/pm-nominee-resigns (Former Justice Ahn made US$ 1.6 million within half a year after he had retired from the Supreme Court of Korea. The suspicion arose that he might earned much money through his influence and connections with incumbent former-colleagues under a long-denounced practice known as "jeongwanyewu").

37 Dong-hwan Ko, "Women Should Not Talk Too Much, Says Judge," *The Korea Times*, October 6, 2013.

38 There were some cases where parties lost in trials revengefully attacked the judges who reached negative decisions. Annie I. Bang, "Crossbow Attack Shocks Judiciary," *Korea Herald*, April 5, 2010.

39 For research on the jury system, refer to Ahn and Han, *supra* note 27, at 23 footnote 1. It was "The Committee for Propelling Judicial Reform" established by ex-president Dae Jung Kim, succeeded as "The Committee for Propelling Reform on Judicial Institution (CPRJI)" established by ex-president Moo-Hyun Roh. On the other hand, the Supreme Court of Korea also established "The Committee on Judicial Reform" which co-worked with CPRJI regarding the introduction of jury trial.

40 Park, *supra* note 4, at 546, 550–2. He argued that the prestige of the United States and its legal institution in Korea has deeply influenced the decision that Western-styled jury trial shall be implemented. However, the initial influence of Anglo-American jury trial was much less than his analysis. More than half of major supporters of Korean civil participation institution had Korean-based legal educations.

41 Lay judge system, or saiban-in seido, has been implemented in Japan since 2009. Jennifer McNulty, "Nations Embracing Jury System as Part of 'Wave of Judicial Reform,' Says UC Santa Cruz Expert," *University of California Santa Cruz*, November 14, 2007, http://news.ucsc.edu. Taiwan has adopted a quasi-jury system into criminal trial after serious consideration. *Taiwan Today*, "Commentary: Taiwan's Quasi-Jury System Inches toward Balancing Judges' Power," August 5, 2011, http://taiwantoday.tw.

42 The CPCTA of 2007 was enacted in June 1, 2007 as Law no. 8495.

43 Article 55 section 1 of the CPCTA of 2007 stipulated that the Civil Judicial Participation Committee will work for deciding a final form of civil participation in judicial decisions.

44 Court/Committee of Civil Participation in the Judiciary (CCPJ), *supra* note 9, at 50, 77.

45 Article 9 (1) of CPCTA states that a judge can decide not to go to a jury trial for the following reasons: (1) suspicion of jury's unfairness, severe difficulty in securing attendance of jury, (2) accomplice (who is co-defendant)'s unwillingness to have a jury trial, and (3) judge's own consideration that a jury trial is inappropriate.

46 Refer to Decision of Supreme Court of Korea, April 26, 2012, 2012ko1225; January 31, 2013, 2012ko13896.

47 Article 46 section 2, 3.

48 The CCPJ was affiliated to the Supreme Court of Korea. The 2013 revision has not passed the legislative process of National Parliament, and is still pending.

49 Article 5 subsection 3 of the 2013 revision bill.

50 Article 46 of the bill.

51 The same article.

52 Currently, the bench should deal with cases with severe legal penalties, such as capital punishment or imprisonment for life or of not less than a one-year imprisonment. In addition, other laws such as Public Election Act and Cure Detention Act attribute violation of the laws to the jurisdiction of the bench. The current CPCTA allows a defendant to place a petition for jury trial in all cases qualified for a bench trial.

53 Notice from Minister of Justice, 2013–88, December 31, 2013.

54 Court/Committee of Civil Participation in the Judiciary (CCPJ), *supra* note 9, at 109–10.

55 Article 296–2 of Criminal Procedure of Korea.

56 Constitutional Court, November 26, 2009. Decision 2008hunba 12.

57 Han and Park, *supra* note 35, at 61–3; Court/Committee of Civil Participation in the Judiciary (CCPJ), *supra* note 9, at 45.

58 Neil Vidmar and Valerie P. Hans, *American Juries: The Verdict* (Amherst: Prometheus Books, 2007), 150 (citing Valerie Hans' study of 382 felony jury trials in four jurisdiction from 2000 to 2001 which showed that juries were much more lenient than judges).

59 The around 80 percent agreement rate between judge and jury was the same in Larry Heuer and Steven Penrod's study over ninety-three criminal trials in thirty-three states in 1990. Vidmar and Hans, *supra* note 58, at 150.

60 Vidmar and Hans, *supra* note 58, at 148–9.

61 *Ibid.*

62 Hye-Jin Chang, "Defendants Who Experienced Civil Participation in Criminal Trial Negative to CPCT," *Beomnyulsinmun*, December 19, 2011.

63 Tae-Hum Cho, "Pan-geomsa Nunchiboyeo Gungmin-chamyeo-jaepan Gipi [Avoiding Civil Participation in Criminal Trial so as to Creep up the Judge/ Prosecutor's Sleeve]," KBS News, September 20, 2011, https://news.kbs.co.kr/news/pc/view/view.do?ncd=2358904.

64 Article 9 section 1 prescribes that a court may decide that jury trial cannot be operated in such cases as (1) jury's attendance cannot be secured due to danger or threat to life or bodily safety of jury or their relatives, (2) an accomplice of a defendant does not want jury trial, or (3) a judge consider jury trial improper on any other reason.

65 Oh Geol Kwon, "A Study on the Korean Jury Trial," paper presented at the East Asia Law and Society Conference, 2011, 4.

66 Sangjoon Kim, "The First Three Years of Implementation of a Jury System in Korea: Judge-Jury Agreement in Criminal Cases," paper presented at the East Asia Law and Society Conference, 2011, 11–12.

67 In 13 cases (2.7 percent), juries' opinions on sentences were stricter than judges'. Meanwhile, twenty-three cases (4.7 percent) showed the opposite result. Han and Park, *supra* note 35, at 62–3.

68 The Supreme Court of Korea, 2009Do14065. It was confirmed in a recent case of the Supreme Court. The Supreme Court of Korea, 2010Do4450. The jury unanimously decided that the defendant was not guilty of intended murder due to lack of intent to murder, and that, since the defendant had treated axes for twenty years, the fact that he imposed very light harm on the victim demonstrated that he did not want to murder the victim. The presiding judge accepted the verdict and ruled in favor of the defendant. However, the appellate court revoked the decision by holding that defendant's intent was murder because the defendant followed the victim and wielded

the dangerous weapon, an axe. In response to the appeal, the Supreme Court of Korea overturned the appellate court's decision.

69 Kim, *supra* note 66, at 2.

70 Currently, those who want to become a shadow jury can register in advance of a trial through the website of the Supreme Court of Korea. Refer to the following website: https://ecfs.scourt.go.kr/psp/index.on.

71 Refer to Article 5, Section 2.

72 Kwon, *supra* note 65, at 6. The defendant cannot refuse the judicial decision.

73 Korea's Constitution Article 26 protects the defendant's right to a *bench* trial. A mandatory jury trial will be against Article 26, so will be exposed to constitutional challenge. In other words, as jury are not judges but laymen without professional legal training, the people's right to trial by a *professional* judge under Article 26 can be infringed if a jury trial is compulsorily imposed, regardless of the defendant's opinion.

74 Constitutional Court of Korea, 11.26. 2009, 2008Hunba12 (en banc). The author emphasized the phrase with *italic* and underlined style.

75 Jae Jung Kim, "Widening Civil Participation in Criminal Trial: Court Willing but Prosecutor Unwilling," *Kookminilbo*, August 25, 2011, 10; Kim, *supra* note 66, at 9–11. Actual results of research indicated that jury trials produced more acquittals, 5 percent more, than bench trials. A survey of several groups regarding binding power of jury verdict indicated that defendants expressed the highest agreement out of other groups, such as jurors, judges, and laymen.

76 Kwan-soon Chang, "Chief Justice Yang Considers the Adoption of Civil Participation in Civil Trials," *CBS*, September 26, 2011.

77 Ten jurors were gathered by an in-advance advertisement and voluntary application through the main homepage of the district court, and their opinions were delivered to a bench despite having no legal power. The jurors delivered their opinions regarding a plaintiff's request for compensatory damages. The bench, several days after receiving the closed-door opinions, announced a sentence. Bong-Chul Kim, "Ulsan District Court Operating Pilot Jury Trial in Civil Procedure for the First Time," *Kyung-Sang Ilbo*, March 20, 2013, http://m.ksilbo.co.kr.

78 Meanwhile, only around 10 percent of all jury decisions are not reflected by holdings with reasons.

79 Somali pirates, who hijacked a Korean-owned vessel in the Arabian Sea and attempted to skill Korean crew, were caught by Korean Navy, faced criminal trial by jury in 2011, Pusan, South Korea. The similar piracy case in Japan went through criminal trial by six lay judges along with three professional judges. Masami Ito, "Somali Pirates' Trials Highlight Role of Interpreters," *The Japan Times*, March 21, 2013, https://www.japantimes.co.jp/news/2013/03/21/national/crime-legal/somali-pirates-trials-highlight-role-of-interpreters.

Bibliography

Ahn, Kyong Whan, and In Sup Han. *Jury & Civil Participation in the Judiciary*. Seoul: Jipmoon, 2005.

Bae, Ji-sook. "Korean Judge Suspected of Taking Lawyer Bribes." *Korea Herald*, December 29, 2012. https://www.koreaherald.com/article/10352913.

Bang, Annie I. "Crossbow Attack Shocks Judiciary." *Korea Herald*, April 5, 2010.
Chae, Sang Woo. *A Study on People's Participation in Criminal Procedure*. Master's thesis, Kun San National University Graduate School, 2009.
Chang, Hye-Jin. "Defendants Who Experienced Civil Participation in Criminal Trial Negative to CPCT." *Beomnyulsinmun*, December 19, 2011.
Chang, Kwan-soon. "Chief Justice Yang Considers the Adoption of Civil Participation in Civil Trials." *CBS*, September 26, 2011.
Chung, Min-uck. "PM Nominee Resigns." *The Korea Times*, May 28, 2014. https://www.koreatimes.co.kr/southkorea/20140528/pm-nominee-resigns.
Cho, Tae-Hum. "Pan-geomsa Nunchiboyeo Gungmin-chamyeo-jaepan Gipi [Avoiding Civil Participation in Criminal Trial so as to Creep up the Judge/Prosecutor's Sleeve]." *KBS News*, September 20, 2011. https://news.kbs.co.kr/news/pc/view/view.do?ncd=2358904.
Committee of Civil Participation in the Judiciary (CCPJ). *2013 Hearing Kits for Determining Final Form of Participatory Trial*. Seoul: CCPJ, February 18, 2013.
Constitutional Court of Korea. "Jurisdiction-Statistics." Accessed July 20, 2025. https://english.ccourt.go.kr/site/eng/jurisdiction/caseLoadStatic.do.
Dobrovolskaia, Anna. "Japan's Past Experiences with the Institution of Jury Service." *Asian-Pacific Law & Policy Journal* 12, no. 1 (2010): 1–23.
Elrod, Jennifer Walker. "Is the Jury Still Out?: A Case for the Continued Viability of the American Jury." *Texas Tech Law Review* 44 (2012): 303–26.
Encyclopedia Britannica. "Jury." Accessed July 20, 2025. https://www.britannica.com/topic/jury.
Forsyth, William. *History of Trial by Jury*. London: John W. Parker and Son, 1852.
Fukurai, Hiroshi, and Valerie P. Hans. "Special Feature: The Future of Lay Adjudication in Korea and Japan." *Yonsei Law Journal* 3, no. 1 (May 2012): 25–45.
Han, In Sup, and Sang Hoon Han. *Civil Judicial Participation*. Gyeonggido: Kyungin, 2010.
Han, Sang Hoon, and Kwangbai Park. "Citizen Participation in Criminal Trials of Korea: A Statistical Portrait of the First Four Years." *Yonsei Law Journal* 3, no. 1 (2012): 54–67.
Ito, Masami. "Somali Pirates' Trials Highlight Role of Interpreters." *The Japan Times*, March 21, 2013. https://www.japantimes.co.jp/news/2013/03/21/national/crime-legal/somali-pirates-trials-highlight-role-of-interpreters.
Kim, Bong-Chul. "Ulsan District Court Operating Pilot Jury Trial in Civil Procedure for the First Time." *Kyung-Sang Ilbo*, March 20, 2013. http://m.ksilbo.co.kr.
Kim, Jae Jung. "Widening Civil Participation in Criminal Trial: Court Willing but Prosecutor Unwilling." *Kookminilbo*, August 25, 2011.
Kim, Jong Bok, "Korean Civil Service System." In *Introduction to the Law and Legal System of Korea*, edited by Sang Hyun Song, 239–41. Seoul: Kyung Mun Sa, 1983.
Kim, Sangjoon. "The First Three Years of Implementation of a Jury System in Korea: Judge-Jury Agreement in Criminal Cases." Paper presented at the East Asia Law and Society Conference, 2011.
Kim, Sangjoon. *Research on American Jury Trial*. Seoul: Ewha Women's University Press, 2003.
Ko, Dong-hwan. "Women Should Not Talk Too Much, Says Judge." *The Korea Times*, October 6, 2013.
Kwon, Oh Geol. "A Study on the Korean Jury Trial." Paper presented at the East Asia Law and Society Conference, 2011.

Lee, Jae-Sang. *Criminal Procedure*. 2nd ed. Seoul: Pakyongsa, 2008.
McClung, Megan Healy. "A Brief History of the Jury." *CBA Record* 19, no. 3 (March 2005): 35–6.
McNulty, Jennifer. "Nations Embracing Jury System as Part of 'Wave of Judicial Reform,' Says UC Santa Cruz Expert." *University of California Santa Cruz*, November 14, 2007. http://news.ucsc.edu.
Park, Kiljun. "Problems Concerning the Reform of Legal Education in Korea." *Korean Journal of Comparative Law* 6 (1978): 55–91.
Park, Ryan Y. "The Globalizing Jury Trial: Lessons and Insights from Korea." *The American Journal of Comparative Law* 58, no. 3 (2010): 525–82.
Ramirez, Deborah A. "The Mixed Jury and the Ancient Custom of Trial by Jury De Medietate Linguae: A History and a Proposal for Change." *Boston University Law Review* 74, no. 4 (1994): 777–818.
Song, Sang Hyun, ed. *Introduction to the Law & Legal System of Korea*. Seoul: Kyung Mun Sa, 1983.
Taiwan Today. "Commentary: Taiwan's Quasi-Jury System Inches toward Balancing Judges' Power." August 5, 2011. http://taiwantoday.tw.
Turner, Ralph V. "The Origins of the Medieval English Jury: Frankish, English, or Scandinavian?" *Journal of British Studies* 7, no. 2 (1968): 1–10.
University of Missouri–Kansas City. "Criminal Procedure in Ancient Greece and the Trial of Socrates." Accessed July 2025. https://www.famous-trials.com/socrates.
Vidmar, Neil, and Valerie P. Hans. *American Juries: The Verdict*. Amherst: Prometheus Books, 2007.
Vogler, Richard. *A World View of Criminal Justice*. Farnham: Ashgate Publishing, 2006.
Weaver, Russell, Leslie Abramson, John Burkoff, and Catherine Hancock. *Principles of Criminal Procedure*. St. Paul: West Academic Publishing, 2007.

A version of this chapter was previously published under the title "Transplanting Jury Trials in South Korean Legal Soils: Comparative Analysis with Jury Trials in the United States" in Asian Criminology 11 (2016): 111–133.

7

Judge–Jury Interaction in Deliberation

Enhancement or Obstruction of Independent Jury Decision-Making?

Jae-Hyup Lee and Jisuk Woo

Introduction

Jury trials were first introduced in 2008 in Korea.[1] The Korean jury system, as envisaged in the Act for Civil Participation in Criminal Trials of 2007 [*Gukminui hyeongsajaepan chamyeoe gwanhan beoprul*] (hereinafter the Act), incorporates elements of both the US-style system and the German lay assessor system to be implemented during an initial five-year experimental phase (Han 2009).[2] The idea of utilizing the two primary styles of lay participation was to experiment with each of them in the Korean context in order to come up with the most appropriate model.

Since its introduction in 2008, a total of 1,464 jury trials were held by the end of the year 2014, and the number of jury trials has consistently increased from year to year (NCA 2015).[3] The rapid increase in the number of jury trials demonstrates the successful implementation of the jury system. Indeed, the evaluation by the Committee on Civil Judicial Participation (the "Committee") on the performance over the five-year experimental period was generally positive. The Committee recommended a final format of the Korean jury system to the National Assembly, which was meant to facilitate the jury system. It consists of some major changes to the system in relation to the jury deliberation. First, the jury verdict becomes de facto binding, meaning the court must respect the jury verdict, unless it is clearly contrary to the Constitution or statutory law. The jury opinion on the sentencing remains advisory. Second, the decision-making rule of the verdict is strengthened to require a three-fourths majority to reach a verdict.[4] If the three-fourths majority is not reached, the court nevertheless renders a judgment with reference to the jury opinions. Third, the number of jurors can either be seven or nine, but not five.[5] Upon this recommendation, the minister of justice submitted a bill revising the existing Act.[6]

As reflected in the recommendation by the Committee, the past five years of experiences were evaluated as a success, and the jury system is expected to be improved and more widely used. Indeed, the jury verdicts and the judge's rulings matched in 92.8 percent of the time (NCA 2015).[7] This is a much higher matching rate than that observed in the US studies (Kalven and Zeisel 1966; Eisenberg et al. 2005). Such a high matching rate may increase the general public's belief in the jury system, one of the most important legislative purposes of the Korean jury system.[8] Moreover, the national statistics show that relatively small gaps were found between the majority opinion of the juries and the sentencing judgment. In 89.3 percent of the cases, the majority of sentencing opinions of the jury and the sentencing judgment did not differ much—two years of imprisonment at most (NCA 2015).

The main reason for the public distrust of the judiciary in criminal trials before the introduction of the jury system in Korea has to do with the discrepancy between the court judgment and the public's legal consciousness, including sentencing, so infusing lay perspectives into the court judgments is regarded as the most important function of the jury system. The important question then, is how the lay perspectives are infused with the professional judgments. Given the nonbinding status of the jury verdict in the Korean jury system, the verdicts do not directly affect the final disposition of the case. There are several ways the common sense of the lay people interacts with the professional judgments, however. First of all, jurors are provided with a case overview, which includes information related to the case summary, relevant criminal codes, and previous judgments.[9] So jurors are assisted by the bench. In addition, more direct interaction is made during the deliberation itself because oftentimes the judge and the jury discuss the case together.

One of the most distinctive features of the Korean jury system is that the judge must provide information or opinions during the jurors' conviction deliberation when the jurors cannot reach a unanimous verdict.[10] Jurors can also request the judge's opinion by a majority vote any time during deliberation.[11] This means that many jury verdicts end up being reached after jurors' discussion with the judge. So, it may be likely that these judge interventions during deliberations will shape the final verdicts. In this context, the high matching rate of jury verdicts and court judgments may be a reflection of the joint deliberation when the jury is deadlocked.

This unique feature of the Korean jury system provides rare opportunities to examine the interaction of the lay people and the judge in deliberation. Some may worry that the intervention of judges may hinder the jurors' independent judgment, and consequently, make jurors dependent on the judge's opinion (Lee, E. 2009). Although the law mandates that judges not make a statement of guilty or not guilty when they discuss the trial with the jurors,[12] we cannot rule out the possibility of influence, without knowing exactly what is happening during deliberation.

Will the judge's intervention enhance the jurors' understanding of the case and the law, and subsequently lead to an informed and reasoned verdict? Or will it unduly interfere with their independent decision-making? When the opinions of jurors and judges drastically differ, how are jurors to reconcile such a discrepancy? What are the main areas of disagreements? Will there be a situation of jury nullification in the Korean jury system? This paper explores these questions through direct observation and the content analysis of the shadow jury deliberations in actual cases in Korea.

Method

The present chapter used the data we collected for the shadow jury deliberation study[13] that was conducted in two phases, between November 2010 and July 2011 (18 cases),[14] and between January 2012 and June 2012 (20 cases).[15] Two types of shadow jury groups were selected. One group was composed of juror candidates who were not selected during the *voir dire* ("research jury"). Another group was composed of people who were recruited by the court to serve as shadow jurors ("participatory jury").[16] In any given trial, therefore, one or two shadow jury groups were studied other than the real jury. We tried to match the number of the shadow jury to that of the real jury. However, it did not always match, due to the availability of the juror candidates who were willing to serve as shadow jurors.

We were first interested in the quality of deliberation. The participatory jury was relatively younger, more homogeneous, and more knowledgeable in law than the research jury: for example, students attending the same law school, workers in the same workplace, or trainees at the Judicial Research and Training Institute. However, there was no meaningful difference in gender distribution between these two jury groups.

We tried to make the environment of shadow jurors and that of real jurors as similar as possible. The shadow jury sat through the trial, retired, and then reached a verdict in parallel to the real jury. They were also given the case overview, just like the real jurors. They were assigned different rooms for deliberation in secret. When the judge's intervention was needed, an associate judge of the three-judge panel went into each room to discuss the case with the shadow jurors.[17] The shadow jurors remained until the final court judgment was rendered, oftentimes until late at night.[18]

Our research team was composed of lawyers and social scientists assisted by graduate students. We observed the trials from the beginning to the end, and then videotaped the shadow jury deliberations. We conducted a content analysis of the jury deliberation and investigated which factors might have influenced the nature of the deliberation. We paid attention to the jurors' demographic characteristics, their level of motivation in participating, political views, and also the composition of the jury such as the number of the jurors, their gender, profession, and how homogeneous or diverse the jury was. The role of the foreperson and his or her interaction with participants in debate and discussion was also noted. We also took survey questions from the shadow jurors three times at different stages: pre-deliberation, post-deliberation, and post-judgment. We created verbatim transcripts of thirteen deliberations, and conducted six in-depth interviews with shadow jurors after deliberation.

Rationality in Jury Deliberation

We are first interested in knowing how Korean jurors discuss fact-finding and sentencing and whether any meaningful deliberation happens in the process before investigating whether the judge's intervention enhances or hampers the jurors' deliberation. In other words, we examined the quality of deliberation of Korean jurors first.

In order to describe the dynamics of jury deliberation and its rationality, we used six criteria: instruction comprehension, evidence review, factual focus, systematic participation, informational influence, and the exclusion of emotion.[19] These six criteria were further divided into twenty variables for measurement. More importantly, we compared the performance of the two shadow jury groups. We believed the participatory jury would be a good reference group for the research jury because they were younger, more educated, and had stronger cognitive wants (e.g., more interested in the trial or the jury system), so their quality of deliberation would be higher. If the research jury's quality of deliberation was not substantially inferior to that of the participatory jury, then we could project that the real jury's quality of deliberation would be at an appropriate level because the research jury was regarded as the most approximate reflection of the real jury.

There are five variables that were derived from our direct observation of the deliberation process: the misunderstanding of legal concepts, the mixing of conviction/sentencing elements, the number of times evidence was cited, the amount of speech, and the amount of emotional speech. These were measured by the amount of speech by the jurors. For example, the misunderstanding of legal concepts means the amount of speech where the jurors were confused about the legal concepts such as the beyond a reasonable doubt or "*dolus eventualis*" (awareness of the likely outcome of an action). All the other variables were derived from the survey response. For instance, the level of understanding the law in the proceeding and jurors' recollection of the judge's instruction were measured by asking "[w]as the judge's instruction or explanation as to the law of the case difficult" and "[w]as it difficult to recollect the judge's instruction during deliberation," respectively.

Overall, our observations and analysis reveal that the "research jury" did not seem inferior to the "participatory jury" in terms of the rationality of jury deliberation even though the participatory jurors were younger, more educated, and more interested in the jury system to begin with. In terms of the t-test, the research jury scored less in three variables and more in four variables. In all other thirteen variables, no statistically meaningful differences were found (Lee et al. 2013b).

On the one hand, the research jury more frequently mixed the conviction elements with the sentencing elements in deliberation, made more emotional statements, and relied less on evidence in discussion. On the other hand, the research jury tended to recall the judge's instruction better and paid closer attention to the court proceedings. They also participated more actively in the deliberation and considered other jurors' opinions more widely and openly (Lee et al. 2013b). Although in general the research jury did not seem inferior to the participatory jury in terms of the rationality of jury deliberation, the results also suggest there is room for improvement for better jury deliberation.

This analysis of the quality of deliberation suggests that jurors understand the judges' instructions well, and understand and recollect the evidence of the case well. Generally, jurors speak sufficiently and participate in deliberation actively. The deliberation proceeded in an open and equitable manner. However, they tend to pay closer attention to the court proceedings rather than to the deliberation while finding facts, and this tendency leads to less evidence-based discussion. In some cases, a few jurors dominated the deliberation process and emotional factors often dominated the deliberation.

Intervention of Judge in Deliberation

Based upon the findings of the previous section on the deliberation quality, we now focus on how the judge's intervention during deliberation affects jurors' decision-making. The three areas in which the research jury scored less than the participatory jury (mixing conviction/sentencing elements, more emotional statements, less reliance on evidence) are very relevant in our discussion on the jury–judge joint deliberation. While some of these weaknesses of the research jury deliberation can be self-corrected, we can expect that these tendencies can be changed through the intervention of the judge in the deliberation. Indeed, many Korean judges who have presided over jury trials have stated that jurors asked for the judge's opinion because they had difficulty differentiating the factual determination and the legal interpretation (Moon 2013). Moreover, the sentencing procedure is highly technical and requires scientific and professional knowledge, so jurors may need more guidance from the judge.

Misunderstanding the Legal Concepts and Mixing Conviction/Sentencing Elements

Jurors typically confuse or misunderstand the key legal concepts and principles, such as "presumption of innocence," "beyond a reasonable doubt," "*dolus eventualis*" and consequently misapplied them during the deliberation. About 11.2 percent of the jurors we studied showed this tendency. One study found that Korean judges were not always clear in their explanations of the elements or degrees of a crime (Park et al. 2008). Another study suggested replacing obscure legal terminology with plain Korean language and to develop standardized jury instruction manuals to improve effective jury instructions (Oh 2007). A recent empirical study shows that a change in the jury instructions, such as adding more explanations and examples, made a difference in jurors' understanding of legal concepts such as "beyond a reasonable doubt" (Kim et al. 2011).

On Beyond a Reasonable Doubt

Juror #1: When we decide the matter of guilt, I think about the defendant as a person … his/her life … how the life can be changed by our decision. Considering all the circumstances, I personally think the defendant stole the purse …

Juror #2: You think the defendant committed a crime.

Juror #1: But there is no positive material evidence. Without such evidence, when we return the verdict ... what if the person did not steal it? ... how much will he suffer emotionally? That's what I am concerned about.

Juror #3: Yes, I think so too.

Juror #1: I think there is a 99% chance that the defendant did commit a crime.

Juror #3: Yes, but that 1% chance ...

Juror #1: If there is 1% chance he did not commit a crime, and if this can be confirmed, I would like to support that 1% chance. For his life. (Case II-14)[20]

As the juror above mentions, jurors tend to require a higher level of burden of proof than judges. Unlike judges who decide criminal cases on a daily basis, jurors have never been in a situation in which their judgments can decide somebody's fate. This pressure makes jurors extra-cautious in finding the defendant guilty. At the same time, they have been exposed to a popular TV drama that features a state-of-the-art scientific investigation of crime and they frequently expect a high level of material evidence.

On Presumption of Innocence

In the next case, the dominant theme of the deliberation was the presumption of innocence. On the one hand, the jurors seemed to ask for almost 100 percent burden of proof and they assumed that circumstantial evidence must be excluded from consideration. Therefore, any evidence presented by the prosecution was discarded if it did not confirm guilt. On the other hand, for victims' actions, some matters unrelated to the case were used as a basis; such as "a pregnant woman drank and smoked" or "the victim herself might have inflicted a searing wound by a cigarette." Anything that may not have supported the victim's statements was also discarded. The judge tried to remedy the error:

Juror #3: This wound can be fabricated later.
Judge: Is that a reasonable doubt?
Juror #3: It is based on experience.
Judge: The wound does not seem to come from the cigarette spark.
Juror #2: It was ten days after the victim was wounded, but the wound looks like a rash.
Judge: Then it was a bit seared. Then you can admit the battery but other things were inflated?
Juror #1: The burden of proof rests on the prosecution, right?

Judge: It seems much skewed (inclined). It is impossible to prove 100% when there is only the defendant and the victim. The statements of the defendant must be considered rationally by comparing the statements of the victim. You can only admit the battery but nothing else? The doubt must be reasonable.

Juror #6: The victim said she was drunk while she was pregnant.

Judge: (interrupting) That is her propensity, but can it be a reason not to believe what she was saying?

Juror #6: She was thinking about abortion, I guess. ...

Judge: Her behavior may be blameworthy but that does not make her statement less credible. The presumption of innocence does not mean the prosecution must prove the guilt 100%. If the defendant's argument is not reasonable, the victim's statement can be credible. If it is credible, this can be accepted as evidence.

Juror #4: I think the principle [of the presumption of innocence] we st[uck] to was too rigid, then.

Judge: Sometimes the principle can hinder finding the truth. Actually, defendants choose jury trials because jurors, as nonprofessionals, tend to adhere to the principle too much. They request an unduly high level of proof. (Case II-18)

Judge: Actually, the presumption of innocence, I think, can be too skewed. Prosecution should establish the guilt beyond a reasonable doubt. Where there are only the victim's and the defendant's statements available without positive proof, however, the prosecution cannot establish the guilt 100%. If we require the prosecution to produce evidence that can establish the guilt 100%, almost all the defendants will be acquitted. Of course, the presumption of innocence is the fundamental principle in criminal procedure. But sometimes jurors stick to the principle too rigidly by requesting too [great a] level of proof, and this eventually leads to the acquittal of the defendant. Of course, the opposite result can occur as well. (Case II-18)

Even though the judge's role is not to convince or persuade the jurors to reach a verdict in a particular direction, we may expect that the judge's intervention will contribute to lessen jurors' strict adherence to the presumption of innocence principle and the level of proof required to rebut the presumption.

On Dolus Eventualis

In Korea, jurors are provided a case overview in writing from the beginning of the trial[21] so their understanding of the legal concepts and relevant statutory provisions can be enhanced. But the way they are presented is sometimes complicated without an explanation by the judge. A frequent example is the defendant's criminal intent, as is illustrated by the following exchange. Here, the judge explains that the scope of intent is broader than what lay people might think, using the legal terminology "*dolus eventualis.*"

Judge: There exists an area in between definite intent and negligence: a person is aware that some event will occur. Let's assume that I live in a high-rise apartment with a veranda. Someone passes by underneath the veranda. I drop something, without pointing at a particular person. Even though I did not intend to injure someone, I am aware someone might be hit in a congested city in such a situation. Someone can die. I realize if I drop a very heavy object, someone might be accidentally hit and killed. So even though you don't have definite intent to kill, if you do an act knowing that your act can possibly lead to someone's death, you have intent to kill by *dolus eventualis*.

Juror #3: How can we determine whether a person is aware of such a possibility?

Judge: That's why we need to examine the objective circumstances. If you look at the case overview material the court provided, under the section "intent to kill" you can see relevant Supreme Court cases and an explanation about how to make decisions in this matter. The motive of crime, types of weapons used, method of the crime, wounds, and other relevant circumstances can provide a basis to ascertain the defendant's subjective intent. (Case I-7)

After the judge retired, jurors once again discussed the intent to kill. One juror started to broaden the scope of the intent and accepted the defendant's guilt by using the concept of *dolus eventualis*.

Juror #1: I thought this matter over. Anyway, the arrow was turned toward the victim whether or not it was definitely aimed at him. At the victim's testimony, what was contested was whether the arrow passed over his head. The arrow hit the wall about 2 meters above the ground. If we assume the defendant is about 180 cm tall, without his avoidance, he could have been hit. The defendant, at the moment he shot the arrow, must have known, even if [sub]consciously, that the arrow might hit the victim and kill him. So, under the *dolus eventualis*, I can accept his intent to kill. (Case I-7)

Mixing Conviction/Sentencing Elements

In Korean jury trials, procedures for verdict determination and sentencing are not separately managed. Frequently, evidence that is relevant to sentencing is introduced before the jury reaches its verdict. Evidence that is not necessarily relevant in determining the verdict—such as diminished capacity due to intoxication, the number of blows causing the bodily injury, or the defendant's prior criminal record—may influence the jurors' ruling on the facts. Some have suggested dividing jury trials into two separate phases, one to determine the verdict and the other for sentencing (Han 2008; Park 2012).

We examined whether sentencing-related matters were used by jurors in rendering judgment on the guilt of the defendant. If sentencing issues were introduced by jurors during the deliberation on guilt, we considered whether this was corrected through deliberation: in other words, whether the jurors recognized they were mixing sentencing issues in the conviction phase of the trial, and if they deliberately stopped doing that. Among the cases we observed in the first phase of the study, for instance, jurors mixed sentencing matters into the conviction deliberation in nine cases (50 percent). However, eight of these cases were corrected through deliberation, as in the example below:

> Juror #5: I think the defendant is guilty, based on what I saw during trial. But if the defendant is found guilty, he will face an aggravated sentence.
>
> Juror #3: The crime the defendant committed requires aggravation, it's true. But right now, we are supposed to decide whether the defendant is guilty or not. Other matters must be discussed during the sentencing deliberation, after we find the defendant guilty. (Case I-5) At the individual level, we also looked at each juror's situation to determine how many of them mixed together the distinct matters of conviction and sentencing during deliberation. In our first phase study, for instance, sixteen (14.2%) out of 113 jurors mixed them in arguments (see Table 7.1). Twenty-two (19.5%) jurors mentioned the defendant's criminal record during the conviction deliberation.

This illustrates that jurors sometimes reach the conviction verdict by considering sentencing matters. It is because the conviction and the sentencing proceedings are not separated in the Korean jury trial. Therefore, when the jurors are not sure of the defendant's guilt, some minority jurors join with other jurors for the guilty verdict by lowering sentencing, even though they think the defendant is innocent. Similarly, in Arizona civil jury cases, the jurors who opposed liability argued for lower awards than some other members who favored liability. This so-called fusion or spillover from damages to liability judgments occurs when jurors use damage information to judge the likely negligence of the defendant's actions (Diamond et al. 2012).

It is not easy for the jurors to separate conviction and sentencing, even though the judge instructs them not to consider them together. Empirical research has

Table 7.1 Frequency of Combining Conviction and Sentencing Considerations

Variables	Value	Frequencies (%)
Confusion of guilt-sentencing	Yes	16 (14.2%)
	No	97 (85.8%)
Mentioning prior criminal records	Yes	22 (19.5%)
	No	91 (80.5%)
Total		113 (100.0%)

Source: Jae Hyup Lee, et al. 2013a, "What's Happening in the Jury Room: Analyzing Shadow Jury Deliberations in Korea," *Journal of Korean Law* 13 (1): 41–68.

demonstrated the biasing effect of the information related to the sentencing, especially the criminal record of the defendant (Eisenberg and Hans 2009). However, mixing the factual determination with the sentencing judgment is not only a problem for jurors. Judges likewise may not always separate the factual determination factors and the sentencing factors in their judgments.

Emotional Statements

It is generally believed that each deliberation should be guided by logic and reason rather than emotion. However, emotions do play important roles in decision-making in general (Damasio 1994) as well as within a legal setting in particular (Feigenson and Park 2006). Moreover, excluding emotion completely would be very difficult in practice, and may not even be desirable. In our study, about 23 percent of jurors made sympathetic comments and exhibited emotional attitudes. Comments such as "if the defendant is found guilty, the defendant and his family may experience hardship," or "the defendant's miserable early childhood and upbringing contributed to the commission of the crime"[22] show jurors' emotion. As the juror in the excerpt below mentions, the consequence of the verdict is often considered with emotions:

> Juror #4: It would be difficult for me to punish (by verdict) the defendant simply as a matter of law, knowing there exists no mechanism in our society to support the defendant's living after he comes back from prison. Can we the people make judgment on the defendant strictly on the basis of law? Even if we hold the defendant guilty, we should be cautious in considering adequate sentencing for the defendant. (Case I-9)

A judge mentions that jurors' sympathetic attitudes are often manifested during sentencing deliberation.

> Judge: It is rare to see jurors' opinions on sentencing converge like this. I typically get sentencing opinions in murder cases from 10 years in prison to … even 2 1/2 years in prison with suspension. Jurors tend to be swayed by defendants' stories that they were wrongfully charged. Such jurors might be sympathetic to the defendant and even think the defendant should be the victim instead. That's why the jurors provide opinions like the suspended sentence. (Case I-12)

Generally speaking, the jury deliberation is based not only on the legal reasoning and the evidence, but also on non-legal factors. For example, the personal factors of the defendant or the family surroundings may sometimes be considered and may not unduly affect reasonable judgment. One scholar divided the deliberation process into the rational deliberation model and the relational deliberation model. He argued that emotion can oftentimes deepen the discussion and induce more participation (Ryfe

2002). Empathy is said to enhance the seriousness of a juror's commitment to the deliberation process (Pettys 2007). So, the involvement of emotion will not create a problem in all cases.

> Juror #1: As I said before, it is an emotional appeal. six years … I think three years after the full reduction is still too harsh. The function of punishment is rehabilitation, right? I don't think the defendant will be rehabilitated after serving the sentence. I think he will be much more rehabilitated in a society than in prison. First of all, the prison has not functioned well for him; he has not been rehabilitated after serving prison many times. In terms of the habitual character of the crime, hmmm … I think the evidence establishes the habitual crime. But the reason why I did not accept the habitual character was that, because of his limited cognitive function, he could not think that he was violating the law. So I did not think he was habitually stealing. But the law should not discriminate in application; it should be applied with a fair and objective standard. In that sense, I can recognize the habitual character. However, three years is so harsh … even after the discretionary reduction … I have a lot of difficulty in rendering a decision like this. … I remember an American movie, is it "Born to Kill"? It looks like the jury system was created to infuse common sense, the way the community feels. In the movie, jurors deliberated so hard, emotionally, I mean. In the end, the jurors made an emotional decision, and the defendant was acquitted. (Case I-13)

Sometimes this anecdotal or empathetic consideration will make the issue clearer and help to legitimize jurors' conviction determination. Therefore, the emotional factor will not hinder the reasoned decisions but clarify in the particular context.

Our inquiry was not focused on the frequency of the emotional statements. Rather, we were particularly interested in evaluating whether jurors found it difficult to make a legally correct decision due to their emotions. We tried to evaluate this undue influence in making a legally correct decision. Our observation suggests that jurors' emotions sometimes obstructed their ability to make decisions. In the case of the "diminished capacity," jurors frequently recognize it in order to lower sentencing, instead of finding the fulfillment of the legal elements.

> Juror: I would like to accept the diminished capacity but it is not easy. The defendant looks like a habitual criminal. If we do not recognize the diminished capacity, he will be sentenced to more than six years. I think this is too severe, so I would like to vote for not guilty because of this harsh sentencing. I know I may be emotional. If I should exclude the emotional consideration, I would rather go for a guilty verdict and try to reduce the sentencing. But I still think the defendant's behavior does not seem to qualify as a habitual crime, so at the moment I would like to vote for a not-guilty

verdict. I haven't completely made up my mind, so I will think about it more. (Case I-13)

The juror in the above case finds it difficult to reach a guilty verdict because the sentence imposed will be unduly severe if the habitual crime is recognized. The discrepancy between laypeople's perception of the proper sentence and the actual sentence imposed by the court is explained by a judge in the following segment:

Judge: Finding the diminished capacity is difficult. Indeed, there are many gray areas. As the prosecution pointed out, the diminished capacity argument sometimes functions as a tool to reduce the sentencing, especially when the law requires a stringent sentencing. For instance, the minimum sentence for the bodily injury resulting from robbery is seven years. If the court gives a full reduction, it could be reduced to three and one-half years without suspension. But there are many types of it. Let's say a college kid who got drunk from a Christmas Eve party tried to steal something at a convenience store. The clerk saw it and in the course of preventing the kid, got bruised. By definition, a bodily injury occurred resulting from robbery. Three and a half years in prison for that college kid even after the full reduction … rather harsh punishment for the kid. So in that case, the court asks "Did you get drunk? So drunk that you did not know what you were doing?" In this way, the diminished capacity due to intoxication can be used to further reduce the sentence. I don't think it is a right thing to do, but is frequently practiced. I think the diminished capacity argument might have been introduced at today's case as a tool for reducing sentencing. So, I suggest you to think about this matter not from the perspective of sentencing. Insanity must only be accepted when the defendant suffers a total lack of awareness or control of his action. If the defendant suffers a lesser amount of awareness or control, then the diminished capacity can be accepted. (Case I-9)

As we have seen, sentencing is one of the most frequent areas where the juror's sympathy and emotions are engaged. Indeed, the public distrust of the judiciary in criminal trials had focused on the sentencing issue, so lay participation in sentencing deliberation was inevitable from the start (Han 2006). It has long been claimed that some Korean judges make sentencing decisions arbitrarily and so are not consistent. In the following deliberation segments, jurors discuss the sentencing with a judge. The judge then admits the existence of a discrepancy between the public perception of the proper sentencing and the mandatory sentencing, but explains this may have more to do with some "populist" special laws enacted by the National Assembly.

Juror #1: The nature of the crime is not trivial and the defendant has committed larceny a number of times in the past, but I don't think he committed a crime serious enough to put him in prison for seven years or longer. So, I cannot vote for guilty of the bodily injury resulting from robbery.

Juror #2: I think so too, like most jurors in this room.
Juror #1: For example, even if committed as a self-defense, those who kill a person in self-defense will only serve a minimum of three years. Stealing 40,000 won (USD 40) and beating a person, then the defendant is sentenced to seven years? That's absurd. (Case I-12)
Juror #2: Oftentimes politicians who were convicted with bribery or something receive ten years in prison. Then after a few years, they are released, and then reinstated. Now a seven-year prison sentence for the defendant in this case, in comparison with these people, seems to be unduly harsh. All sentencing decisions must be equitable, but I am not sure the court rightly applies this principle.
Judge: In some sex crimes, especially the widely publicized ones, sentencing decisions for more than ten years of prison are not rare. This sentencing may be higher than some murder cases. I am not saying murder cases, in all cases, must be punished more severely than sex crimes. But I cannot deny some special laws have been promulgated in response to public opinions, and therefore have generally stricter sentencing provisions. For example, An Act of Punishment of Violence, etc. has it that for most crimes under the Act, the minimum sentence is one year or two years or three years. So, if someone raises disturbance at night with a bat and injures someone, he may face a three-year sentence. (Case I-18)

Through this deliberation process, lay people can raise their opinion that the sentencing provisions in some laws are not in line with their legal consciousness, and they have subsequently brought about occasional acquittal of the defendants. This apparent mismatch of the jury verdict and the law has functioned as a de facto nullification. Records show that there is little discrepancy between jurors' opinions and the judge's sentencing decisions (NCA 2015). It may be that the judges take the jurors' opinions into consideration, or it may be that the jurors and the judges independently tend to reach similar conclusions about sentencing. It also led to an opportunity for lawmakers to reflect on their views in the revision of the sentencing provisions.

Change of Opinion

Judge intervention in the deliberation can enhance jurors' understanding. Our results indicate that there are few undue influences of the judges' explanation and opinion on the jurors' independent decision-making. In considering the effect of judges' participation on jury panels as a whole, there was only one case where all jurors changed their opinion about the defendant's guilt after the judge's intervention. In two cases, half of the jurors changed their opinions. One or two jurors changed opinions in three cases. But in almost all the other cases, each juror's position on the defendant's guilt did not change.

On the individual level, we have divided judges who intervened at the jury deliberation into three groups in accordance with the style of their discussion with jurors: (1) information-delivering type; (2) opinion-introducing type; and (3) conclusion-inducing type (see Table 7.2).[23] The percentages of judges, respectively, were 64.6 percent (information-delivering type), 29.2 percent (opinion-introducing type), and 6.2 percent (conclusion-inducing type). Notably, when the judge was a conclusion-inducing type, all jurors changed their decisions after discussions with the judge. In the case of opinion-introducing type judges, 30.3 percent of jurors changed their positions. In the case of information-delivering type judges, 23.3 percent of jurors changed their decisions. Therefore, the evidence indicates that when a judge interjects his or her opinion strongly during the deliberation, jurors are more likely to follow the judge's opinion, although we cannot provide any conclusive generalization due to the limited number of cases.

To illustrate the possibility of influence of the judge on the jury deliberation, in one instance, a judge expressed his opinion after hearing jurors' opinions and the supporting evidence. He distinguished assault with apprehension and mentioned that assault is easily accepted. Eventually the judge's explanation led to jurors' acceptance of guilty of assault. The judge then explained that jurors and the judges thought similarly on the guilt of the defendant.

> Judge: I will explain the legal concept of assault and arrest. Assault is straightforward. If someone makes another apprehended by whatever means, assault is established. There are many ways to make people apprehended, by words or by actions. Did the victims get apprehended before leaving the elevator or did they leave without apprehension? If the former, then there is assault. But here they left the elevator. That may be what the defendant

Table 7.2 Jurors' Change of Positions and the Type of Judges in Deliberation

Types of judges	Frequency %	Jurors changed position?		Total
		Yes	No	
Information-delivering	Frequency	17	56	73
	%	23.3%	76.7%	100.0%
Opinion introducing	Frequency	10	23	33
	%	30.3%	69.7%	100.0%
Conclusion inducing	Frequency	7	0	7
	%	100.0%	.0%	100.0%
Total	Frequency	34	79	113
	%	30.1%	69.9%	100.0%

x^3=17.871, df=2, p=.000

Source: Jae Hyup Lee, et al. 2013a, "What's Happening in the Jury Room: Analyzing Shadow Jury Deliberations in Korea," *Journal of Korean Law* 13 (1): 41–68.

intended. He may have wanted to tie the hands of the victims with the cable string so that they could not move.

Juror #4: It is problematic to tie them with a cable string. Even if he did, this will not lead to a situation to restrain the victims.

Judge: Restraint is a different concept that is beyond the scope of assault. If the victims are restrained, then the arrest applies. The crime of arrest means restraining a person from moving; assault in most cases stops before arrest. Generally, a person assaults another tries to move or does something, then after assault, he will take other actions. In that case, the arrest applies. Suppose someone assaults in order to arrest, but couldn't. The victim ran away, being apprehended. Assault is established when someone is apprehended by whatever means. It is one of the least serious crimes, which can be easily thought of. (Case I-7)

Several changes occurred after the introduction of the jury system to court proceedings in Korea. The prosecution and the defense must present their cases in order to convince the jury using simpler terminology in a more concentrated and adversarial manner than non-jury trials. At the same time, however, jurors evaluate the professionals in the courtroom (judges, prosecutors, and the defense attorneys) when they form opinions about the case. Our survey result indicates the role of the judges is a determining factor in shaping the jurors' perception of the fairness of the trial (Woo et al. 2013). So when jurors think they would be more assisted by the judge during the deliberation, their recognition of the fairness of the trial improved.

Besides this positive effect of the judge's intervention, we have noted another aspect of interaction. Sometimes judges are affected by jurors as well. The judge's statement below implies that the influence can go in both directions, including from the juror to the judge.

Judge: I went downstairs and thought about it. After I watched three jurors (out of five) having difficulty accepting the habitual character of the crime, I thought maybe the court has been too lenient in accepting it. Recognizing the habitual character makes such heavy impacts on the defendant. (Case I-13)

Through interaction with lay jurors during the deliberation, judges can reexamine the matters that are often overlooked or missed if they discuss the case only with professional judges. This two-way influence will then further the legislative purpose of the Act, that is, joining common sense and lay perspectives with professional judgment. Indeed, many presiding judges of the jury trial have indicated they were impressed by jurors' performance in the jury room, as is manifested in the segment below.

Judge: Four people are in favor of not-guilty and one person finds the defendant guilty. ... The result is similar to that of our judge panel. One judge found for guilty. ... Our panel has held about ten jury trials, and over 200 jury trials countrywide. Some worried about how well jurors perform their duty, as

> they are not professionally trained. But if we look at the results, jury verdicts match with court decisions nine out of ten times. As we hold more jury trials, we judges come to realize that the jury system is quite a good institution. Of course, it is an arduous process, but jurors become more knowledgeable about the law and understand better about the trial process. In turn, courts can get [the] public's opinion which can be useful for judgment. (Case I-7)

Conclusion

In this chapter, we tried to infer the actual jury deliberation process from examining shadow jury deliberations. We found the quality of deliberation of the Korean shadow jury was generally high. Misunderstanding law and the intermingling of facts relevant to conviction or sentencing were not as frequent as many people expected. Moreover, when such problems occurred, they were most often corrected through the intervention of other jurors or judges. Most judges were helpful in assisting jurors to reach a verdict in the jury room. They provided explanations on the key legal principles with examples and cases, answered jurors' questions about difficult legal concepts, and interacted with jurors in discussing appropriate sentencing. With judges' proper guidance and oversight, jurors were less likely to mix conviction and sentencing considerations. In addition, juror deliberations on sentencing provided the opportunity to combine the common sense of the lay people with the judge's decision-making.

In Korean jury trials, the judge's intervention during the deliberation of jurors seems to have functioned to enhance the jurors' informed judgments, rather than to obstruct their independent judgments. The results show that the collaborative deliberation amongst jurors and judges in sentencing, and in some cases in conviction, will mutually benefit both. In turn, jurors will contribute to the credibility of the judiciary while the judges will reflect upon their decisions in accordance with the legal consciousness of the lay people.

Notes

1 For a general overview of the background and history of the Korean jury system and the relevant legal provisions, *see* Lee, J. (2009) and Lee (2010).

2 During this period, the jury verdict is advisory. A major reason why the jury verdict in Korea is advisory is to avoid a potential constitutional challenge. Because Article 27(1) of the Korean Constitution gives one the right to be tried by a judge, a binding jury verdict may conflict with this right by putting the fate of the defendant in the hands of lay people (Daehanminguk Hunbeob [Constitution of the Republic of Korea] 1987).

3 The number of jury trials was 64 in 2008, 95 in 2009, 162 in 2010, 253 in 2011, 274 in 2012, 345 in 2013, and 271 in 2014.

4 Currently, jurors can render a verdict based on a simple majority. The Act, article 46(3).

5 Depending on the severity of the case and the defendant's plea, the number of jurors in a Korean jury trial can be five, seven, or nine. The Act, article 13(1). In practice, five jurors were seldom used (6.4 percent) (NCA 2015).

6 On December 31, 2013, the Ministry of Justice posted a bill for public comments. Beopmubu Gonggo 2013-288. At the time of this chapter's publication, legislation is under review by the National Assembly for passage.

7 Among the 105 cases in which the verdict and the ruling did not match, the jury verdict was not guilty and the judges' verdict was guilty in 97 cases. For an empirical analysis of the jury–judge decision matching, *see* Kim et al. (2013).

8 The two main legislative purposes were to increase democratic participation of the lay people and to enhance the credibility of the judiciary. The Act, article 1(1).

9 Providing a case overview is a unique feature of the Korean system. Although it is not specified in the Act, this has been the consistent practice of the court.

10 The Act, article 46(3).

11 Judges provide their opinions to the jurors, although they should not make a statement of guilty or not guilty. After the judges and the jurors have discussed the guilt of the defendant together, the jurors, again outside of the presence of the judges, render a verdict based on a simple majority. The Act, article 46(2) and article 46(3).

12 Gukminui hyeongsajaepan chamyeo e gwanhan gyuchik, article 41(5).

13 This study was commissioned by the National Court Administration of the Supreme Court of Korea.

14 The results of the first phase study were published in Lee et al. (2013a).

15 The results of the second phase study were published in Lee et al. (2013b) and Woo et al. (2013).

16 In Korea, a number of district courts around the country started a "shadow jury program" in September 2010, in order for people to actually experience the judicial process through voluntary participation. The court intended to improve the public perception of the judiciary's credibility through this program. So far the program has been successfully administered. The Seoul Central District Court, for instance, has administered the shadow jury program more than thirty times since January 2011. More than 400 people volunteered to become shadow jurors (Seoul Central District Court 2011). We categorized this shadow jury group as "participatory jury" in our study.

17 All jury trials in Korea are conducted by a three-judge panel.

18 In one instance, the jury deliberation was completed around 3:00 am.

19 The first five criteria are very similar to those used in Devine et al. (2007).

20 Case II-14 refers to the case number 14 that we observed in our Phase II study. The numbering throughout this chapter follows the same rule.

21 A sample case overview (or juror's guide) that is used in a Korean court can be found in the Appendix in Hans (2014).

22 In the United States, jurors in capital cases are permitted to consider such "mitigating circumstances" in the sentencing phase. For further discussion on jury sentencing in the United States, *see* Hans et al. (2015).

23 If the judge simply provides the information related to the case at hand or informs jurors about how similar cases are handled by courts, such style is regarded as "information-delivering." If the judge provides his or her opinion by saying "I think … " or "[I]n my opinion … " then we categorized it as "opinion-introducing." When the judge's opinion is expressed strongly, then it is regarded as "conclusion-inducing."

On one such occasion, the judge said "if the defendant is found not guilty under the circumstances, we can say that justice does not prevail in this case."

Bibliography

Beopmubu Gonggo [Ministry of Justice Public Notice] 2013-288. Effective February 12, 2016. http://making.law.go.kr/lmSts/ogLmPp/17936.

Daehanminguk Hunbeob [Constitution of the Republic of Korea]. 1987. Effective February 12, 2016. http://www.law.go.kr/lsInfoP.do?lsiSeq=61603&urlMode=engLsInfoR&viewCls=engLsInfoR#0000.

Damasio, Antonio. *Descartes' Error: Emotion, Reason, and the Human Brain*. New York: Putnam, 1994.

Devine, Dennis J., Jennifer Buddenbaum, Stephanie Houp, Dennis P. Stolle, and Nathan Studebaker. "Deliberation Quality: A Preliminary Examination in Criminal Juries." *Journal of Empirical Legal Studies* 4, no. 2 (2007): 273–303.

Diamond, Shari Seidman, Beth Murphy, and Mary R. Rose. "The 'Kettleful of Law' in Real Jury Deliberations: Successes, Failures, and Next Steps." *Northwestern University Law Review* 106, no. 4 (2012): 1537–608.

Eisenberg, Theodore, and Valerie P. Hans. "Taking a Stand on Taking the Stand: The Effect of a Prior Criminal Record on the Decision to Testify and on Trial Outcomes." *Cornell Law Review* 94, no. 6 (2009): 1353–90.

Eisenberg, Theodore, Paula L. Hannaford-Agor, Valerie P. Hans, Nicole L. Waters, G. Thomas Munsterman, Stewart J. Schwab, and Martin T. Wells. "Judge-Jury Agreement in Criminal Cases: A Partial Replication of Kalven and Zeisel's The American Jury." *Journal of Empirical Legal Studies* 2, no. 1 (2005): 171–206.

Feigenson, Neal, and Jaihyun Park. "Emotions and Attributions of Legal Responsibility and Blame: A Research Review." *Law and Human Behavior* 30, no. 2 (2006): 143–61.

Gukminui hyeongsajaepan chamyeoe gwanhan beopryul [Act for Civil Participation in Criminal Trials]. Act No. 8495, June 1, 2007 (S. Kor.).

Gukminui hyeongsajaepan chamyeo e gwanhan gyuchik [Rule for Civil Participation in Criminal Trials]. Sup. Ct. Rule No. 2107, October 29, 2007.

Han, In Sup."Hangukui Baesimwonjaepan [Criminal Jury Trials in South Korea: Issues and Initial Experiments]." *Seouldaehakgyo Beophak* [Seoul Law Journal] 50, no. 2 (2009): 681–710.

Han, Sang Hoon."Gukminchamyeojaepanjedoeui Jeongchakbanghyang [Recent Developments and Suggestions for the New Civil Participation in Criminal Trials System in Korea]." *The Justice* 106 (2008): 483–534.

Han, Sang Hoon. "Gukminui Hyeongsajaepanchamyeojedo Ipbeopnonui [Legislative Discussion on Civil Participation in Criminal Trials]." *Beopgwa Sahoe* [Law and Society] 30 (2006): 303–16.

Hans, Valerie. "Reflections on the Korean Jury Trial." *Journal of Korean Law* 14, no. 1 (2014): 81–115.

Hans, Valerie P., John H. Blume, Theodore Eisenberg, Amelia Courtney Hritz, Sheri L. Johnson, Caisa Elizabeth Royer, and Martin T. Wells. "The Death Penalty: Should the Judge or the Jury Decide Who Dies." *Journal of Empirical Legal Studies* 12, no. 1 (2015): 70–99.

Kalven, Harry, and Hans Zeisel. *The American Jury*. Boston: Little, Brown, 1966.

Kim, Ji Hoon, Eun Jung Lee, and Sang Hoon Han. "Haprijeok Uisimui Yeoji Eopneun Jeungmyeong Gijune Daehan Baesimwonui Ihaedo Yeongu [Study on Mock Juror's Understanding of Proof beyond a Reasonable Doubt Standard]." *Beophakyeongu* [Yonsei Law Review] 21, no. 2 (2011): 1–42.

Kim, Sangjoon, Jaihyun Park, Kwangbai Park, and Jin-Sup Eom. "Judge-Jury Agreement in Criminal Cases: The First Three Years of the Korean Jury System." *Journal of Empirical Legal Studies* 10, no. 1 (2013): 35–53.

Lee, Eun Jung. "Hyeonhaeng Gukminchamyeojaepanjedoui Naeyonggwa Munjejeom: Ilbonui Jaepanwonjedowaui Bigyoreul Jungsimuro [The Substance and Problems of the New Citizen Participation Criminal Trials System: A Comparison with Japan's Lay Judge System]." *Beophaknonchong* [Hanyang Law Review] 26, no. 1 (2009): 405–26.

Lee, Jae Hyup. "Getting Citizens Involved: Civil Participation in Judicial Decision-Making in Korea." *East Asia Law Review* 4, no. 2 (2009): 177–207.

Lee, Jae Hyup. "Korean Jury Trial: Has the New System Brought about Changes?" *Asian-Pacific Law and Policy Journal* 12, no. 1 (2010): 58–71.

Lee, Jae Hyup, Jisuk Woo, June Woong Rhee, Jeong Min Choi, and Hyunki Shin. "What's Happening in the Jury Room: Analyzing Shadow Jury Deliberations in Korea." *Journal of Korean Law* 13 , no. 1 (2013a): 41–68.

Lee, Jae Hyup, Jisuk Woo, and June Woong Rhee. "Baesimwon Pyeonguiui Hapriseonge Gwanhan Yeongu: Gukminchamyeojaepaneseoui Geurimja Baesim Pyeongui Bunseok [A Study on the Rationality of the Jury Deliberation: Analysis of the Shadow Jury Deliberations in Korean Jury Trials]." *The Justice* 139 (2013b): 208–49.

Moon, In Seob. "Gukminchamyeojaepan Baesimwone Daehan Silmujeok Jeobgeun [Practical Approach on Jurors of Jury System]." *The Justice* 135 (2013): 173–200.

National Court Administration. *2008–2014 Gukmin Chamyeo Jaepan Seonggwabunseok* [Analysis of Performance of the Civil Participatory Criminal Trials, 2008–2014]. Seoul: National Court Administration, 2015.

Oh, Geol. "Baesimwonui Pandanneungryeok [The Ability of Juries to Find Fact]." *The Justice* 96 (2007): 124–38.

Park, Hee Jin. "Baesimwon Yanghyeonge Gwanhan Jaengjeom Geomto [Study on Selected Issues of Jury Sentencing]." *Hyeongsajeongchaekyeongu* [Korean Criminological Review] 90 (2012): 41–74.

Park, Misuk, Jeongmin Yi, Jitae Hwang, Gwangjun Kim, Hyeonggwan Chu, and Yuseok Yim. *Gukminchamyeojaepane Daehan Chamgwanmit Josayeongu* [A Study of the Jury Trial System in Korea]. Seoul: Korean Institute of Criminology, 2008.

Pettys, Todd. "Emotional Juror." *Fordham Law Review* 76, no. 3 (2007): 1609–40.

Ryfe, David. "The Practice of Deliberative Democracy: A Study of 16 Deliberative Organizations." *Political Communication* 19, no. 3 (2002): 359–77.

Seoul Central District Court. *Gukminchamyeojaepan Geurimjabaesim Chamyeo Annaemun* [A Guide to Shadow Jury Program]. Seoul: Seoul Central District Court, 2011. Effective February 28, 2015. http://newsletter.seoulbar.or.kr/system/webzine/viewDownFile.php?id=167.

Woo, Jisuk, June Woong Rhee, and Jae Hyup Lee. "Jaepanui Gongjeongseonge Daehan Insige Yeonghyangul Michinun Yoine Daehan Yeongu [The Effects of Trial Procedure Factors and Deliberation Factors on the Perception of Fairness about the Trial—Based on Shadow Jurors' Experiences at Jury Trials in Korea]." *Seouldaehakgyo Beophak* [Seoul Law Journal] 54, no. 4 (2013): 261–89.

This chapter was previously published under the same title in Oñati Socio-Legal Series 6, no. 2 (2016): 179–196.

8

Diversity, Dialogue, and Deliberation

An Empirical Investigation of Age, Gender, and Meaningful Decision-Making in Korean Juries

Jisuk Woo and Justin D. Levinson

Introduction

American legal discourse has long supported the importance of achieving diversity on juries.[1] Representative juries, in which individuals from a wide range of backgrounds, life experiences, and perspectives participate in deliberation and decision-making, reflect American values of equality, opportunity, and fair treatment for all citizens.[2] The US Supreme Court, reflecting these values, has repeatedly acknowledged that the representativeness of the American jury is as an important element of a litigant's right to a fair trial.[3]

Scholarly interest in jury diversity in the United States reflects this historical belief that diversity promotes just trial outcomes. Until the past fifty years, however, it was less clear whether and how this belief is realized in jury deliberation processes. Empirical studies have now provided meaningful insight into the connection between representativeness, justice, and participation, and largely support the contention that the best juries possess meaningful diversity.[4] Outside of the American context, however, it is unclear whether and how diversity promotes, or perhaps hinders, jury deliberations. This knowledge gap is heightened in non-Western cultural contexts, such as in East Asia. Because "jury-style" systems have emerged in locations such as Taiwan,[5] Japan,[6] and Korea,[7] the cultural context of Western-validated empirical assumptions must be recognized and pursued. Cultural psychological research, for example, has shown differences between Eastern and Western cultures, in areas such as understanding of causation and intentionality,[8] conceptions of conflict tolerance,[9] and view regarding the appropriateness of severe punishment.[10] It has not been studied yet, however, how much these cultural differences may reflect or perhaps challenge the conclusions made by American scholars, including previous findings that (1) diversity of background adds to the quality of deliberations, and (2) better quality deliberations involve meaningful participation by the most jurors possible.

In this chapter, we seek to determine the role of diversity in Korean jury deliberations and contribute to a nascent field of empirical literature focusing on

East Asian juries. Furthermore, we investigate whether speech diversity,[11] in addition to age and gender diversity,[12] affects the quality of jury deliberations. To pursue these goals, we coded and analyzed data from a unique study[13] of full video recordings of thirty-two shadow juries that sat in for nineteen actual criminal cases in Korea.[14] The remainder of the chapter is structured as follows: the second section begins by considering the diversity of American juries, from a theoretical and empirical perspective. It notes the differing American theoretical perspectives regarding fair cross section and cultural experience, and describes studies documenting the important role of diversity in decision-making. It concludes by contextualizing this American work in Korea, where juries are a new part of the legal system, having been introduced to criminal trials in 2008. The third section turns to examine the role of juror engagement and speech in deliberations. It reviews empirical research from American juries and describes the different theories of jury deliberations, highlighting what makes these juries most effective. The fourth section presents the methods and materials of the empirical study we designed. We conducted an in-depth analysis of demographic and speech diversity in Korean jury deliberations, using full-length videos of thirty-two jury deliberations in nineteen real cases, as part of a program sponsored by the National Court Administration of Korea. The fifth section presents the results. We found that age and gender diversity harmed the efficacy of Korean jury deliberation, while speech diversity predicted success. The last section contextualizes these results, looks toward future research, and concludes.

Diversity and the Jury: Theory and Empirical Evidence from the United States

The jury has long been a core component of the American legal system, but scientific interest in jury decision-making processes has emerged only recently. Until the 1950s, the idea of using empirical studies to understand legal assumptions had not yet emerged. Since the 1990s, there has been a relative explosion of empirical methods in legal analysis. Yet, relevant data on jury diversity is still less robust than commentators might hope, partly due to the difficulty researchers face in accessing and analyzing realistic jury deliberations.[15] Nonetheless, because of the long-held American view that the representativeness of diverse groups in the jury is an essential element of the defendant's right to a fair trial, some research has focused on evaluating whether diversity indeed leads to fairer trial outcomes.

Scholars have investigated the effect of jury diversity using a variety of methods. Leslie Ellis and Shari Diamond found, for example, that jury diversity indeed promotes the sense of a fair trial.[16] Ellis and Diamond found that when citizens were provided with the description of a trial involving an all-White jury and a Black defendant, those citizens perceived a guilty verdict to be less fair than when they were told that the verdict was given by a mixed-race jury.[17] Diversity has also been found to promote juror satisfaction with the deliberation and verdict. Nancy Marder, in her research on demographic diversity (gender, race, and age) in deliberations, found that jurors who participated in more diverse juries reported being more satisfied with the deliberations and the verdict.[18]

Other empirical studies of jury diversity in the United States have examined how gender plays a role in the deliberation process.[19] An empirical study by Marder on cultural diversity and deliberations found that some types of diversity, such as gender and age, can make a positive difference in the tone and thoroughness of deliberations.[20] Gender had the strongest effect on deliberations.[21] As the jury became more gender diverse, the tone became less hostile, more harmonious, and jurors became more supportive of each other.[22] Furthermore, as gender diversity increased, the jurors perceived the deliberations to be more thorough.[23] In addition, jurors were also more satisfied with their deliberations, their jury experience, and their verdict.[24] Marder suggested that courts should strive for petit juries that contain an equal or almost equal number of men and women.[25]

Studies using mock trials similarly concluded that more diversity resulted in more thorough deliberation. Samuel Sommers found that racially heterogeneous groups (with white and Black jurors) deliberated longer and considered a wider range of information than did racially homogeneous groups (with white jurors only).[26] Sommers also pointed out that these differences did not solely result from Black participants adding different perspectives to the discussion, but also because white participants raised more case facts, made fewer factual errors, and were more amenable to the discussion of race-related issues when they were in a diverse group versus in an all-white group.[27] Sommers concluded that racially diverse groups were more thorough and competent than homogeneous ones: "Jury representativeness can be more than a moral or Constitutional ideal; it is sometimes an ingredient for superior performance."[28] This finding suggests that jury diversity is not only important for equal access and legitimacy, but also an important element that changes the dynamics of the deliberation process. This leads us to think that it would be worth examining the ways in which the diversity of the jury influences the deliberation process more systematically.

Another core element of American research on jury diversity is the size of the jury, in that larger juries potentially allow for more diversity to manifest within a diverse society. Shari Diamond and colleagues analyzed jury selection and composition in 277 civil jury trials and found that jury size had a substantial effect on minority representation.[29] In their study, twelve-member juries included more minority representation than six-member juries.[30] Diamond concluded that reducing jury size would negatively influence representation of minorities on the jury and criticized contemporaneous reform efforts to reduce the jury size.[31] William Schreckhise and Charles Sheldon found in their study on juries in Washington, DC, that supplementing juror source lists with driver's license and state identification card lists, rather than exclusively using voter registration lists, resulted in greater diversity.[32]

These studies have made important contributions to the literature on jury diversity by analyzing mock trial deliberations using objective criteria. In Korean juries,[33] the study we present similarly employs a diversity-based approach, applying concepts of demographic and speech diversity to real trials.

Balanced Participation, Sufficient Engagement, and Quality of Deliberation

To contextualize our empirical study of diversity and deliberation in Korean jurors, we next consider the dynamics of the deliberation process. We ask: what do the best juries do when deliberating and how can one measure these qualities? In pursuing this inquiry, we seek to further engage empirical studies of jury deliberation by evaluating how particular elements of the deliberations, such as speech diversity and argument engagement, are related to overall jury success.

Empirical studies measuring the quality of deliberations have been plentiful, but still less common than one might expect, despite historically prominent discussions in the literature indicating that dynamics of deliberations can influence their outcomes.[34] In American juries, Reid Hastie and colleagues have led the way in developing a model of jury decision-making, which characterizes two differing, yet dominant, styles of deliberations: verdict-driven and evidence-driven.[35] Verdict-driven deliberations occur when jurors announce their position about the case at the beginning of the discussion, followed by citations to evidence in support of that specific position.[36] On the other hand, evidence-driven deliberations occur when jurors' opinions are expressed late in the group discussion and evidence is first reviewed without reference to the verdict categories.[37] Researchers have found that evidence-driven deliberations generally have higher levels of participation and include wider-ranging discussions.[38] In contrast, verdict-driven deliberations feature early and frequent polling, and harbor pressures to conform to the majority. Interestingly, they also include a greater likelihood of a hung jury.[39]

Despite the research favoring evidence-driven deliberations, scholars who study American juries found that verdict-driven juries are more common than evidence-driven juries. Furthermore, researchers who have developed their own theories of deliberation have identified a general leniency bias whereby jurors' first ballots tend to predict final verdicts.[40] The famous jury researchers Harry Kalven and Hans Ziesel even concluded, on the basis of survey data from 225 actual jury trials, that "the real decision is often made before the deliberation begins."[41] In this context, jurors who actively participate by making comments and arguments based on evidence make deliberations a meaningful fact-finding process. Despite research showing the importance of jurors' first impressions, other studies have found more optimistic results. For example, Neil Vidmar and Shari Diamond concluded that American jurors indeed pay close attention to the content of the evidence, including expert testimony.[42]

In their reflective look at decades of work on jury decision-making, Dennis Devine and colleagues suggested five process-oriented criteria for evaluating the performance of a jury as a whole: instruction comprehension, evidence review, factual focus, systematic participation, and informational influence.[43] Employing these criteria, Devine and colleagues conducted post-trial surveys from jurors and legal professionals associated with 197 criminal jury trials in Indiana and evaluated their criteria, ultimately reaching mixed conclusions.[44] On the positive side, study results showed that a strong majority of the juries reported that they indeed reviewed the evidence thoroughly and understood their instructions. However, less positively, data on systematic participation, maintaining a factual focus, and openness to opinion changes based on informational influence suggested uneven participation and a verdict-driven deliberation style.[45]

In one of the few empirical jury studies in Korea, Jae-Hyup Lee and colleagues employed Devine and colleagues' criteria to examine the rationality of jury deliberations of Korean juries.[46] Lee and his colleagues found that Korean shadow jurors mostly understood the judge's instructions, and understood and recalled the evidence presented at trial. The jurors also paid close attention during the court proceedings and actively participated in deliberations. On the other hand, the degree of evidence-based review seems to have been relatively low, as the jurors tended to vote very early rather than wait until they had fully discussed the facts and evidence of the case. The observations in Lee and colleagues' study suggest that although there is room for improvement in Korean jury deliberations, the overall quality of deliberations was high, considering Korea only introduced the jury system five years before the study. More encouragingly, the deliberations of older or less educated jurors were equal in quality to those of jurors who were younger, more educated, and had a preexisting interest in the jury system. Notably, both the Devine and Lee studies relied on self-reports from jurors, which provided more insight into how the jurors perceived the jury experience, rather than how they actually deliberated. Recognizing the need to build upon self-report studies by employing observational methods, the study we devised focuses on direct observation of each juror's communication behavior to determine the quality of deliberations.[47]

Scholars have also examined how American individual jurors' behavior may influence the overall quality of deliberations. One of the biggest challenges to quality deliberations seems to be passive jurors, who are often completely disengaged from the deliberation process. Diamond and Casper studied when jurors are more likely follow the model of "active information processor" rather than the "jury as a passive participant" by looking at when and how often jurors follow judicial instructions.[48] They found, as expected, that active jurors are those who participate in evidence interpretation, as well as actively communicate with other jurors.[49] Sarah Tanford and Steven Penrod build on these concepts by suggesting that further study should include a coding-based examination of dynamics of communication and static content categories.[50] Dynamics of communication, for example, can be observed by measuring several different criteria, such as by examining communications based upon what communications theorists call "two-way" or "multi-way" interactions.[51] Building upon this scholarship, the study we designed for Korean jurors focuses on the interactivity of juror communication. Specifically, we examined how frequently jurors make comments in response to other jurors' comments or arguments.

Jürgen Habermas's idea of a deliberative public sphere is also relevant to assessing what constitutes meaningful deliberation.[52] Deliberative theorists agree that deliberations should stress rational, critical arguments (or, at least, reasoned arguments).[53] Deliberative theorists and practitioners of the jury system are generally wary of the role of emotion, in contrast to reason, in jury deliberations.[54] Their focus on reasoned arguments, however, does not mean that jury deliberations should exclude emotion altogether. Studies have found that emotion deepens deliberations, encourages more participation, and motivates further deliberations.[55] Andrea Hickerson and John Gastil found, in their survey study of over 3,000 jurors, that experiencing emotion was fairly constant for both men and women. In addition, balancing reason and emotion may be the key for a positive juror experience.[56]

When South Korea was in the process of introducing the jury system for the first time in its history, one of the strongest arguments used to oppose the jury system asserted that Korean people tend to be overly emotional, to the extent that making reasoned arguments and reaching consensus in a rational manner is impossible.[57] Lee and colleagues' study of shadow jurors examined how often jurors made overly emotional comments that inhibited the rational discussion necessary for fact-finding. The researchers found that such comments were actually not very common.[58] A juror's ability to make reasoned arguments and engage in logical thinking is an important element that increases the quality of deliberations. Our study examines how jurors use logic and reason instead of simply arguing their thoughts and positions without any basis besides emotion.[59]

Based on the foregoing theories and empirical findings, we believe that one meaningful way that the quality of deliberations can be assessed empirically is by measuring how much each juror comments on the evidence of the case, responds to other jurors, and uses logic and reason in his or her arguments. We therefore devised a study that employed such measures and attempted to address the following questions in the context of Korean juries:

1. How does age and gender diversity influence the quality of jury deliberations?
2. How does speech diversity influence the quality of jury deliberations?
3. How does the level of argument engagement influence the quality of jury deliberations?

Empirical Study

Building upon the theories and empirical findings regarding diversity and quality of jury deliberations in America and Korea, we designed a study to consider the deliberation dynamics that influence the quality of deliberations of Korean juries. First, we examined whether and how age and gender diversity are associated with the quality of deliberations. Next, we investigated whether and how speech diversity, an important parameter of the dynamics of jury deliberations, influenced the quality of Korean jury deliberations. We predicted that, first, diverse juries would demonstrate better performance, and second, that more speech diversity during the deliberation process would be associated with higher quality of jury deliberations. We also explored whether and how argument engagement was associated with the relationship between speech diversity and deliberation quality. In this section, we describe the methods, materials, and results of the study.

Data Collection

Our methods and statistical analysis draw upon the data we collected for the shadow jury deliberation studies that were conducted with the official cooperation of the National Court Administration of Korea ("NCA"). The NCA coordinated with the courts to set up shadow juries consisting of real juror candidates who were not ultimately selected during voir dire. In addition, a number of district courts in Korea started their own shadow jury programs beginning in September 2010, in order for people to actually experience the judicial process through voluntary participation. These courts intended to improve the public perception of the judiciary's credibility through this program.[60] In each trial included in our study, one or two shadow jury groups were formed in addition to the actual jury. Some groups were composed of juror candidates who were summoned by the court to serve as jurors, but were not selected during voir dire (we refer to each such panel as a "venire jury"). Other groups of shadow jurors were composed of people who were directly recruited by the court to serve as shadow jurors (each such panel, a "recruited jury").[61]

The shadow jurors observed the trial, participated in jury deliberations, and reached a verdict in parallel to the real jury. Shadow jurors were also given the same bench memo (facts, legal issues, etc.) provided to the real jury. After the conclusion of the court proceeding, they were assigned different rooms in the same court and were engaged in the same process of jury deliberations in secret. When the judge's intervention was needed, an associate judge of the three-judge panel went into each room to discuss the case with the shadow jurors.[62] The shadow jurors remained until the final court judgment was rendered, frequently late into the night. The research team observed the trials from beginning to end, and then videotaped the shadow jury deliberations. The team did not intervene in the deliberations in any way other than observing and recording the process, in order to preserve the objectivity of the research.

A total of thirty-two shadow juries of nineteen trial cases were set up and operated between January 2012 and June 2012 in cities across the country including Seoul, Ulsan, Gwangju, Jeonju, and Chuncheon. We included both types of shadow jury groups (venire juries and recruited juries) in the study. Through this process, 108 jurors in venire juries and 134 jurors in recruited juries (a total of 242 jurors) participated in the deliberation process. The number of jurors in each shadow jury varied from four to twelve members.[63] Our research team created verbatim transcripts of all the deliberations and conducted a content analysis of the jury deliberations.[64] Three coders watched the videos and read the transcripts together until they reached a mutually agreed upon coding, or categorization of data, and then each coder analyzed the videotapes and the transcripts separately (Table 8.1).[65]

Characteristics of the Jurors

In order to collect the sociodemographic characteristics of the jurors, a survey was conducted after deliberations. Of the 242 jurors, 43.8 percent were men and 56.2

Table 8.1 Composition of Juries for Research

Area		Venire jury	Recruited jury	Total
		Number of jurors (Number of jurors in videotape, if different)	**Number of jurors (Number of jurors in videotape, if different)**	
1	Seoul Central	7	7	14
2	Seoul Central	12	A 11 / B 7	30
3	Changwon	9	8	17
4	Cheongju	5	6	11
5	Seoul East	6	8	14
6	Seoul North	8	8	16
7	Ulsan	7	9	16
8	Gwangju	8	7	15
9	Cheongju	4	5	9
10	Seoul South	0, jury not made	A 7 / B 9	16
11	Gwangju	7	4	11
12	Seoul South	8 (0, no videotape)	7	7
13	Seoul North	5	4	9
14	Gwangju	6	9	15
15	Jeonju	5	11 (0, no videotape)	5
16	Chuncheon	7	11	18
17	Seoul North	6	0, jury not recruited	6
18	Seoul Central	5 (0, no videotape)	7	7
19	Seoul Central	6	15 (0, no videotape)	6
	Total	121 (108)	160 (134)	242

Note: Not enough potential jurors were left to make a venire jury in one of the trials. Recruited jurors were not recruited in one of the trials. Videotaping was not possible due to the circumstances of the court in four of the trials.

percent were women. By age, jurors included persons in their twenties or younger (56.4 percent), thirties (15.3 percent), fifties (14.4 percent), forties (7.2 percent), and sixties or older (6.8 percent). One of the reasons for the large number of individuals in their twenties is that many of the recruited jurors were college students. The level of education of the jurors tended to be high, as 52.2 percent had a college education or higher, 41.8 percent had a high school education, and only 6.0 percent received a middle school education or lower.

Main Variables and Measurements

We used variables at both the jury panel level and the individual juror level, as described below.

Table 8.2 Demographic Characteristics

		Number	Percentage
Gender (not available-8)	Male	103	43.8
	Female	132	56.2
Age (not available-6)	20s or younger	133	56.4
	30s	36	15.3
	40s	17	7.2
	50s	34	14.4
	60s and older	16	6.8
Education (not available-10)	Middle school graduate or lower	14	6.0
	High school graduate	97	41.8
	College graduate or higher	121	52.2

Independent Variables (Diversity and Engagement)

In order to measure the "demographic diversity" of jury composition, we used the following formula.

$$\text{Demographic Diversity} = \mathit{fl}\sum_{i=1}^{x}(r_i \times \ln(r_i))$$

$$r_i = \text{percentage per group}$$

We divided jurors into four groups according to gender and age: Males in their twenties and thirties, Males in their forties and older, Females in their twenties and thirties, and Females in their forties and older.[66] We put natural logarithms on r_i, where r_i was the percentage per group and obtained entropy by calculating Σ. When the calculated value is close to 1, all four groups exist in each jury, indicating higher demographic diversity. When the number is far from 1, the jury consists of only one or two of the groups, indicating a greater similarity in the jurors' gender and age in the group and thus, less demographic diversity.

In order to measure the "speech diversity" of each jury, which means how evenly each juror spoke during the deliberation, we used the following formula.

$$\text{Speech Diversity} = -\frac{\sum_{i=1}^{n}(r_i \times \ln(r_i))}{\ln(n)}$$

$$r_i = \text{percentage of individual utterances}$$

$$n = \text{number of jurors}$$

We obtained a value representing entropy by calculating the natural logarithms and Σ of r_i, where r_i was the percentage of individual utterances. A greater entropy value indicates greater uncertainty regarding who will make a comment. A low entropy value is observed when one or two jurors dominate the conversation and it becomes

Table 8.3 Values of the Jury-Level Variables

	N	Minimum	Maximum	Average	SD
Demographic diversity	32	0.00	1.35	0.89	0.29
Speech diversity	32	0.79	1.18	0.92	0.06
Argument engagement	32	1.00	3.00	2.14	0.65

predictable which individual will speak. Conversely, the entropy value is high when many jurors speak, as the uncertainty of who will speak is also high. If the total number of jurors of Σ becomes large, entropy will also be a high value. In order to control the size of the juries in comparing speech diversity, we divided the Σ by the number of the jury. Therefore, the speech diversity among the jurors becomes high when the entropy becomes high. The closer this calculated value is to 1, the more evenly speaking is distributed amongst the jurors during the deliberations.

We also measured the level of "argument engagement" by examining how many times a juror's remarks and other jurors' replies were exchanged on each issue. The standard by which engagement is measured is whether comments and replies were exchanged more than three times. The level of argument engagement is measured with three levels: (1) no engagement (no reply), (2) medium engagement (three or fewer exchanges), and (3) strong engagement (more than three exchanges). The values of each of the jury level variables are presented in Table 8.3.

Dependent Variables (Quality of Deliberation)

The research team analyzed each juror's behavior during deliberation. The unit of analysis is every utterance of each juror. An "utterance" is measured as an instance when a juror verbalized a substantive and intelligible sentence lasting at least five seconds. A short interjection such as "yes" or "agree" was not coded as an utterance. An unclear expression of opposition such as "uh-" was not coded as an utterance either. On average, each juror made 10.63 utterances, and the maximum number of a single juror's utterances was 41. The highest number of average utterances of the jurors in a single deliberation was 25.83, and the lowest number of average utterances in a deliberation was 1.55.

We defined the quality of deliberations to depend on the number of meaningful utterances made during the deliberations and the characteristics of such utterances. The quality of deliberations was measured by how often each juror made remarks using supporting evidence, how often the jurors cited and commented on other participants' arguments, and how often the jurors used logic and reasoning in making their arguments.

For each utterance, we coded whether it included evidence that supported the juror's argument. Each juror made an average of 4.71 utterances that included evidence, and the highest number of such utterances with evidence for a single juror was 28 (Table 8.4).

Table 8.4 Values of the Individual-Level Variables

	N	Minimum	Maximum	Average	SD
Evidence	242	0	28	4.71	4.261
Commenting on other participants	242	0	8	1.86	1.365
Logic and reasoning	242	0	16	3.18	2.434
Quality of deliberation	242	0	52	6.34	6.467

We also coded if the utterance included commenting on another participant's argument. For example, an utterance is coded as commenting on other participants if the utterance specifically supported, opposed, or added a supplementary explanation after citing arguments of the judge, prosecutor, lawyer, witness, or other jurors. Jurors made on average 1.86 utterances that commented on other participants, and the highest number of comments on other participants made by a single juror was 8. Finally, we also coded if each utterance used logic or reasoning to support the juror's argument. The jurors made an average of 3.18 remarks with logic and reasoning, and the highest number of remarks with logic and reasoning made by a single juror was 16. The quality of deliberations was determined by adding these three kinds of meaningful utterances made by each juror. The jurors averaged 6.34 quality remarks during deliberation. There were jurors who did not make any of these utterances throughout deliberations. The highest number of quality utterances made by a single juror was 52.

Results

Gender and Age Diversity and Quality of Deliberations

First, we examined the quality of deliberations, demographic diversity, and speech diversity between venire juries and recruited juries. While the number of utterances did not vary, the quality of deliberations differed between the two groups (Table 8.5). The average values of the quality of deliberations were 4.76 in venire juries and 7.62 in recruited juries ($t=-3.715$, $df=211$, $p=0.000$).[67] The fact that the quality of deliberations in recruited juries is higher is arguably because these jurors were recruited though a voluntary application process through the homepage of the Supreme Court. Respondents tended to be active citizens who are interested in the jury trial system, as well as law students, who began the process with more knowledge of the trial process. Demographic diversity was lower in the recruited jury group (0.74 compared to 1.08), likely for the same reason ($t=-10.802$, $df=242$, $p=0.037$). This clear distinction between the characteristics of the venire juries and the recruited juries suggests a need for us to consider these two groups separately in examining the effect of diversity on the quality of deliberations. Speech diversity did not differ between the venire jury and the recruited jury groups ($t=2.302$, $df=240$, $p=0.519$).

Table 8.5 Values of the Jury-Level Variables of Different Groups

Variable	Group	N	Mean	SD
Quality of deliberations***	Venire jury	108	4.76	4.10
	Recruited jury	134	7.62	7.65
Demographic diversity*	Venire jury	108	1.08	0.21
	Recruited jury	134	0.74	0.26
Speech diversity	Venire jury	108	0.92	0.04
	Recruited jury	134	0.92	0.07

*** $p < 0.001$, * $p < 0.05$.

Correlation of the Variables

We examined the correlation of the variables and found that the type of jury group (venire or recruited) is correlated with demographic diversity, speech diversity, and the quality of deliberations (Table 8.6). Recruited juries had less demographic diversity and higher quality of deliberations. Demographic diversity and speech diversity were also positively correlated in that higher demographic diversity corresponded to higher speech diversity. Speech diversity was also positively correlated with argument engagement and quality of deliberations.

Diversity and Quality of Deliberations

We examined how demographic diversity and speech diversity influence the quality of deliberations. We found that both of them influence the quality of deliberations ($F=11.54$, $p=0.001$, and $F=56.26$, $p=0.000$, respectively), and that the correlation between the two variables also influences the quality of deliberations ($F=6.89$, $p=0.009$; Table 8.7). When the level of demographic diversity is low, the quality of deliberations was higher than when the level of demographic diversity is high, regardless of the level of speech diversity of the group. Contrary to literature in the United States focusing on the benefits of diversity within American juries, the results of our study in Korea demonstrated that the level of demographic (age and gender) diversity and the quality of deliberations were negatively correlated. However, speech diversity was positively correlated with the quality of deliberations. The higher the level of speech diversity, the higher the quality of deliberations was. The quality of deliberations was at the highest level when demographic diversity was low and speech diversity was high (Figure 8.1). This result may be driven by the fact that the recruited jury group, consisting of volunteer applicants, was less diverse but more knowledgeable and interested in the jury trial process. Therefore, we decided to examine the two groups separately in conducting our analyses of the relationship between diversity and the quality of deliberations.

Table 8.6 Correlation of Variables

	Jury group	Demographic diversity	Speech diversity	Argument engagement	Quality of deliberations
Jury group	1	−0.572**	−0.051	−0.080	0.220**
Demographic diversity	−0.572**	1	0.206**	−0.122	−0.079
Speech diver-sity	−0.051	0.206**	1	0.222**	0.385**
Argument engagement	−0.080	−0.122	0.222**	1	0.076
Quality of deliberations	0.220**	−0.079	0.385**	0.076	1

** $p < 0.01$

Table 8.7 Quality of Deliberations by Demographic Diversity and Speech Diversity

	Sum sq	df	Mean sq	F	p-value
Speech diversity	1,813	1	1,813	56.26***	0.000
Demographic diversity	372	1	372	11.54***	0.001
Speech diversity * dem. diversity interaction	222	1	222	6.89**	0.009
Residuals	7,671	238	32		

*$p < 0.05$, ** $p < 0.01$, *** $p < 0.001$

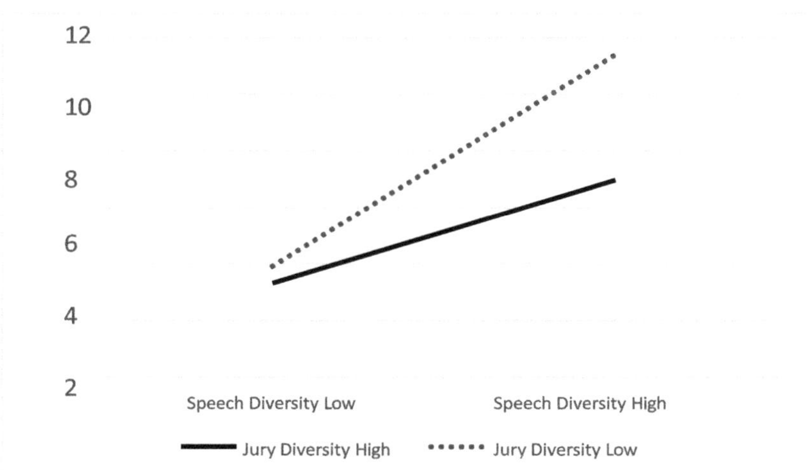

Figure 8.1 Quality of Deliberations by Demographic Diversity and Speech Diversity.

Demographic Diversity and Quality of Deliberations

Demographic diversity (age and gender) negatively influenced the quality of deliberations (F=7.37, p=0.006; Table 8.8). Jury group characteristics (whether the jury was a recruited jury or venire jury) also influenced the quality of deliberations, such that (F=5.53, p=0.020; Table 8.8) the quality of deliberations was higher in the recruited jury group than in the venire jury group (Figure 8.2). There was no interaction effect of demographic diversity and jury characteristics on the quality of deliberations. However, the negative relationship between demographic diversity and the quality of deliberations was found only in the venire jury group (Figure 8.2).

Table 8.8 Quality of Deliberations by Demographic Diversity and Jury Group

	Sum sq	df	Mean sq	F	p- value
Demographic diversity	295	1	295	7.37***	0.007
Jury group	221	1	221	5.53*	0.020
Demographic diversity * jury group interaction	48	1	48	1.20	0.274
Residuals	9,571.1	238	40.215		

*$p < 0.05$, ** $p < 0.01$, *** $p < 0.001$

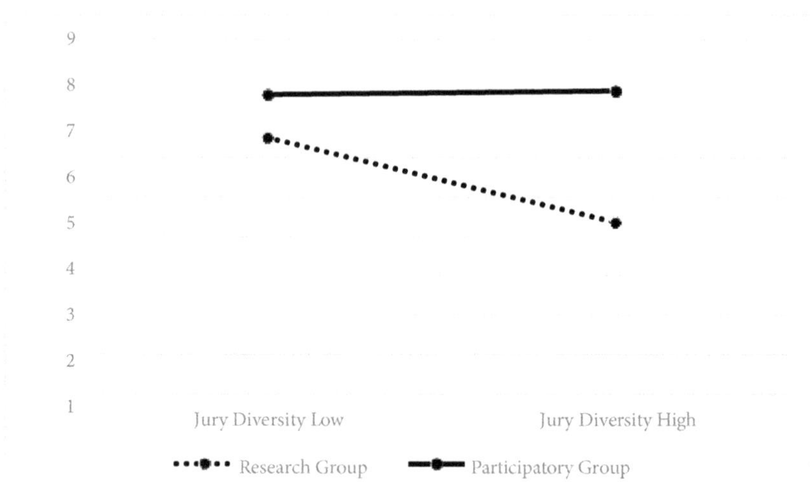

Figure 8.2 Quality of Deliberations by Demographic Diversity and Jury Characteristics.

Speech Diversity and Quality of Deliberations

Both speech diversity and the characteristics of the jury (recruited or venire jury) influenced the quality of deliberations (F=56.60, p=0.000 and F=8.53, p=0.004, respectively; Table 8.9). When jurors spoke more evenly, as opposed to one or two jurors dominating the discussion, the jurors tended to engage in better deliberations by more often providing evidence, commenting on other participants' arguments, and using logic and reasoning. In addition, the interaction of speech diversity and the characteristics of the jury influenced the quality of deliberations (F=11.45, p=0.001; Table 8.9), such that the quality of deliberations was the highest for juries that consisted of recruited jurors and are engaged in a high level of speech diversity (Figure 8.3). Jurors in a jury with more speech diversity engaged in better deliberations in terms of providing evidence, commenting on other participants' arguments and using logic and reasoning in making their arguments.

Table 8.9 Quality of Deliberations by Speech Diversity and Jury Group

	Sum sq	df	Mean sq	F	p- value
Speech diversity	1,813	1	1,813	56.60**	0.004
Jury group	273	1	273	8.53***	0.000
Speech diversity * jury group interaction	367	1	367	11.45***	0.001
Residuals	7,625	238	32		

* p < 0.05, ** p < 0.01, *** p < 0.001

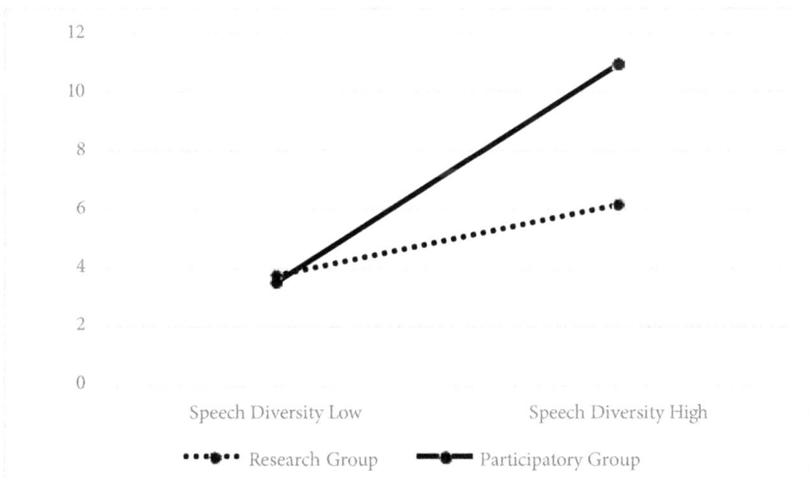

Figure 8.3 Quality of Deliberations by Speech Diversity and Jury Characteristics.

Interaction Effect of Argument Engagement

When we examined how argument engagement and speech diversity influenced the quality of deliberations, we found that higher speech diversity correlated with higher quality of deliberations (F=54.65, p=0.000; Table 8.10). Argument engagement itself was not found to influence the quality of deliberations. However, the interaction effect of argument engagement and speech diversity was striking (F=8.33, p=0.000; Table 8.10). When speech diversity was high, the quality of deliberations was the highest when argument engagement was mid-level (Figure 8.4). When there was no argument engagement regarding each issue, the quality of deliberations was at the lowest level. At the other extreme, when there was a strong level of engagement, such as more than three separate speech interactions on the issues, the quality of deliberations was also low. In contrast, the quality of deliberations was at its highest level when the speech interactions were exchanged between one and three times. This finding indicates that when jurors commented evenly among themselves, they tended to provide more evidence, comment more on other participants, and use more logic and reasoning. But these indicia of quality deliberations became less common when arguments became more heated through a high level of argument engagement.

When speech diversity was low, on the other hand, the relationship between argument engagement and the quality of deliberations followed a generally opposite pattern. When there was no engagement, the quality of deliberations was low (Figure 8.4). But when there was a moderate degree of engagement, the quality of deliberations became even lower. Quality of deliberations was highest when there was strong level of engagement. When the jurors did not make remarks evenly, only strong engagement through extended exchanges was able to induce the jurors to provide more evidence, comment on other participants, and use more logic and reason. This sharply contrasted with the finding that, when jurors spoke more evenly, moderate engagement enhanced the quality of deliberations, while strong engagement reduced the quality of deliberations.

Table 8.10 Quality of Deliberations by Speech Diversity and Argument Engagement

	Sum sq	df	Mean sq	F	p-value
Argument engagement	63	2	32	0.97	0.381
Speech diversity	1,781	1	1,781	54.65***	0.000
Argument engagement*speech diversity interaction	543	2	272	8.33***	0.000
Residuals	7,691	236	33		

* $p < 0.05$, ** $p < 0.01$, *** $p < 0.001$

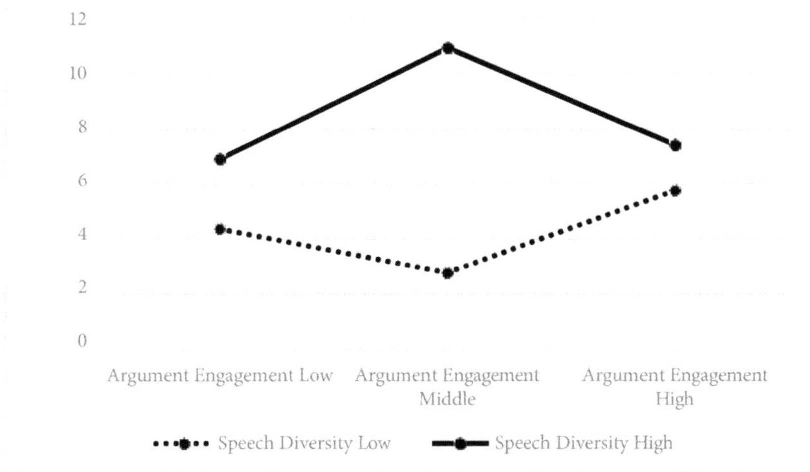

Figure 8.4 Quality of Deliberations by Speech Diversity and Argument Engagement.

Discussion and Conclusion

In our study of a rich and unique data set of Korean jury deliberations, we focused on examining the dynamics of jury deliberations and attempted to enhance the understanding of a neglected aspect of decision-making: the deliberation process. We were interested in whether and how both the structure of jury composition and the dynamics of the deliberation processes influenced deliberation quality. To that end, we examined how demographic diversity and speech diversity influenced the quality of deliberations. Our findings demonstrated that gender and age diversity negatively influenced the quality of deliberations. These findings contrasted with studies of American juries that have demonstrated the benefits of diversity.

This result suggests that, in Korea, there may be factors that inhibit quality of deliberations in juries that consist of different genders and diverse age groups. Although this was not studied directly, informal observation of deliberations revealed possible reasons that might prevent quality deliberations. When a jury consisted of some male and some female jurors, one or two of the male jurors often dominated the discussion, to the preclusion of participation by other jurors. This male dominance during deliberations seemed to occur more when the female jurors were younger than the dominant male jurors, but less frequently when the jury consisted of mostly male jurors. Future research is needed to reach a definitive conclusion regarding the occurrence of this male dominance and how it affects the quality of deliberations.

More interesting is the finding that this negative relationship between gender and age diversity and quality of deliberations did not occur in recruited juries where jurors were younger, more educated, and more interested in the jury system. In a jury of more knowledgeable and interested jurors, minimal diversity did not generate a low level of deliberation quality. It is difficult to suggest direct policy implications from this finding, because juries cannot (and should not) be engineered to consist only of younger, more educated, and more interested people. Facing a rather contrary demand to promote quality deliberations of juries consisting of members from a broad spectrum of society, we suggest that further research into the dynamics of the deliberation processes is needed to seek an explanation for why demographic diversity produces a contrary result (lower-quality deliberations) in juries with certain characteristics, but not in the case of juries with other characteristics. Future research should evaluate the possible role of the jury moderator, and in particular measuring how the moderator's behavior influenced the dynamics of the deliberation process.

We also found that speech diversity is an important factor that promotes better deliberations. When jurors were able to talk more evenly among themselves, they provided more evidence in making arguments, commented more frequently on other participants' arguments, and used more logic and reasoning in making their arguments. On the other hand, when one or two jurors dominated the discussion process, the jurors altogether in the group tended to provide less evidence, use less logic and reasoning, and comment less on the views of other participants. This positive relationship between speech diversity and the quality of deliberations sustained across different jury groups with different characteristics. This finding suggests that more attention should be given to the dynamics of deliberation processes of Korean juries, because age and gender diversity is not sufficient in itself to achieve better deliberations, and may even hinder quality deliberations. We found that when jurors do not take turns and do not provide opportunities for each juror to express thoughts and opinions, jury diversity does not necessarily lead to a more meaningful deliberation with more evidence, reasoning, and responsive comments. The dynamics of deliberation, rather than the age or gender diversity of the jury, appear to be the key determinants of deliberative quality.

Speech diversity also promoted high-quality deliberations in relation to the level of argument engagement. When jurors made remarks more evenly among themselves, a moderate level of engagement promoted quality deliberations. When certain jurors made asymmetrically more remarks than others, however, very strong levels of engagement (such as more than three commenting exchanges on each issue) were needed for jurors to provide more evidence, logic, and reasoning and to comment on other participants' remarks. Thus, quality deliberations are not only associated with speech diversity but also with argument interactions. Further study is needed to explore how the level of active engagement during deliberations influences their quality, but this finding provides us with another reason to focus on the ways in which Korean jury deliberations unfold, not on who the jurors are.

The results of this study present important implications for a country where a jury system is not an embedded historical asset but an imported system. Especially in a country that has different cultural underpinnings from the United States and other Western countries, cultural factors should be given greater consideration, and it is possible that more active intervention will be needed to educate jurors. The results of our study seem to reflect the cultural tendency of Korea—or perhaps East Asian countries more generally—for fluid conversation to be difficult in mixed gender and mixed age groups. Younger people are discouraged to speak out in front of older people, and oftentimes conversation is dominated by the oldest person in the group. This phenomenon is compounded if the group consists of both male and female members. Women tend to be discouraged from being outspoken in general, especially in front of people with whom they are not familiar, and younger women seem to feel this pressure to an even greater extent. Therefore, courts may be able to promote better deliberations by designing the juror's guide and other instruction materials with this cultural factor in mind and explaining the importance of balanced participation to the jurors. The role of the jury moderator may also be critical in this regard.

Our study also provides more general implications for the jury system. Previous literature on American jury diversity has focused its policy recommendations on the jury selection process, but jury diversity seems to interact with other factors that also influence the deliberation process. It would be worthwhile in the Korean context to consider different procedural elements that could encourage each juror to be more evenly and actively engaged in the deliberations, thus promoting more meaningful arguments and conclusions through the deliberation process. Considering the moderator selection process more systematically and improving the juror's guide are examples of such elements, and additional targeted research on the jury deliberation process in more detail would provide further insight as to how jury deliberations can be of higher quality.

Another contribution of our study may come from the heretofore rare methodology of videotaping actual deliberations of shadow jurors who were potential jurors from the venire (rather than the college students often recruited in mock jury studies), and who participated in the actual trial process in the same way as actual jurors. With a research design devised to imitate actual jury deliberations as much as possible, we revealed that juries with more diverse age and gender jurors do not necessarily engage in higher-quality deliberations, but juries in which jurors speak more evenly among themselves do produce a higher quality of deliberations.

Notes

1 This work was supported by the National Research Foundation of Korea Grant funded by the Korean government (NRF-2014028257). Any opinions, findings, conclusions, or recommendations expressed in this material are those of the authors and do not necessarily reflect the view of the NRF. We thank Professor June Woong Rhee of the Department of Communication at Seoul National University and Jae-Hyup Lee of the School of Law at Seoul National University for consultation on data analysis and helpful comments. Kaitlyn Iwashita provided research assistance.

2 Eric Y. Cornwell and Valerie Hans, "Representative through Participation: A Multilevel Analysis of Jury Deliberations," *Law & Society Review* 45 (2011): 667–98.

3 *See* Peters v. Kiff, 407 U.S. 493 (1972); Taylor v. Louisiana, 419 U.S. 522 (1975); Duren v. Missouri, 439 U.S. 357 (1979).

4 Cornwell and Hans, *supra* note 2, at 667–8; Nancy Marder, "Juries, Justice, and Multiculturalism," *Southern California Law Review* 75 (2002): 659, 726; Samuel Sommers, "On Racial Diversity and Group Decision Making: Identifying Multiple Effects of Racial Composition on Jury Deliberations," *Journal of Personality and Social Psychology* 90 (2006): 597, 600–12.

5 *See* Kuo-Chang Huan and Chang-Ching Lin, "Rescuing Confidence in the Judicial System: Introducing Lay Participation in Taiwan," *Journal of Empirical Legal Studies* 10 (2013): 542.

6 *See* Kent Anderson and Emma Saint, "Japan's Quasi-Jury (Saiban-in) Law: An Annotated Translation of the Act Concerning Participation of Lay Assessors in Criminal Trials," *Asian-Pacific Law & Policy Journal* 6 (2005): 233; Masahito Inouye, "Introduction of the Saiban-in System and Reformation of Criminal Procedure in Japan," *Seoul Law Journal* 55 (2014): 441.

7 *See* Jae-Hyup Lee, "Getting Citizens Involved: Civil Participation in Judicial Decision-Making in Korea," *East Asia Law Review* 4, no. 2 (2009): 177; Jae-Hyup Lee, "Korean Jury Trial: Has the New System Brought about Changes?" *Asian-Pacific Law and Policy Journal* 12, no. 1 (2010): 58.

8 Justin D. Levinson, "Mentally Misguided: How State of Mind Inquiries Ignore Psychological Reality and Overlook Cultural Differences," *Howard Law Journal* 49 (2005): 1.

9 Richard E. Nisbett and Takahiko Masuda, "Culture and Point of View," *Proceedings of the National Academy of Sciences* 100, no. 19 (2003): 11163.

10 Levinson, *supra* note 8.

11 "Speech diversity" means how evenly each juror spoke during the deliberation.

12 Note that there is little racial and ethnic diversity in Korea. Ethnicity and race are not even factors that are surveyed in the Korean national census. In 2016, 3.9 percent of the population of Korea were foreign nationals, half of whom were Chinese. Bo-bae Lee, "Gugnae Chelyu Oegug-in 200 Manmyeong Dolpa … 2021 Nyeon 300 Man Jeonmang [Over Two Million Foreigners in Korea … Predicted to Reach Three Million by 2021]," *Yonhap News*, July 27, 2016, https://www.yna.co.kr/view/AKR20160727075600004?section=search.

13 Few empirical studies of juries have had access to real criminal trials. Due to the collaboration between the Supreme Court of Korea and scholars at Seoul National University, a "shadow jury" program was established whereby mock jurors were present for actual trials.

14 South Korea instituted a jury system for the first time in its history in January of 2008, when the Act for Civil Participation in Criminal Trials of 2007 was first implemented. The policy goal of this legislation was to increase democratic participation and reinforce the democratic legitimacy of the judicial process, and to enhance the transparency and credibility of the judiciary. For more details about the Korean jury system, *see* Sangjoon Kim et al., "Judge-Jury Agreement in Criminal Cases: The First Three Years of the Korean Jury System," *Journal of Empirical Legal Studies* 10 (2013): 35–53; Jae-Hyup Lee et al., "What's Happening in the Jury Room?: Analyzing Shadow Jury Deliberations in Korea," *Journal of Korean Law* 41 (2013): 41. As in the US jury system, deliberations are secret, but the Supreme Court of Korea and scholars at Seoul National University collaborated in creating a "shadow jury program" to facilitate empirical research. This chapter relies upon data collected during shadow jury research.

15 Dennis J. Devine et al., "Deliberation Quality: A Preliminary Examination in Criminal Juries," *Journal of Empirical Legal Studies* 4 (2007): 273, 304.
16 Leslie Ellis and Shari S. Diamond, "Race, Diversity, and Jury Composition: Battering and Bolstering Legitimacy," *Chicago-Kent Law Review* 78 (2003): 1033, 1060.
17 *Ibid.* at 1043–8.
18 Marder, *supra* note 4, at 659.
19 Andrea Hickerson and John Gastil, "Assessing the Difference Critique of Deliberation: Gender, Emotion, and the Jury Experience," *Communication Theory* 18, no. 2 (2008): 281, 290–303; Sommers, *supra* note 4, at 597–612.
20 Marder, *supra* note 4.
21 *Ibid.* at 659.
22 *Ibid.* at 701.
23 *Ibid.*
24 Marder did not find that race diversity had any effect. *Ibid.*
25 *Ibid.* at 703.
26 Sommers, *supra* note 4, at 597–612.
27 *Ibid.* at 606.
28 *Ibid.* at 608.
29 Shari S. Diamond et al., "Achieving Diversity on the Jury: Jury Size and the Peremptory Challenge," *Journal of Empirical Legal Studies* 6 (2009): 441.
30 *Ibid.* at 435.
31 *Ibid.* at 427.
32 William D. Schreckhise and Charles H. Sheldon, "The Search for Greater Juror Diversity: The Case of the U.S. District Court for the Eastern District of Washington," *Justice Systems Journal* 20, no. 1 (1998): 95, 112.
33 The Korean jury system, implemented in 2008, incorporates elements of both the US-style system and the German lay assessor system. The adoption of the jury system in Korea was mainly driven by participatory democratic concerns. The two main purposes of the Korean jury system are to reinforce the democratic legitimacy of the judicial process and to enhance the transparency and credibility of the judiciary. The Korean jury trial is limited to certain type of criminal cases and is only invoked upon the defendant's choice. Jury verdicts are advisory in nature. The number of jurors varies according to the severity of the case; it can be five, seven, or nine. The more severe the case is, the more jurors are appointed. Jurors discuss the guilt of the defendant in secret and try to reach a unanimous verdict. If the jurors cannot reach a unanimous verdict, they must hear the judges' opinion. After the judges and the jurors have discussed the guilt of the defendant together, the jurors, again without the presence of the judges, enter a verdict based on a simple majority. If the defendant is found guilty, then Korean jurors discuss the sentence with the judge and each juror submits his/her sentencing opinion individually. *See* Lee (2010), *supra* note 7.
34 Reid Hastie, Steven D. Penrod, and Nancy Pennington, *Inside the Jury* (Cambridge: Harvard University Press, 1983); James H. Davis et al., "Order Effects in Multiple Decisions by Groups: A Demonstration with Mock Juries and Trial Procedures," *Journal of Personality and Social Psychology* 47 (1984): 1003–12; John H. Davis et al., "Effects of Straw Polls on Group Decision Making: Sequential Voting Pattern, Timing, and Local Majorities," *Journal of Personality and Social Psychology* 55, no. 6 (1988): 918–26; Shari S. Diamond et al., "Juror Decisions during Civil Trials: Studying an Arizona Innovation," *Arizona Law Review* 45, no. 1 (2003): 1–81; James A. Holstein,

"Jurors' Interpretations and Jury Decision Making," *Law and Human Behavior* 9 (1985): 83, 90–100; Sarah Tanford and Steven D. Penrod, "Jury Deliberations: Discussion Content and Influence Processes in Jury Decision Making," *Journal of Applied Social Psychology* 16 (1986): 322–47.

35 Hastie et al., *supra* note 34, at 163.

36 *Ibid.*

37 *Ibid.*

38 Devine et al., *supra* note 15, at 622–5.

39 Hastie et al., *supra* note 34, at 163.

40 *Ibid.*; Harry Kalven and Hans Zeisel, *The American Jury* (Chicago: University of Chicago Press, 1966); Robert MacCoun and Norbert Kerr, "Asymmetric Influence in Mock Jury Deliberation: Jurors' Bias for Leniency," *Journal of Personality and Social Psychology* 54 (1988): 21–33; Marla Sandys and C. Dillehay, "First-Ballot Votes, Predeliberation Dispositions, and Final Verdicts in Jury Trials," *Law and Human Behavior* 19 (1995): 175, 180–95.

41 Kalven and Zeisel, *supra* note 40, at 488.

42 Neil Vidmar and Shari S. Diamond, "Juries and Expert Evidence," *Brooklyn Law Review* 66, no. 4 (2001): 1121, 1180. These positive attentional effects may be less prominent in legal cultures like Korea, where jurors are less familiar with the ways that jury trials progress, and thus may not know to focus on expert testimony, for example. When formulating our own study on Korean jurors, we were therefore particularly interested in the ways jurors would talk (or not talk) about evidence during deliberations.

43 Devine et al., *supra* note 15, at 273–80.

44 *Ibid.*

45 *Ibid.*

46 Jae-Hyup Lee, Jisuk Woo, and June Woong Rhee, "Baesimwon Pyeonguiui Hapriseonge Gwanhan Yeongu: Gukminchamyeojaepaneseoui Geurimja Baesim Pyeongui Bunseok [A Study on the Rationality of the Jury Deliberation: Analysis of the Shadow Deliberations in Korean Jury Trials]," *The Justice* 139 (2013): 208 (adding one more criterion to Devine et al.'s five criteria, a cultural aspect of Korean society: exclusion of emotion).

47 Devine et al., *supra* note 15, at 273–80; Lee et al., *supra* note 46, at 140.

48 Shari S. Diamond and Jonathan D. Casper, "Blindfolding the Jury to Verdict Consequences: Damages, Experts, and the Civil Jury," *Law and Society Review* 26, no. 3 (1992): 513, 520–57.

49 *Ibid.* at 513–63.

50 Tanford and Penrod, *supra* note 34, at 322–47.

51 John Fiske, *Introduction to Communication Studies* (London: Routledge, 1990); William W. Wilmot, *Dyadic Communication* (New York: McGraw-Hill, 1987).

52 Jürgen Habermas, *The Theory of Communicative Action: Reason and the Rationalization of Society*, trans. Thomas MacCarthy (Boston: Beacon Press, 1985); Jürgen Habermas, *The Structural Transformation of the Public Sphere*, trans. Thomas Burger (Cambridge: MIT Press, 1991).

53 Joshua Cohen, "Deliberation and Democratic Legitimacy," in *The Good Polity: Normative Analysis of the State*, ed. Hamlin and Pettit (Oxford: Blackwell, 1989), 17–34.

54 Simon Thompson and Paul Hoggett, "The Emotional Dynamics of Deliberative Democracy," *Policy and Politics* 29 (2001): 352–64; Lee et al., *supra* note 46, at 208–30.

55 David Michael Ryfe, "The Practice of Deliberative Democracy: A Study of 16 Deliberative Organizations," *Political Communication* 19 (2002): 359–77; Bas van Stokkom, "Deliberative Group Dynamics: Power, Status, and Affect in Interactive Policy Making," *Policy and Politics* 33 (2005): 387, 400–9.

56 Hickerson and Gastil, *supra* note 19, at 597–612.

57 Kim et al., *supra* note 14, at 35–53; Lee et al., *supra* note 14, at 43.

58 Lee et al., *supra* note 46, at 232 (in the study, a juror said, "The poor defendant could not help acting that way due to his childhood experience, so his dad, not the defendant, should be the one to be punished." Another juror said, "If the defendant goes to jail, what is going to happen to other family members? I feel sorry for him and the family. I do not want to see him punished." Yet another juror said, "I feel sick that she drank and smoke while she was pregnant. I know that kind of a person. She could have burned her skin with her own cigarette").

59 We did not include the absence of emotion as an indicator of quality deliberations, as previous research suggested that emotion itself does not necessarily conflict with reasoned arguments. *See generally* Ryfe, *supra* note 55; van Stokkom, *supra* note 55; Hickerson and Gastil, *supra* note 19.

60 The shadow jury program has been successfully implemented. About 16,000 people have participated in the shadow jury program for the past ten years since the program began on January 1, 2008. Se-hyeon Lee, "2017 Nyeon Beob-Won Jeonsigwan Gihoegjeonsi 'Gugminchamyeojaepan' Gaemag [Opening of the Shadow Jury Program Planned for the 2017 Court Exhibition]," *Beomnyulsinmun*, September 19, 2017, https://www.lawtimes.co.kr/news/121099.

61 Both venire jurors and recruited jurors were paid KRW 50,000.

62 All jury trials are conducted by a three-judge panel in Korea. As with the judge's intervention in the shadow juries, in real trials Korean jurors summon judges in similar situations.

63 Actual Korean juries consist of five, seven, or nine members. The size of the shadow jury panels deliberately varied from the size of actual juries, as we wanted to examine the effect of different panel sizes on jury deliberations.

64 The length of deliberation ranged from 24 to 104 minutes.

65 Not enough potential jurors were left to make a venire jury in one of the trials. Recruited jurors were not recruited in one of the trials. Videotaping was not possible due to the circumstances of the court in four of the trials.

66 Due to the study population consisting of shadow jurors who tended to be young, we did not break down age categorizations further.

67 We used ANOVA (analysis of variance) for these statistical analyses.

Bibliography

Anderson, Kent, and Emma Saint. "Japan's Quasi-Jury (Saiban-in) Law: An Annotated Translation of the Act Concerning Participation of Lay Assessors in Criminal Trials." *Asian-Pacific Law & Policy Journal* 6 (2005): 233–89.

Cohen, Joshua. "Deliberation and Democratic Legitimacy." In *The Good Polity: Normative Analysis of the State*, edited by Hamlin and Pettit, 17–34. Oxford: Blackwell, 1989.

Cornwell, Eric Y., and Valerie Hans. "Representative through Participation: A Multilevel Analysis of Jury Deliberations." *Law & Society Review* 45 (2011): 667–98.

Davis, James H., R. Scott Tindale, Dennis H. Nagao, Verlin B. Hinsz, and Bret Robertson. "Order Effects in Multiple Decisions by Groups: A Demonstration with Mock Juries and Trial Procedures." *Journal of Personality and Social Psychology* 47 (1984): 1003–12.

Davis, James H., Mark F. Stasson, Kaoru Ono, and Suzi Zimmerman. "Effects of Straw Polls on Group Decision Making: Sequential Voting Pattern, Timing, and Local Majorities." *Journal of Personality and Social Psychology* 55, no. 6 (1988): 918–26.

Devine, Dennis J., Jennifer Buddenbaum, Stephanie Houp, Dennis P. Stolle, and Nathan Studebaker. "Deliberation Quality: A Preliminary Examination in Criminal Juries." *Journal of Empirical Legal Studies* 4 (2007): 273–304.

Diamond, Shari Seidman, Destiny Peery, Francis J. Dolan, and Emily Dolan. "Achieving Diversity on the Jury: Jury Size and the Peremptory Challenge." *Journal of Empirical Legal Studies* 6 (2009): 425–49.

Diamond, Shari S., and Jonathan D. Casper. "Blindfolding the Jury to Verdict Consequences: Damages, Experts, and the Civil Jury." *Law and Society Review* 26, no. 3 (1992): 513–63.

Ellis, Leslie, and Shari S. Diamond. "Race, Diversity, and Jury Composition: Battering and Bolstering Legitimacy." *Chicago-Kent Law Review* 78 (2003): 1033–60.

Fiske, John. *Introduction to Communication Studies*. London: Routledge, 1990.

Habermas, Jürgen. *The Structural Transformation of the Public Sphere*. Translated by Thomas Burger. Cambridge: MIT Press, 1991.

Habermas, Jürgen. *The Theory of Communicative Action: Reason and the Rationalization of Society*. Translated by Thomas MacCarthy. Boston: Beacon Press, 1985.

Hastie, Reid, Steven D. Penrod, and Nancy Pennington. *Inside the Jury*. Cambridge: Harvard University Press, 1983.

Hickerson, Andrea, and John Gastil. "Assessing the Difference Critique of Deliberation: Gender, Emotion, and the Jury Experience." *Communication Theory* 18, no. 2 (2008): 281–303.

Holstein, James A. "Jurors' Interpretations and Jury Decision Making." *Law and Human Behavior* 9 (1985): 83–100.

Huag, Kuo-Chang, and Chang-Ching Lin. "Rescuing Confidence in the Judicial System: Introducing Lay Participation in Taiwan." *Journal of Empirical Legal Studies* 10 (2013): 542–79.

Inouye, Masahito. "Introduction of the Saiban-in System and Reformation of Criminal Procedure in Japan." *Seoul Law Journal* 55 (2014): 441–73.

Kalven, Harry, and Hans Zeisel. *The American Jury*. Chicago: University of Chicago Press, 1966.

Kim, Sangjoon, Jaihyun Park, Kwangbai Park, and Jin-Sup Eom. "Judge-Jury Agreement in Criminal Cases: The First Three Years of the Korean Jury System." *Journal of Empirical Legal Studies* 10 (2013): 35–53.

Lee, Bo-bae. "Gugnae Chelyu Oegug-in 200 Manmyeong Dolpa … 2021 Nyeon 300 Man Jeonmang [Over Two Million Foreigners in Korea … Predicted to Reach Three Million by 2021]." *Yonhap News*, July 27, 2016. https://www.yna.co.kr/view/AKR20160727075600004?section=search.

Lee, Jae-Hyup. "Getting Citizens Involved: Civil Participation in Judicial Decision-Making in Korea." *East Asia Law Review* 4, no. 2 (2009): 177–207.

Lee, Jae-Hyup. "Korean Jury Trial: Has the New System Brought about Changes?" *Asian-Pacific Law and Policy Journal* 12, no. 1 (2010): 58–71.

Lee, Jae-Hyup, Jisuk Woo, and June Woong Rhee. "Baesimwon Pyeonguiui Hapriseonge Gwanhan Yeongu: Gukminchamyeojaepaneseoui Geurimja Baesim Pyeongui Bunseok [A Study on the Rationality of the Jury Deliberation: Analysis of the Shadow Deliberations in Korean Jury Trials]." *The Justice* 139 (2013): 208–49.

Lee, Jae Hyup, Jisuk Woo, June Woong Rhee, Jeong Min Choi, and Hyunki Shin. "What's Happening in the Jury Room?: Analyzing Shadow Jury Deliberations in Korea." *Journal of Korean Law* 41 (2013): 41–68.

Levinson, Justin D. "Mentally Misguided: How State of Mind Inquiries Ignore Psychological Reality and Overlook Cultural Differences." *Howard Law Journal* 49 (2005): 1–35.

MacCoun, Robert, and Norbert Kerr. "Asymmetric Influence in Mock Jury Deliberation: Jurors' Bias for Leniency." *Journal of Personality and Social Psychology* 54 (1988): 21–33.

Marder, Nancy. "Juries, Justice, and Multiculturalism." *Southern California Law Review* 75 (2002): 659–726.

Nisbett, Richard E., and Takahiko Masuda. "Culture and Point of View." *Proceedings of the National Academy of Sciences* 100, no. 19 (2003): 11163–70.

Ryfe, David Michael. "The Practice of Deliberative Democracy: A Study of 16 Deliberative Organizations." *Political Communication* 19 (2002): 359–77.

Sandys, Marla, and Ronald C. Dillehay. "First-Ballot Votes, Predeliberation Dispositions, and Final Verdicts in Jury Trials." *Law and Human Behavior* 19 (1995): 175–95.

Schreckhise, William D., and Charles H. Sheldon. "The Search for Greater Juror Diversity: The Case of the U.S. District Court for the Eastern District of Washington." *Justice Systems Journal* 20, no. 1 (1998): 95–112.

Sommers, Samuel. "On Racial Diversity and Group Decision Making: Identifying Multiple Effects of Racial Composition on Jury Deliberations." *Journal of Personality and Social Psychology* 90 (2006): 597–612.

Stokkom, Bas van. "Deliberative Group Dynamics: Power, Status, and Affect in Interactive Policy Making." *Policy and Politics* 33 (2005): 387–409.

Tanford, Sarah, and Steven D. Penrod. "Jury Deliberations: Discussion Content and Influence Processes in Jury Decision Making." *Journal of Applied Social Psychology* 16 (1986): 322–47.

Thompson, Simon, and Paul Hoggett. "The Emotional Dynamics of Deliberative Democracy." *Policy and Politics* 29 (2001): 352–64.

Vidmar, Neil, and Shari S. Diamond. "Juries and Expert Evidence." *Brooklyn Law Review* 66, no. 4 (2001): 1121–80.

Vidmar, Neil, Shari S. Diamond, Mary R. Rose, and René Stemple Ellis. "Juror Discussions during Civil Trials: Studying an Arizona Innovation." Arizona Law Review 45, no. 1 (2003): 1–83.

Wilmot, William W. *Dyadic Communication*. New York: McGraw-Hill, 1987.

This chapter was previously published under the same title in Asian-Pacific Law & Policy Journal 19, no. 1 (2017): 23–48.

Part Four

Law in Transition

Legal Norms, Justice, and the Contradictions of Global Reform

9

Contract Law and Insolvency Law, Continuity or Discontinuity

On a Recently Proposed Amendment to Korean Insolvency Law

Joon-Kyu Choi

Introduction

Insolvency law deals with insolvent debtors' emergent situations within insolvency proceedings. Contract law usually focuses on debtors' legal relationships outside insolvency proceedings. To achieve the objectives of insolvency law, doctrines of contract law may be modified when applied within the debtor's insolvency proceedings. However, arbitrary, excessive, or ill-founded changes are not permitted. This is because the freedom of contract principle may be violated through bad modifications, and groundless distinctions can trigger opportunistic behavior among interested parties. In principle, private autonomy should be respected within insolvency procedures, just as it is outside of them. The doctrines of contract law should continue to be applied within insolvency proceedings without modification unless such changes are justified by written law or unwritten legal doctrines. This chapter employs the term "continuity" to denote the application of contract law without modification in insolvency proceedings, while "discontinuity" is utilized to signify the modification of contract law within such proceedings.

When an insolvency procedure[1] begins, the creditor is prohibited from enacting individual enforcement against the bankrupt debtor, and the debtor's voluntary payment to the individual creditor is also banned. Insolvency procedures "freeze" the legal relationships surrounding the bankrupt debtor. Such a standstill or stay is required to ensure fair repayment to all general creditors under the comprehensive "execution and distribution" procedure (i.e., insolvency procedure) administered by a trustee and monitored by the insolvency court.

As a natural result of the standstill, the bankrupt debtor's nonperformance of contractual obligations continues or occurs anew during the insolvency procedures. This raises two questions: (1) Can the creditor claim damages resulting from such nonperformance? (2) Can the creditor terminate the contract based on the bankrupt debtor's nonperformance resulting from the mandatory standstill imposed by the insolvency procedures?

To address such issues, this chapter analyzes two types of contracts—executory and non-executory—and introduces the recent, preliminarily[2] proposed amendment to the Korean Debtor Rehabilitation and Bankruptcy Act (DRBA). This chapter is organized as follows: in the second section, the aforementioned two issues with non-executory contracts are examined. In the third section, the legal relationships governed by executory contracts are analyzed, and problems with the current DRBA articles concerning executory contracts are pointed out. In the fourth section, we introduce the Korean Ministry of Justice's (MOJ) proposed amendment to the DRBA concerning executory contracts, and the two previously mentioned issues with executory contracts are reviewed. Finally, the last section provides a summary of the argument and an epilogue.

Situation 1. A Bilateral Contract under Which Unfulfilled Obligations Remain Solely with One of the Contracting Parties

The Basic Structure of a Non-Executory Contract

In this section, we focus on bilateral contracts under which unfulfilled obligations remain solely with one of the contracting parties: the bankrupt debtor. This contractual relationship can be called a "closed and decided relationship" because one contract party's (the creditor's) obligation has been fully performed prior to the initiation of the debtor's insolvency proceeding, and only a one-way relationship from the creditor to the bankrupt debtor remains. Among the various legal aspects of contractual relationships, only one contractual claim takes precedence, and the other aspects take a back seat.

Let's consider an example. A television (TV) sale contract was signed on February 8, 2023. The sale price was $500. The buyer paid $500 in advance to the seller on the day of the contract's conclusion. The due date for the seller to fulfill their duty of transferring ownership of the TV is February 20, 2023. However, on February 15, 2023, before the due date for the seller to fulfill their duty to transfer ownership of the TV, the seller's insolvency proceeding is initiated, with the seller's contractual obligation remaining unfulfilled.

The buyer's claim to ownership transfer is then classified as an insolvency claim subject to the *pari-passu* principle. This claim is subject to a standstill under the insolvency proceedings. During the insolvency procedure, the creditor's claim to specific performance may not be fully realized as in an individual civil execution procedure initiated outside insolvency procedures. This is because this claim is subject to the *pari-passu* principle, which means that all creditors are treated equally in the distribution of the debtor's assets. In bankruptcy procedures,[3] a contractual claim to ownership transfer is converted into a monetary claim, which is paid according to the distribution ratio.

The Creditor's Claim to Damages: Continuity

In this case, can the buyer claim damages for the delay in the seller's specific performance[4] during bankruptcy procedures? The prevailing opinion is that the buyer cannot.[5] The reason for this is that the seller's nonperformance is a result of the standstill mandated by insolvency law (*Wirkung ipso iure*) and is not caused by the seller (insolvent debtor) themselves. Thus, there is no fault on the part of the seller for their nonperformance, and they cannot be blamed for their inability to perform.

But this reasoning is ill-founded. The direct cause of the insolvent debtor's nonperformance is the mandatory standstill from which the debtor cannot deviate. However, the fundamental and proximate cause of the debtor's nonperformance is their poor financial situation, which led to the initiation of the insolvency proceedings. The debtor has control over their own financial conditions outside of the insolvency proceedings and could have avoided becoming bankrupt. Therefore, the debtor is to blame for their nonperformance under the bankruptcy procedures. The nonperformance of the debtor is their own fault, and as a result, they should bear responsibility for any damages arising from delayed contractual performance under the bankruptcy proceedings in the form of a subordinate bankruptcy claim.[6]

The Creditor's Termination Right: Discontinuity

This raises a second question: can the buyer terminate the TV sale contract on account of the seller's nonperformance after the opening of the bankruptcy procedures? Under Korean Civil Code, a creditor can principally terminate a contract on account of a debtor's nonperformance only if the debtor is at fault for their nonperformance.[7] A creditor cannot terminate a contract when the debtor is not to blame for their nonperformance. Therefore, if we admit the insolvent debtor's fault during bankruptcy proceedings, it is a logical answer to the second question that the buyer can terminate the TV sale contract. In principle, the doctrines of contract law should also be respected within the insolvency proceedings (which comprises continuity). It seems that there is no reason to deviate from the doctrines of contract law.

However, the author advocates discontinuity on this issue. In other words, the buyer's (creditor's) termination right should not be respected within the insolvency proceedings.[8] The main arguments for discontinuity are as follows:

First, in principle, insolvency creditors'[9] "new"[10] termination rights should also be subject to a standstill or pause. In other words, insolvency proceedings should also freeze insolvency creditors' "new" termination rights. One of the objectives of a "freeze" during insolvency proceedings is to (1) stabilize the legal situation of the insolvent debtor as of the commencement of the insolvency procedures and (2) respect this fixed situation as the status quo to protect the interests of all general insolvency creditors, namely, those of the insolvency estate. If we admit an individual insolvency creditor's termination right during the insolvency procedures, we have to sacrifice the total interests of all general insolvency creditors and accept the losses of the insolvency estate for the sake of the interests of the individual creditor, who can exercise new termination rights.[11] This is contrary to the purpose of a "standstill" or "freeze" during insolvency proceedings.[12]

Second, respecting an individual creditor's termination right may make insolvency procedures too complex and cause delays, as every creditor who wishes to terminate a contract would need to have their eligibility to do so reviewed. Additionally, these requirements may involve ambiguous concepts, such as "fundamental nonperformance" and an "adequate additional period after the creditor's demand notice." Therefore, discontinuity is desirable to simplify and efficiently carry out insolvency procedures, in which speed is often crucial.

Third, a creditor's termination right is not a natural right to be guaranteed at any time without reservation. This right can be restricted if it is deemed necessary and if such a limitation is justified by balancing the interests of the individual creditor with those of the insolvency estate. In the context of this chapter, it is important to differentiate between a creditor's termination right and a creditor's compensation claim to expectation damages. The latter is considered the most basic right of a creditor against a debtor's default and should, in principle, be guaranteed. Any attempt to restrict this fundamental right must be supported by strong reasoning. However, in the case of a termination right, such a strong justification is not required. The creditor's restitution interests in an insolvency claim can be brought into question only when the creditor has performed their contractual obligations in advance without waiting for the counterparty's performance. In such a scenario, the creditor has willingly assumed the risk of the debtor's financial distress by performing their obligations in advance and waiving the plea for contemporaneous performance. Consequently, there is no compelling reason to protect the restitution interests of such a risk-taking creditor who wishes to recover the value of work already completed as an insolvency claim. Legal relationships surrounding performance fully completed in advance should be treated as established and completed (i.e., closed and decided) relationships.

The author acknowledges that there may not be a single correct answer to this issue. The three arguments mentioned above are policy-based and include a degree of tautology rather than logic. However, if one were to choose between continuity and discontinuity, discontinuity appears preferable for both practical and theoretical reasons.

Situation 2. Executory Contracts

The Basic Structure of an Executory Contract

In this section, we will discuss executory contracts. An executory contract is a bilateral contract in which continuing obligations exist on both sides of the contract at the time the insolvency procedures commence. Unlike Situation 1, an executory contract is an indeterminate and open-ended relationship in the sense that neither party has fully received what was initially expected from the contract, and the ultimate fate of the contract hinges on additional decisions made by one of the contract parties (i.e., the trustee of the insolvent debtor).

Let's consider an example. On February 8, 2023, a contract for the sale of a TV was signed with a sale price of $500. Both the seller's obligation to transfer ownership of the TV and the buyer's obligation to pay $500 must be satisfied by February 23, 2023, with both obligations to be performed simultaneously on that day. However, the seller's insolvency proceeding commences on February 15, 2023, with both parties' obligations still outstanding.

In this case, the key is held by the trustee in the insolvency procedures, and the seller's trustee has two options—fulfillment or termination—under DRBA Articles 119 and 335. If the trustee chooses to fulfill the executory contract, both contractual obligations—to pay $500 and transfer ownership of the TV—should be performed simultaneously, as if the seller were not undergoing bankruptcy procedures. The buyer's claim is not an insolvency claim subject to standstill, and thus, the claim is not monetized. As a result, the seller's trustee can voluntarily transfer ownership of the TV to the buyer even if the seller is involved in insolvency procedures. Moreover, as a common-interests creditor, not as an insolvency creditor, the buyer can freely exercise their contractual rights against the seller's trustee during the insolvency procedures.[13] If the trustee opts to terminate the sale contract, it is retroactively considered null and void,[14] and restitution may be ordered if any contractual obligations have already been performed before the termination.

Problems with the Trustee's Termination Right: Discontinuity

The trustee's termination right,[15] conferred by the DRBA, contains certain loopholes that are inconsistent with the principles of contract law. According to contract law, the defaulting party does not have the right to terminate a contract.[16] The trustee's termination right poses a significant problem, as it allows the bankrupt debtor to escape from a bad bargain. If the termination is granted to the bankrupt debtor, the creditor may be forced to restitute what they received, even if the contract is a winning contract from the creditor's viewpoint and the creditor does not wish to terminate it. It is unconvincing to argue that the final outcome of the executory contract should be determined by the bankrupt debtor, who failed to fulfill their own contractual obligations. The breaching debtor is undeserving of such a privilege.

Let's examine the following example. A contract governing stock sales was signed on February 8, 2023. The sale price was $4 per stock, and a total of 100 stocks were sold, resulting in a total sale price of $400. The buyer paid $100 in advance to the seller. At the time of the opening of the buyer's bankruptcy proceedings, the parties had respective obligations to pay the remaining $300 and transfer ownership of the 100 stocks. However, the market price of the stock sold had dropped dramatically to $0 per stock. In this situation, the stock sale contract became a losing contract from the buyer's perspective. Consequently, the buyer's trustee may wish to terminate the stock sale contract based on DRBA Article 335. If the stock sale contract is terminated, the seller must return $100 and can claim expectation damages of $400[17] as an insolvency claim. If the distribution ratio under the bankruptcy procedures is 1 percent, the seller, as an insolvency creditor, will receive a total of $4 ($400 × 0.01).

The outcome would be significantly different if the trustee were granted a rejection right instead of a termination right. With a rejection right, the trustee would not have the power to terminate the executory contract but would only be able to declare that the bankrupt debtor did not fulfill their contractual obligations (namely, the duty to pay the remaining stock price: $300). In this scenario, the seller would be able to keep the $100 already received and make a claim to expectation damages of $300 as an insolvency claim without being forced to restitute what they had already received. If the distribution ratio dictated by the bankruptcy procedures was 1 percent, the seller would ultimately receive a total of $103 ($100 + $300 x 0.01).

The Korean DRBA's termination system requires creditors to return what they have already received only because of the bankrupt debtor's fault, even if the creditors do not wish to do so. This results in unjustifiable losses for the creditors and is a significant and fundamental problem with the current DRBA. To address this problem, it is necessary to follow the example of countries such as Germany,[18] France,[19] and the United States[20] and provide the trustee with the rejection right instead of the termination right. Thus, an amendment to the current DRBA is required. In the upcoming section, we will explore the rejection system in detail while reviewing the recent proposals to amend the DRBA.

The MOJ's Proposed Amendment to the DRBA

Conflicting Views on the Legal Effect of a Trustee's Rejection

In December 2020, the Korean MOJ established a committee tasked with proposing amendments to the DRBA. The committee's mandate was to comprehensively address issues related to improving and modernizing Korean insolvency law to the fullest extent possible. The committee was active from January 2021 to February 2022, for approximately one year, and comprised nine members, namely, one judge, four professors, and four lawyers.[21] The head of the committee was Professor Han Min from the School of Law at Ewha Women's University.

The committee unanimously resolved to substitute the trustee's termination right with a rejection right. Additionally, they unanimously determined that the legal effect of a trustee's rejection of a continuous contract during insolvency proceedings, such as a lease or rental contract, is a termination *ex nunc*.[22] However, the committee members expressed differing views regarding the legal effect of a trustee's rejection of a noncontinuous contract, such as a land sale or building construction contract. Six members contended that the trustee's rejection is not different from the debtor's nonperformance outside of the insolvency proceedings. Thus, after the trustee's rejection, the creditor may choose the final fate of the contract on the basis of contract law doctrines, as in instances when the debtor breaches their contractual obligations outside the insolvency proceedings.[23] This majority view advocated for "continuity," maintaining that contract law ought to be respected within insolvency procedures as well as outside of them. In contrast, three members upheld the notion of "discontinuity." This minority view posited that a trustee's rejection right constitutes not only nonperformance of the debtor's contractual obligations but also an inherent and specific right in insolvency law to liquidate an executory contract. According to the minority view, when a trustee chooses to reject an executory contract, any open and ongoing relationships governed by the executory contract must cease in the current state and be liquidated *ex nunc*. As a result, the creditor's termination right based on the debtor's nonperformance is not respected.[24] The detailed differences between these two conflicting views are as follows.

The Majority Opinion: Continuity

According to the majority opinion, which advocates for continuity, a creditor holds the power to determine the fate of an executory contract following the trustee's rejection. The creditor has three options.

1. They can claim expectation damages as an insolvency claim without terminating the contract. This option is preferable to the creditor when the contract is a winning contract for their interests.
2. They can terminate the contract *ex tunc* and assert a restitution claim as an insolvency claim. The creditor may also claim expectation damages if possible. This option is preferable to the creditor when the contract is a losing contract for their interests.
3. They can take no action. The creditor may prefer this final option when expectation damages are negative, but they want to retain what they have already received from the bankrupt debtor prior to the opening of the insolvency proceedings.

In the case of cross-border insolvencies, the legal matters related to options 1, 2, and 3 are decided according to the *lex contractus*, not the *lex fori concursus*. This means that the legal matters—such as the creditor's ability to terminate the executory contract, the conditions that must be met for the creditor to terminate the contract, the legal effect of terminating the contract, and the method of calculating the amounts of expectation damages and restitution interests—are determined based on the governing laws of the executory contract rather than the laws of the jurisdiction in which the relevant insolvency court is situated.

The Minority Opinion: Discontinuity

According to the minority opinion, which advocates for discontinuity, the trustee's rejection finally determines the fate of an executory contract, and the creditor does not have the right to choose. Rejection is the sole method of liquidating an executory contract under insolvency procedures. Following the trustee's rejection, the executory contract is liquidated *ex nunc*. The precise definition of "liquidation *ex nunc* of a noncontinuous contract" is as follows:

1. Restitution takes place prospectively from the moment of the trustee's rejection. Hence, any performance made by the debtor after the trustee's rejection must be returned by the creditor (restitution).[25]
2. The performance made before the opening of the insolvency proceedings can be retained by the creditor, unless this is avoided by the trustee. Nonetheless, the "profit" generated by such performance and enjoyed by the creditor can be considered when calculating the creditor's expectation damages. The calculation of the creditor's final damages includes the deduction of the value of the amount already received from the total original expectation damages.
3. If the final damages amount to less than zero after deducting the profit already received from the original expectation damages, or if the total and original expectation damages are already negative, then the creditor is required to restitute the excess value received from the debtor's performance prior to the commencement of the insolvency proceedings.

In the case of cross-border insolvencies, the method of liquidating an open and executory contract is determined by the *lex fori concursus*, while the calculation of expectation damages and interpretation of the scope and meaning of contractual obligations is determined by the *lex contractus*.

Two Amendment Proposals Based on Two Conflicting Views

Both of the conflicting members proposed an amendment based on their own perspectives, but the majority opinion (continuity) ultimately prevailed as the committee's proposal. Now, let's examine the content of these two amendment proposals. Along with the introduction of the amendment proposal, a brief comment will be added.

Continuity (the majority opinion and adopted proposal)

Article 121[26] (rejection of an executory contract)

(1) In the event that the trustee refuses to perform an obligation in accordance with Article 119, the counterparty has the right to seek compensation for any damages incurred as an insolvency creditor.

(2) In the event that the counterparty terminates the contract due to the trustee's refusal to perform which is based on the paragraph (1), the counterparty shall not be entitled to claim the return of what has been provided to the bankrupt debtor, but may enforce their right of as an insolvency creditor. However, this provision shall not apply when the counterparty is entitled to exercise the right of reclamation[27] under other provisions of this Act.

(3) Notwithstanding paragraph (2), in the event that the counterparty who has terminated the contract has already received performance from the debtor, the

counterparty may assert their rights with respect to the counter-performance already provided to the debtor, in accordance with the subsequent subparagraphs:
1. In the event that the trustee exercises the right to claim the return of performance already provided to the counterparty;
a) if the counter-performance already provided to the debtor is among the bankrupt debtor's property, the counterparty shall assert their right of reclamation and claim the return of such property.[28]
b) if the counter-performance already provided to the debtor is not among the bankrupt debtor's property, the counterparty shall claim its value as a common-interests creditor.[29]
2. In the event that the trustee chooses not to exercise the right to claim the return of performance already provided to the counterparty,
the counterparty, as an insolvency creditor, shall claim the repayment of an amount obtained by the debtor after deducting the value of the performance already provided to the counterparty.
(4) The set-off of monetary claims and obligations held by the counterparty arising from paragraphs (1), (2), and (3) is allowed, regardless of the other provisions of this Act.

Article 121, paragraph (1) outlines the primary and most common method of liquidating an executory contract (option 1): a claim for expectation damages is made as an insolvency claim without terminating the contract. The minority opinion also includes this paragraph.

Article 121, paragraph (2) describes the legal consequences that arise when a creditor terminates a contract (option 2). Upon termination, the creditor is generally precluded from seeking the return of any items previously provided to the debtor, as the creditor's restitution claim is deemed an insolvency claim subject to the *pari-passu* principle. However, the creditor can seek the return of the object itself during the insolvency procedures exceptionally when the creditor is authorized to assert the right of reclamation based on other provisions of the DRBA.[30] It is important to note that Article 121, paragraph (2) applies only in cases in which the creditor has provided something to the debtor before the initiation of the insolvency procedures, but the debtor has not yet given anything to the creditor.

In cases where a bilateral contract is terminated, each contract party may be obligated to restitute any objects received or the corresponding value if both parties have partially fulfilled their contractual obligations before the commencement of the debtor's insolvency proceedings. These two obligations for restitution are also based on the contemporaneous-performance relationship, much like the two reciprocal contractual obligations of an executory contract. These legal relationships of a terminated contract are the mirror images of those of an executory contract. Thus, a bilateral-restitution relationship can be called a "quasi-executory contract." Given that the trustee has an option between fulfilling or rejecting the executory contract, the trustee who chooses to reject the executory contract should also have a second opportunity to choose either fulfillment or rejection under the bilateral-restitution relationship. Article 121, paragraph (3) stipulates this.

The fulfillment of a bilateral-restitution relationship means that the trustee desires the return of something previously given by the debtor to the creditor before the opening of the insolvency proceedings. In this scenario, the creditor's right to restitution should be protected as if the debtor and creditor were not part of the insolvency proceedings. Therefore, the creditor's right to restitution should be elevated and classified as a right of reclamation or a common-interest claim, neither of which is subject to the *pari-passu* principle. Within the insolvency procedures, the creditor can freely exercise these rights without restriction against the trustee, and the trustee can also voluntarily fulfill these obligations. Article 121, paragraph (3), subparagraph 1 outlines these legal relationships.

The rejection of a bilateral-restitution relationship implies the monetary liquidation of a quasi-executory contract. As an insolvency claim, the creditor can claim restitution of the value already received by the debtor. In calculating the final amount of the creditor's restitution claim, the value already received by the creditor should be deducted. Article 121, paragraph (3), subparagraph 2 stipulates these legal relationships.

Article 121, paragraph (4) permits recoupment when calculating the amount of the creditor's insolvency claims under paras. (1), (2), and (3). This provision aims to exclude the rules of the DRBA (Article 145, 422) that permit a set-off only under strict conditions during insolvency proceedings when calculating a monetary claim by a creditor that arises after a trustee's rejection. Paragraph (4) is also necessary in the minority opinion. However, the amendment proposal of the minority opinion does not include a provision similar to paragraph (4). This is because the minority opinion supposes that recoupment is naturally and obviously allowed, even if there is no legal provision explicitly stating that such recoupment is permitted.

It is worth noting that the aforementioned proposal does not specify the legal consequences that ensue when a creditor opts for inaction (option 3). The majority opinion's approach to the legal effect remains uncertain regarding cases in which a creditor who has already received partial performance refrains from taking an action subsequent to the trustee's rejection. As we will see in the fourth section, this is one of the significant shortcomings of the majority opinion.

Discontinuity (minority opinion)

Article 121[31] (rejection of an executory contract)

(1) In the event that the trustee refuses to perform an obligation in accordance with Article 119, the counterparty has the right to seek compensation for any damages incurred as an insolvency creditor.

(2) In the event that the counterparty has been found to receive something in excess after the liquidation of an executory contract subsequent to the trustee's

refusal to fulfill the obligation based on Article 119, the counterparty must return the excessive value.

The proposed amendment of the minority group is quite simple and straightforward, since, according to this opinion, the creditor has no right to choose, and there is only one method for fixing the legal relationship of an executory contract.

Article 121, paragraph (1) outlines the basic and conventional approach of liquidating an executory contract. However, complications may arise when the creditor has been given too much by the debtor prior to the commencement of the insolvency proceedings. Article 121, para (2) addresses this matter by mandating that if the creditor has obtained excessive value from the debtor, the creditor must return the surplus amount to the bankrupt debtor (trustee). In such cases, the creditor's claim to expectation damages does not exist because the contract itself is a losing contract for the creditor (i.e., the expectation damages are less than zero) or the value received by the creditor exceeds the original expectation damages (the creditor has already received a benefit greater than the original expectation damages). The final consequences of the minority opinion are similar to those of termination *ex nunc*.

The Author's Opinion: Discontinuity

The author advocates for "discontinuity," not only in situation 1 (the second section) but also in situation 2. The reasons for discontinuity in situation 2 are as follows:

First, this issue is essentially the same as that in situation 1. Thus, the three justifications[32] mentioned in the second section of this chapter can be applied similarly.

Second, under discontinuity, contractual relationships can be determined earlier and more clearly than under continuity. The primary critique of continuity can be summarized by the following questions: How can a contractual relationship be established when a creditor takes no action following a trustee's rejection? Are there no uncertainties or other complications concerning the final determination of contractual relationships?

The Uncertainty Problem

Let us examine the following example. A contract for the sale of a TV was concluded on February 8, 2023, with a sale price of $500. On the day of the contract's conclusion, the buyer paid $100 in advance to the seller. The parties were respectively obligated to pay the remaining $400 and transfer the ownership of the TV when insolvency proceedings were initiated against the buyer. The trustee rejected the sale contract because the bankrupt buyer no longer needed the TV, and it would be challenging to dispose of it at an advantageous price. At the time of the trustee's decision to fulfill or reject the contract, the market price of the TV had fallen from $500 to $460, thus making this sale contract a winning contract for the seller.[33] However, when calculating the seller's currently available expectation damages, the value of the performance already completed for the seller ($100) should be deducted from the original expected profit of the contract ($40). As the final amount (–$60) is less than zero, the seller can no longer claim any expectation damages. In this case, the seller will not terminate the contract because doing so would necessitate the return of the $100 to the buyer.[34]

In this case,[35] can the creditor retain what they received ($100)? Or should they restitute the excessive value ($60 =100–40) to the trustee? If the creditor is required to restitute the excessive value, what grounds support this decision?

There is uncertainty about this question in the majority opinion. At first sight, it seems reasonable to require the creditor to return such excessive value because the creditor appears to be receiving double or unjust enrichment. However, it seems that there are no legal grounds justifying the claim to the return of excessive value, since the contract is not terminated.[36] As long as the contract exists, the creditor's claim to the sale price remains valid. Consequently, the creditor seems to be authorized to retain the sale price already partially paid.

Outside insolvency proceedings, such problems seldom arise because the creditor's claim is not subject to a standstill; thus, the creditor can freely execute their claims against the debtor through civil enforcement procedures and realize the value of the contract forcibly. Similar issues may arise only outside of insolvency proceedings, when the creditor's attempt to enforce the contract by enacting civil execution procedures against the debtor ends in vain, yet the creditor seeks to retain what they have received from the debtor (buyer) previously.

Even in this situation, it is likeliest that the buyer will voluntarily try to fulfill their contractual obligations. This is because, if the buyer tries to satisfy their contractual obligations, they are always better off than when they take no action. In other words, trying to fulfill contractual obligations is always a dominant strategy for the buyer.[37]

However, during insolvency procedures, a trustee who stands in the shoes of the debtor cannot voluntarily try to satisfy contractual obligations because voluntary payment is generally prohibited under such procedures (due to the standstill). Furthermore, even if such voluntary payment were permitted, the trustee may elect not to fulfill the executory contract. This is because, while attempting to fulfill an executory contract is typically a dominant strategy for a buyer outside insolvency proceedings, it may not always be so for the buyer's trustee.

During insolvency procedures, and especially during bankruptcy procedures, the monetizable value of the TV may hold greater significance than its market value. Furthermore, the costs of the disposition should also be considered.[38] The monetizable value is likely to be substantially lower than the market value. As a result, it may be appropriate for the trustee to reject the executory contract within the bankruptcy procedure, unlike in situations outside of such procedures.

The author's tentative opinion is that, even under the majority opinion, a creditor may be obligated to return the excessive value,[39,40] as suggested by the principles of *condictio ob rem* (*Zweckverfehlungskondiktion*)[41] or an analogical application of Article 537 of the Korean Civil Code, which stipulates that the debtor bears the burden of the contractual risk when the performance of the debtor's obligations becomes impossible through no fault of either party.[42] These two legal doctrines[43] share the notion that a contractual performance already delivered to the creditor can be restituted under certain circumstances, even though the contract itself has not been terminated or rescinded.

The Inconsistency and Imbalance Problem

If we were to accept the premise of the creditor's obligation to return the excessive value, the uncertainty issue would no longer apply in the majority opinion. However, a more significant and substantial issue with the majority opinion is its inconsistency and imbalance.

The obligation of a creditor to return excessive value signifies that the creditor is restricted from enjoying a benefit exceeding the amount of the expectation damages in cases where the debtor has partially performed to the creditor (proposition 1). Similarly, when the creditor partially performs to the debtor, the benefits that the creditor can obtain should also be limited to the expectation damages. To illustrate this point, let us consider the following scenario. A manufacture and sales contract for the supply of mechanical parts was signed on February 8, 2023, with a sale price of $500. The buyer made an advance payment of $100 to the seller on the same day. On February 15, 2023, the seller's insolvency proceedings commenced, with the two parties respectively having the obligations to pay the remaining $400 and transfer the ownership of mechanical parts. At the time of the trustee's choice of fulfillment or rejection, the market price of the mechanical parts fell from $500 to $420.[44] Nevertheless, the trustee rejected the contract because the bankrupt seller was no longer able to manufacture the parts. If the creditor (buyer) seeks expectation damages without termination, they can claim only $20 as an insolvency claim.[45,46] However, if the creditor (buyer) terminates the contract, they can claim restitution of $100 as an insolvency claim.[47] If the majority opinion is adopted, the creditor's termination right, based on the debtor's nonperformance, should be secured within the insolvency procedure as well as outside of it. Therefore, in the above case, the creditor (buyer) can obtain a benefit of $100 as restitution,[48] which exceeds the expectation damages ($20).[49] This result contradicts proposition 1. Proposition 1 should be applicable whenever either the creditor or debtor partially performs. Regardless of which party partially performed before the insolvency proceedings, the principle that the creditor cannot benefit by more than the expectation damages should be applied equally.

If a creditor is obligated to return excessive value, then it would be illogical to grant the creditor the power to choose the fate of an executory contract, since the creditor can escape from a bad bargain through such a power. Neither the debtor nor the creditor should be allowed to escape from bad bargains. Open contractual relationships must be liquidated in an orderly way to the extent necessary for the comprehensive execution procedures established to protect the interests of all general insolvency creditors, and they should not be modified substantially or unnecessarily. Termination *ex tunc* of a noncontinuous contract is a substantial and unnecessary alteration of a contractual relationship.

However, the minority opinion in favor of discontinuity failed to garner sufficient support within the committee. The primary arguments against discontinuity were that (1) it is a rare occurrence for a creditor to have no expectation claims and yet wish to retain an already received benefit without terminating the contract, and (2) there are no comparable foreign insolvency laws that adopt the discontinuity stance. The minority view was criticized for being too radical, risky, and meticulous. The committee expressed considerable apprehension about incorporating a legal provision that deviates from contract law doctrines when the discussion of these matters has yet to mature. Nonetheless, it is questionable whether a logically and legally sound opinion should be discarded solely on the grounds of practical concerns.

An additional proposal was also reviewed that abstained from explicitly stating the legal effect of the trustee's rejection and instead delegated this matter to the court's interpretation of law. However, this proposal was dismissed due to the strong concerns raised by practitioners, including lawyers and judges, who apprehended that this approach could potentially undermine the predictability of contractual relationships.

Summary and Epilogue

The author's main arguments can be distilled as follows:
"In both situations 1 and 2, the creditor should not have the power to terminate the contract on the basis of the bankrupt debtor's nonperformance after the initiation of the insolvency proceedings. In principle, the creditor's power to exercise a new termination right during the insolvency procedures should be constrained to ensure the orderly and unified liquidation of the contractual relationships."

Another question then follows: "Is this proposition a rigid and invariable principle that is rarely or never capable of being opted out of, or is it a default rule that could be waived in certain situations if necessary?"

This is an important and weighty topic that cannot be fully addressed in this chapter, but I will briefly mention my tentative idea, which is in the conception stage. Insolvency procedures as a collective process may differ from formal and traditional civil procedures, which are individual, one-on-one processes. The dichotomy of substantive law and procedural law is mitigated during insolvency procedures, and a strictly formal doctrine based on such a dichotomy may not be desirable. Instead, a more flexible and dynamic legal doctrine can benefit all interested parties participating in such a collective process and contribute to the final objective of the insolvency procedures. Furthermore, discontinuity is an exception that is only justified under insolvency law and not as a general rule. This exceptionality should not be extended ("*Singularia non sunt extendenda*"). Therefore, it seems desirable that the restriction on the creditor's termination right should not be classified as a substantive legal proposition that is fixed and cannot be changed. Rather, it should be regarded as a procedural legal proposition that only applies during insolvency procedures and can even be altered during the procedures if necessary. In other words, it seems desirable for the insolvency court to principally or automatically impose such a restriction on creditors as a "standstill" mechanism, but the court should have the discretion to lift this stay and allow creditors to exercise their termination rights when necessary (e.g., when an executory contract turns out to be unnecessary and harmful to the insolvent debtor's rehabilitation, and the creditor also wants to terminate the executory contract). If we adopt the notion of discontinuity and the corresponding amendments, we may also need to include another provision that confers discretion on the insolvency court to lift the stay and respect the creditor's termination right.

However, it should be noted that this idea is still in its preliminary stage and requires further examination, refinement, and improvement. Finding a satisfactory answer to the question at hand may prove to be challenging, and much work may need to be done before a conclusive response can be reached. This chapter represents only the initial phase of the inquiry.

The author's proposed legislation, which is based on the concept of discontinuity, may be a new and unfamiliar idea that lacks comparable precedents in the insolvency laws of other countries. Therefore, the author welcomes all constructive feedback, critical responses, and insightful comments to facilitate the development of this proposal.

Addendum

I revised one of the opinions asserted in this chapter and provided further analysis in a subsequent article: Joon-Kyu Choi, "Legal Relationship between Two Bankrupt Parties of an Executory Contract," Juris 1, no. 69 (2024): 3–38 (in Korean). The main points are as follows:

(1) If partial performance by either of the two contract parties has been made before the commencement of bankruptcy proceedings, a claim for the return of such performance or its equivalent value is "always" prohibited. Even if one contract party enjoys benefits that exceed its expectation interests due to the partial performance made by the other contract party, a claim for return of the excess is not permitted.

(2) In a lease contract, if the bankrupt lessee's trustee chooses to refuse the executory lease contract, the lease contract should, in principle, be deemed terminated immediately. However, if the lessee has paid partial rent in advance, the lease contract shall be deemed terminated when the rental period corresponding to the rent paid in advance ended after the trustee's rejection. The same principle applies even if both the lessor and the lessee go bankrupt and the lessee's trustee chooses to refuse. In this case, if the lessor's trustee chooses to assume, the lessor's trustee can exercise a claim for expectation damages as a bankruptcy claim. If the lessor's trustee chooses to refuse, no claims can be made against each other.

(3) In the case of bilateral bankruptcy, the effect of assuming executory contracts takes place only if both trustees choose to assume the executory contract. If one trustee chooses to assume and the other trustee chooses to refuse, then the trustee who chose to assume may exercise a claim for expectation damages as a bankruptcy claim against the trustee who chose to refuse. If both trustees choose to refuse, no claims can be made against each other.

Notes

1 In this chapter, the term "insolvency procedure" is used to refer to both the "bankruptcy procedure," which focuses on the liquidation of the bankrupt debtor's assets, and the "rehabilitation procedure," which focuses on the recovery of the debtor or the debtor's business.

2 As of August 8, 2023, this proposal, which was prepared by the Committee for Amendment of DRBA organized under the Korean Ministry of Justice (MOJ), has not been confirmed as the formal proposal of the MOJ.

3 The Korean insolvency procedures are broadly categorized into bankruptcy procedures and rehabilitation procedures. Unlike bankruptcy procedures, insolvency claims are not automatically monetized under rehabilitation procedures. However, similar to bankruptcy procedures, insolvency claims are generally paid equally with other comparable insolvency claims according to the distribution ratio established by the rehabilitation plan. For the sake of convenience of the discussion, the author's argument in the following main text is primarily focused on bankruptcy procedures.

4 Monetization of the contractual claim for specific performance under bankruptcy procedures does not result in the extinguishment of the claim itself. Instead, it entails the conversion of the claim into a monetary claim for the purpose of equal distribution among all insolvency claims. Therefore, the delay of specific performance can still occur within bankruptcy procedures, potentially leading to damages suffered by the buyer.

5 Byung-Dae Park, "Pasanjeolcha ga kyeyakkwankye e michineun younghyang [Impact of Bankruptcy Proceedings on Contractual Relationships]," *Jaepanjaryo* [Court Reference Material] 82 (1996): 455–6 (In Korean); Young-Bo Roh, *Dosanbeob Gangui* [Lecture on Bankruptcy Law] (Seoul: Parkyoungsa, 2018), 228 (In Korean). This prevailing opinion is supposed to be influenced by the prevailing opinion in Japan. Ito Makoto, *Hasanho·Minjisaiseiho* [Bankruptcy Law and Civil Rehabilitation Law], 5th ed. (Tokyo: Yuhikaku Publishing, 2022), 308 (In Japanese).

6 Debtor Rehabilitation and Bankruptcy Act article 446 paragraph 1 subparagraph 2 categorizes "a claim for damages for nonperformance after bankruptcy proceedings" as a subordinate bankruptcy claim. Consequently, a claim for damages resulting from the delay of specific performance under bankruptcy procedures is also considered a subordinate bankruptcy claim. These claims have a low probability of being repaid during the bankruptcy proceedings. In contrast, "a claim for damages for nonperformance after rehabilitation proceedings" is classified as a normal insolvency claim (rehabilitation claim) rather than a subordinate insolvency claim (Debtor Rehabilitation and Bankruptcy Act article 118 subparagraph 3 [S. Kor.]).

7 Minbeob [Civil Code], article 546 (In case of impossibility of contractual obligations) (S. Kor.). In the case of a delay in performing contractual obligations as well, the creditor may only terminate the contract, if the debtor is responsible for their own delay. This is a commonly accepted principle of Korean contract law. Won-Lim Jee, *Minbeobgangeui* [Lectures on Civil Code], 19th ed. (Seoul: Hongmoonsa, 2021), 1413–14 (In Korean).

8 Kamo Akira, a Japanese scholar of civil law, also supports "discontinuity." However, his argument is based on a more doctrinal approach. According to him, one of the requirements for a creditor to terminate a contract, namely, the creditor's demand notice for the debtor's voluntary payment within an appropriate period, cannot be

met during the insolvency proceedings. This is because the insolvency procedure prohibits the debtor from making voluntary payments, thereby rendering such a demand notice fundamentally impossible. Kamo Akira, "Atarashii Kyeyakukaijohosei to Tosantetsuzuki: Tosantesuzukikaishigo ni okeru Kyeyakuaitegatano Hoteikaijokenshutoku no Kahi [New Contract Termination Legislation and Insolvency Proceedings: Whether the Counterparty to a Contract Can Obtain a Statutory Right of Termination after the Commencement of Insolvency Proceedings]," in *Atarashii Kyeyakukaijohosei to Tosan-Saiseitetsuzuki* [New Contract Termination Legislation and Insolvency-Rehabilitation Proceedings] (Tokyo: Shojihomu Co. Ltd., 2019), 230 (In Japanese).

9 "Insolvency creditors," in the present context, mean the creditors whose claims are subject to the *pari-passu* principle under the insolvency proceedings.

10 In this context, the term "new" termination rights denote the rights that emerge subsequent to the initiation of insolvency proceedings. Another issue that may arise is whether "old" termination rights, which were preexisting before the commencement of insolvency proceedings, should also be subject to a standstill. However, this chapter does not delve into this issue which is left for further independent and in-depth study.

11 An insolvency creditor may usually prefer to terminate the contract, when the combined amount of the restitution and compensation claims that would be available after terminating the contract, both of which are insolvency claims, is greater than the compensation claim for expectation damages that would be available without terminating the contract, which is also an insolvency claim. The interests of an individual insolvency creditor and those of the insolvency estate are in a zero-sum relationship, meaning that any gain by one party results in an equal loss to the other party. Therefore, if the termination right is allowed, the insolvency estate loses as much as the individual creditor gains from terminating the contract.

12 The insolvency creditor's claim is analogous to one that has completed extinctive prescription, as the claim retains its existence albeit lacking enforceability. In cases where the statute of limitations has expired for contractual claims, the contract cannot be terminated on the basis of nonfulfillment of those claims. In other words, the contract cannot be terminated due to the nonperformance of time-barred claims.

13 A common-interests creditor is not subject to the *pari-passu* principle.

14 In accordance with the Korean Civil Code, termination of a contract by a creditor has proprietary (*in-rem*) effects. Therefore, a terminated contract is treated as if it had never existed before, and a claim for restitution is considered a proprietary claim in principle. However, these proprietary effects are limited within insolvency proceedings. In such proceedings, an insolvency creditor's claim for restitution is generally considered an insolvency claim subject to the *pari-passu* principle, unless there are "specific" legal grounds justifying the creditor's *in-rem* rights. This is because the principle of equality among general creditors should be particularly respected and emphasized within the insolvency proceedings. Under the insolvency proceedings, creditors seeking restitution for their previously made contractual performance are treated no differently from other general creditors seeking the fulfillment of contractual obligations by the debtor.

15 The Japanese insolvency law also grants the trustee the right to terminate contracts. Regrettably, the adoption of the Japanese termination system in Korean legislation was carried out without adequate and sufficient deliberation.

16 The trustee stands in the shoes of the bankrupt debtor. So, if we deny the bankrupt debtor's termination right, we should also deny the trustee's termination right.
17 There may be controversy over when the standard period for calculating expectation damages is. However, in the above example, it is assumed that the stock price continues to be $0 after falling to $0. In this case, the expectation damages would be $400, regardless of when the base period was selected.
18 Insolvenzordnung [InsO] [Insolvency Law], Section 103 paragraph 2 (Ger.).
19 Code de commerce [C. com.] [Commercial Code], article L614-11-1 (Fr.).
20 11 U.S.C. Section article 365(a).
21 The author participated in this committee as one of nine members.
22 By German legal terminology, a termination ex-nunc is called "Kündigung," and a termination ex-tunc is called "Rücktritt."
23 A standard textbook of German Insolvency Law appears to agree to this opinion (= "continuity"), since it allows the creditor's termination right based on the debtor's nonperformance inside the insolvency procedure. *See* Reinhard Bork, *Einführung in das Insolvenzrecht* [Introduction to Insolvency Law], 9th ed. (Tübingen: Mohr Siebeck, 2019), 103n3 (In German).
24 KPB/Tintelnot InsO, Section103 Rn.15 advocates the same opinion("discontinuity") regarding German insolvency law.
25 The rationale for such restitution can be attributed to the stand-still effect of the insolvency procedure, which entails the prohibition of voluntary payments by the debtor. Furthermore, any performance rendered by the debtor after the commencement of insolvency proceedings but prior to the trustee's rejection may also require restitution, as it falls under the scope of the mandatory stand-still effect of the insolvency procedure.
26 This chapter applies to the rehabilitation procedure. The provisions of the amended article applicable to the bankruptcy procedure (Article 337) are nearly identical to those of the aforementioned article.
27 The right of reclamation means the right to separate the objects that do not belong to the insolvency estate. It can be invoked, when the objects that do not belong to the bankrupt debtor have been included in the insolvency estate. The holder of the reclamation right is not considered an insolvency creditor subject to *pari-passu* principle. This right is referred to as "Aussonderungsrecht" (= the right of separation) in German legal terminology.
28 The remaining "specific things" can be the subject of the reclamation right. However, the money transferred to the counterparty as a means of payment cannot, in principle, be the subject of the reclamation right, due to their fungible nature.
29 Common-interests creditors are defined as creditors who have paid the costs that are beneficial to all insolvency creditors and the insolvency estate. As a consequence, such creditors have the right to recover their costs from the insolvency estate with priority over insolvency creditors, and without any restriction imposed by a standstill within the insolvency proceedings. The common-interests claim is not subject to *pari-passu* principle. This claim is referred to as "Masseforderung" (= the claim for the insolvency estate) in German legal terminology.
30 For example, when the trustee of the bankrupt lessee refuses to pay rent, the creditor(lessor) can terminate the contract and can exercise the right of reclamation over the leased object as an owner.

31 The provisions of the amended article applicable to the bankruptcy procedure (Article 337) are nearly identical to those of the aforementioned article.

32 (1) A creditor's new termination right should be subject to a mandatory standstill imposed by the insolvency procedures. (2) Discontinuity is desirable to simplify and efficiently operate the insolvency procedure. (3) There are no special reasons to protect the restitution interests of a creditor who in advance provided performance to the debtor before receiving an equivalent counter-performance from the debtor.

33 For the sake of the convenience, let us assume that the market price of TV continues to be $460 after falling to $460. *See* note 17. And let's also assume that the seller's expectation damages are solely determined by the difference between the sale price and the market price.

34 If the contract is terminated, the seller can claim for expectation damages in the amount of $40 as an insolvency claim. But the seller must return $100 already received. The overall net effect ($40 as an insolvency claim) on the seller is worse than if the contract had not been terminated and the seller had retained the $100.

35 There may be a similar scenario; the market price of a TV has increased from $500 to $550, thus making the contract a losing contract for the seller. However, the seller may not choose to terminate the contract. This is because the net wealth of the seller if the contract were terminated is worse than that of the seller if they took no action. In the former case, the seller cannot claim for any expectation damage as an insolvency claim, because this contract is a losing contract for the seller, and at the same time the seller should return the $100 already received to the bankrupt debtor(trustee). In the latter case, the seller cannot claim for expectation damages either, but may retain 100$. In this case, the excessive value enjoyed by the seller is $100.

36 Under the majority opinion, only the creditor has the termination right. If the creditor did not exercise such termination right, the contract in principle persists.

37 When the buyer takes no action, they will lose $100. If the buyer takes no action, the buyer's advance payment of $100 becomes useless, resulting in net loss (-$100). And the values of the buyer's remaining contractual obligation (-$400) and claim (+$460) cannot be included in calculating the buyer's final net benefit from the sale contract. Under the assumption made in the main text that the seller cannot execute their contractual claims against the buyer, it becomes definite and final that the buyer's remaining obligation and claim cannot be realized, and the remaining contractual relationships are stuck in deadlock situations (such situations rarely occur outside insolvency proceedings, but always occur inside insolvency proceedings in principle due to the stand-still effect). Therefore, the values of the buyer's remaining obligation and claim cannot be considered as either a loss or a benefit.

However, if the buyer tries to fulfill contractual obligations, they can take less damages. There are two scenarios: (1) If the seller receives the remaining sale price ($400) from the buyer, and transfers the ownership of TV to the buyer, the buyer would lose $40 (because the market price of TV has fallen down from $500 to $460). (2) If the seller refuses to receive the remaining sale price, and transfer the ownership of TV, then the buyer can terminate the contract, based on the seller's nonperformance, and claim for restitution of $100. In this case the buyer would lose nothing.

38 Under insolvency procedures, especially bankruptcy procedures, what matters is the monetary value of the debtor's asset that can be finally attributed to creditors, not the asset's value that can be enjoyed by the owner of such asset.

39 This result is not contradictory to the arguments that a creditor should not be forced to restitute what they have received from the debtor before the opening of the insolvency proceedings. As we have discussed in the third section, while criticizing the current structure of DRBA and urging the introduction of a "rejection system," a creditor should not be forced to restitute. However, at the same time the creditor should accept the consequences, whether gains or losses, of their voluntary decisions to make a contract. The creditor does not deserve windfall or unjustifiable gains.

40 German legal scholar Ludwig Häsemayer characterized such excess value as the creditor's "insolvency gain" and justified claims for its return by analogically applying the provision governing the trustee's avoidance powers. Ludwig Häsemayer, *Insolvenzrecht* [Insolvency Law], 4th ed. (Köln: Carl Heymanns, 2007), Rn. 20–6 (In German).

41 *Condictio ob rem* is one of various types of unjust enrichment claims recognized in German Civil Code (Bürgerliches Gesetzbuch [BGB], Section 812, paragraph 1, sentence 2, http://www.gesetze-im-internet.de/englisch_bgb/index.html (Ger.)). According to *condictio ob rem*, a performance can be restituted if the purpose of a legal transaction (which justified such performance but has not become a part of the contents of the transaction) is frustrated. But there is ongoing debate among Korean legal scholars as to whether such a restitution claim can or should be recognized in Korean law. This is because the Korean Civil Code does not have provisions like Section 812, paragraph 1, sentence 2 of German Civil Code. Some scholars argue that *condictio ob rem* can be recognized as a type of unjust enrichment claim. Others argue that there is no need to recognize *condictio ob rem* as a separate legal concept in Korean law, and that other existing legal doctrines can be used to address similar situations. *See* Jong-Hee Seo, "Budangsamukwanri mit bujinjeong samukwanri wa budangideuk kwaeui kwankye [A Relationship between Unjust Negotiorum-Gestio/Quasi Negotiorum-Gestio and Unjust Enrichment]," *Minsabuphak* 63, no. 1 (2013): 39, 56–7 (In Korean) (positive opinion); Chang-Soo Yang, *Minbupjuhae* [An Exposition of Korean Civil Code], 17th ed. (Seoul: Parkyoungsa, 2005), 176 (In Korean) (negative opinion).

42 According to Korean Civil Code article 537, the debtor can no longer claim their contractual rights against the creditor, when the performing of debtor's corresponding obligations becomes impossible without either party's fault. That is to say, the debtor should restitute what they have received from the creditor in advance, when the performing of debtor's corresponding obligations becomes impossible without either party's fault.

43 One (*condictio ob rem*) is a purely theoretical doctrine and the other is a doctrine based on the written law.

44 For the sake of the convenience, let us assume that the market price of mechanical parts continues to be $420 after falling to $420. *See* note 17. And let's also assume that the seller's expectation damages are solely determined by the difference between the sale price and the market price.

45 The buyer must pay the remaining $400 in exchange for mechanical parts worth $420, therefore the buyer's final expectation damages are $20 (=420-400). Originally the buyer's expectation interests are -$80 (=420-500), because this contract is a losing one for the buyer. However, the buyer paid $100 in advance. If we assume that such prepayment is already completed and irreversible, the buyer can claim for expectation damages of $20 as an insolvency claim.

46 For the convenience of the discussion, it is supposed that other collateral losses, such as the buyer's damages resulting from the delayed production of goods due

to the non-delivery of mechanical parts, are not at issue. Instead, the sole losses suffered by the buyer are the reduction in the market value of the mechanical parts. However, even if there exist some collateral losses on the buyer's side, the problems identified in the main text persist, as the buyer could potentially recover more than the amount of expectation damages, by pursuing a claim for restitution interests.

47 When the contract is terminated, the creditor may also claim for expectation damages, if any. But in this case, the contract is a losing contract to the creditor. Therefore the amount of the creditor's expectation claims is less than zero (-$80).

48 The ultimate result is that the buyer does not experience any nominal gains or losses as they receive the $100 which they had given to the debtor before. However, the buyer's restitution claim of $100 only qualifies as an insolvency claim, and thus the amount they can recover is substantially reduced by the distribution ratio. As a result, the buyer still experiences a loss.

49 If the contract were to be fulfilled, the buyer would ultimately incur a loss of $80, as they entered into a losing contract and their expectation interests amounted to -$80. However, in calculating the buyer's expectation damages as of the current executory stage, it amounts to $20 as insolvency claim. As a result, the buyer can only receive a reduced amount of $20 based on the distribution ratio, and loses $100 of advance payment. If the distribution ratio is 2 percent, the buyer's final net wealth is -99.6$ (=$20x0.02-$100). Such a final outcome is different from the buyer's net wealth when the contract is fully realized as promised which is -$80 (=$420-$500).

Bibliography

Bork, Reinhard. *Einführung in das Insolvenzrecht* [Introduction to Insolvency Law]. 9th ed. Tübingen: Mohr Siebeck, 2019 (In German).

Häsemayer, Ludwig. *Insolvenzrecht* [Insolvency Law]. 4th ed. Köln: Carl Heymanns, 2007 (In German).

Ito, Makoto. *Hasanho·Minjisaiseiho* [Bankruptcy Law and Civil Rehabilitation Law]. 5th ed. Tokyo: Yuhikaku Publishing, 2022 (In Japanese).

Jee, Won-Lim. *Minbeobgangeui* [Lectures on Civil Code]. 19th ed. Seoul: Hongmoonsa, 2021 (In Korean).

Kamo, Akira. "Atarashii Kyeyakukaijohosei to Tosantetsuzuki: Tosantesuzukikaishigo ni okeru Kyeyakuaitegatano Hoteikaijokenshutoku no Kahi." In *Atarashii Kyeyakukaijohosei to Tosan-Saiseitetsuzuki* [New Contract Termination Legislation and Insolvency-Rehabilitation Proceedings], 230. Tokyo: Shojihomu Co. Ltd., 2019 (In Japanese).

Park, Byung-Dae. "Pasanjeolcha ga kyeyakkwankye e michineun younghyang [Impact of Bankruptcy Proceedings on Contractual Relationships]." *Jaepanjaryo* [Court Reference Material] 82 (1996): 455–6 (In Korean).

Roh, Young-Bo. *Dosanbeob Gangui* [Lecture on Bankruptcy Law]. Seoul: Parkyoungsa, 2018 (In Korean).

Seo, Jong-Hee. "Budangsamukwanri mit bujinjeong samukwanri wa budangideuk kwaeui kwankye." *Minsabuphak* 63, no. 1 (2013): 39, 56–7 (In Korean).

Yang, Chang-Soo. *Minbupjuhae* [An Exposition of Korean Civil Code]. 17th ed. Seoul: Parkyoungsa, 2005 (In Korean).

This chapter was previously published under the same title in Journal of Korean Law 22, no. 2 (2023): 295–321.

10

For the World's More Full of Weeping

Why South Korea Should Retroactively Abolish Civil and Criminal Statutes of Limitation Applicable to Illegal International Adoptions

Daniel A. Edelson

Introduction

In the sixty years following the Korean War, South Korea sent up to 200,000 children to adoptive parents in other countries.[1] Although an exact number is not known, advocates believe that some of these children were not eligible for international adoption under either South Korean law or the laws of the countries to which the children were sent. They allege that South Korean adoption agencies, among other abuses, improperly pressured women to relinquish their children, accepted children for international adoption without the consent of both parents, and classified children as orphans using falsified documents. A number of commentators believe that South Korea's former military dictatorships promoted and facilitated the illegal international adoptions for economic reasons and that the adoption agencies in South Korea acted as their agents.

Some adoptees wish to pursue civil remedies in the South Korean courts against the adoption agencies and the South Korean government. They also believe that the South Korean government should criminally prosecute those responsible for orchestrating their illegal adoptions.

But rigid application of South Korea's statutes of limitation would time-bar both civil and criminal cases against defendants allegedly responsible for illegal international adoptions. This chapter proposes that South Korea's courts or its legislature should retroactively abolish, toll, or significantly extend civil and criminal statutes of limitation to enable South Korean courts to decide illegal international adoption cases on their merits.

The chapter is in five sections. The first section discusses the abusive practices that allegedly infect the international adoption industry and accusations of corruption in connection with South Korea's international adoption practices.

In the second section, the chapter briefly discusses how and why common law and civil jurisdictions apply statutes of limitation to bar untimely claims. In addition, the second part discusses criticisms of statutes of limitation, especially where meritorious claims are dismissed. This section also explains how South Korean statutes of limitation, if rigidly applied, will prevent South Korean courts from reaching the merits of illegal adoption cases.

The third section explains why different jurisdictions throughout the world, including South Korea, abolish, extend, or toll statutes of limitation where principles of fairness and justice militate against their rigid application. Jurisdiction typically relax their application of statutes of limitation where plaintiffs were unable, through no fault of their own, to commence a timely litigation.

In the fourth section, the chapter suggests that the principles discussed in the second and third sections favor South Korea abolishing statutes of limitation applicable to illegal international adoptions. In addition, the fourth section argues that changes to South Korea's statutes of limitation should apply retroactively to revive claims that may have already expired. Finally, the last section summarizes the chapter's conclusions and briefly considers alternatives.

International Adoption, Child Laundering, and South Korea

The Business of International Adoption and Allegations of Corruption

In the decades following the Korean War, international adoption, which originated as a charitable movement, became a private industry.[2] The adoption industry is lucrative—prospective parents are willing to pay tens of thousands of dollars to adopt a child from a country other than their own.[3] To meet this demand, adoption agencies operate in countries around the world from which they send thousands of children every year ("sending countries") to adoptive families in other countries, primarily the United States, Canada, and nations in western Europe ("receiving countries").[4]

Both supporters and opponents of international adoption agree that governments and adoption agencies in sending countries sometimes engage in improper conduct, although commentators disagree over the frequency and severity of the misconduct.[5] Critics of international adoption argue that in many cases, purported orphans are actually children who were purchased, cajoled, stolen, or otherwise fraudulently procured from one or both parents.[6] Through a process sometimes referred to as "child laundering," adoption agencies—often in collusion with government officials—furnish children with false documents attesting that they are orphans so that parents overseas will adopt them.[7] When certain sending countries more strictly regulate international adoption to prevent such abusive practices, critics believe that adoption agencies shift their operations to countries with more lax supervision to meet the demand for children in receiving countries.[8]

Advocates contend that illegally exporting babies for profit (or for other motivations) harms both the child and the child's family of origin.[9] Illegally adopted children may, among other things, suffer psychological despair, knowing that they were improperly displaced from their birth families and that their birth identities were erased.[10]

Illegal international adoptions may violate children's human rights, as reflected in such international documents as the United Nations Convention on the Rights of the Child.[11] In fact, some critics argue that in the form that it is practiced today, international adoption is a form of child trafficking.[12] The United Nations General Assembly provides some support for this argument as it identified "false adoption" as a form of human trafficking.[13]

Although this chapter focuses on South Korea, which experts believe alone has sent at least 160,000[14] and as many as 200,000 children overseas for adoption,[15] illegal international adoptions are not limited to any single country.[16] In particular, commentators point to abusive practices in countries including, but not limited to, Cambodia,[17] Haiti,[18] India,[19] and Guatemala.[20]

Allegations of Illegal International Adoptions in South Korea

South Korea is attractive to adoptive parents for a number of reasons, including its reputation as an ethical, safe, and efficient country from which to adopt.[21] In fact, among both critics and advocates of international adoption, South Korea may have the best reputation for reputable practices of any sending country.[22] China, at one point, shared South Korea's sterling reputation, but numerous reports exposed corruption in Chinese adoption practices.[23]

But some advocates believe that South Korea's reputation for corruption-free international adoptions is undeserved.[24] South Korean adoption law, both before and after its recent amendment, requires that parents, if living, consent to the child's placement in adoption.[25] Advocates believe that numerous international adoptions were illegal under South Korean law and inconsistent with international norms because[26] at least one parent did not relinquish the child for adoption under a real name; a person other than the parent relinquished; only one parent relinquished; the child was relinquished for domestic but not international adoption; the signature on the relinquishment form was forged; single mothers were improperly pressured to relinquish their children, told by adoption agencies that it would be impossible for them to raise a child as a single mother in South Korea;[27] and one side of the family, typically the child's paternal grandmother, orchestrated the adoption.[28]

The case of Mr. Yong-moon Kang, who was adopted from South Korea by a US couple in 1983, is illustrative. Unlike most Korean adoptees in recent times who are adopted at age 12–24 months,[29] Yong-moon's father relinquished Yong-moon to an adoption agency when the child was six.[30] Yong-moon's parents were married at the time, and Yong-moon was not an orphan.[31]

As with other South Korean citizens at that time, Yong-moon's name at birth was recorded on his father's family registry (in Korean a Hojeok Deungbon, hereinafter "Hojeok").[32] The Hojeok was kept with the municipal office in his father's hometown.

At the adoption agency's request, the municipal office in the capital city of Seoul created an "Orphan Hojeok Deungbon" stating that Yong-moon was an orphan. Yong-moon's Orphan Hojeok Deungbon was a fabrication as both of Yong-moon's parents were alive and his mother did not authorize his adoption.[33] Yong-moon's fraudulent documentation was not unusual. According to TRACK, adoption files consistently demonstrate that the orphans were furnished with fabricated orphan Hojeoks.[34]

The Role of the South Korean Government in Illegal International Adoptions

Critics allege that the South Korean government shares responsibility for illegal international adoptions. In a major piece published in 1988, Matthew Rothschild described the four adoption agencies that then operated in South Korea as quasi-government institutions.[35] Critics allege that the South Korean military governments directed, approved, and promoted a policy of exporting children for profit.[36] Commentators believe that the autocratic South Korean regimes in the 1970s and 1980s, which were focused on economic expansion, relied on "baby exports" by the international adoption agencies to reduce social costs and to earn US dollars.[37]

As South Korea began democratizing in the late 1980s and worldwide attention focused on South Korea in advance of the 1988 Seoul Olympics, some South Korean children's rights advocates and newspapers publicly criticized the government's role in making South Korea the world's leading "baby exporter."[38] Many South Koreans viewed the number of children sent overseas as a national embarrassment.[39] A decade later, on October 31, 1998, President Dae Jung Kim apologized to South Korean adoptees.[40]

Yet more than twenty years after establishing a democracy and emerging as one of the world's stronger economies, South Korea remained a leading sending country, causing many commentators to question why a modern industrialized country send so many children overseas.[41] In addition, despite South Korea's proliferate use of truth commissions to investigate and document past abuses in South Korea,[42] there was never an investigation into South Korea's international adoption practices.[43] Nor has there ever been any investigation into the role that the government played in facilitating adoptions by, among other things, directing the international adoption agencies and approving documents such as orphan Hojeoks and travel visas.[44]

South Korean Adoptees and Their Search for the Truth

Some South Korean adoptees have traveled to South Korea to learn more about the facts and circumstances underlying their relinquishment and adoption. But adoptees frequently report that adoption agencies and government officials do not provide them with assistance and often frustrate their efforts to discover the truth.[45]

Until 2011, there was no legal framework that guaranteed the right of the adoptee to access his or her birth information. In response to efforts by organizations such as TRACK,[46] South Korea recently amended the Special Law on Adoption Promotion and Procedure (the "Special Adoption Law").[47] The Special Adoption Law nominally allows adoptees to gain access to their birth information from adoption agencies via Korean Adoption Services (KAS), a government entity intended to function as a central authority on all adoptions in South Korea.[48] Despite the amended legislation, many adoptees report that they do not receive adequate and timely responses to requests for information related to their birth and adoption from KAS.[49]

Adoptees who cannot gain access to their birth records from KAS have few options. The law does not provide any recourse to compel KAS to comply with requests for information.[50] Moreover, adoption agencies have refused to turn over information to KAS without any repercussions.[51] For adoptees, it may take years of effort to piece together how their identities were erased so they could be sent overseas for adoption.[52]

Recent Reforms in South Korea

This past decade, particularly between 2004 and 2009, South Korea took steps to restrict international adoption and to promote domestic adoption.[53] During those years adoption from South Korea to the United States dropped from an average prior range of 1,500–2,000 children yearly to approximately 1,000.[54] However, as of 2011 the number of adoptions remained steady and South Korea still ranked as one of the top senders of adopted children to the United States.[55]

On May 24, 2013, South Korea signed the Convention on Protection of Children and Co-operation in Respect of Intercountry Adoption (the "Hague Convention").[56] Although not yet ratified by the South Korean government, the Hague Convention establishes standardized regulations in the international adoption process intended to prevent abuses such as abduction and fraud.[57] Among other things, the Hague Convention requires that a central authority oversee the adoption process[58] in a sending country to prevent improper financial gain. The Hague Convention also requires that each sending country ensures that adopted children are eligible for adoption under that sending country's laws, mandates record keeping, and requires sending countries to create a process to lodge complaints against adoption agencies that violate the Convention.[59]

In addition, the Special Adoption Law[60] addresses abuses in South Korea's adoption system by mandating that every international adoption receive approval from a Korean family court,[61] requires efforts to place children first domestically, not internationally,[62] and is also intended to provide adoptees with better access to their birth records.[63] The law imposes criminal penalties on persons who arrange adoptions without accreditation.[64]

Statutes of Limitation: Why Some Claims Are Time Barred

Statutes of Limitations and Their Application around the World

As a general rule across most jurisdictions, civil and criminal cases must be brought within a certain period of time; otherwise, the claims can never be brought at all. Laws establishing when claims expire are called statutes of limitation. Statutes of limitation eliminate the rights of private plaintiffs to raise their grievances with a court[65] and prevent the state from prosecuting criminal cases.[66]

Both common law and civil law jurisdictions impose statutes of limitation.[67] In the United States, statutes of limitation for civil damages usually begin to run from the time the plaintiff discovers (or should reasonably be expected to discover) that she was injured[68] or when the last act causing the injury is complete.[69]

South Korea's statutes of limitation for civil actions are similar to those of Japan and Germany.[70] The time to bring an action begins to run from discovery of the injury, but there is an outside limit on when the action may be brought regardless of whether the injury is discovered (e.g., plaintiffs must bring a civil action within three years of discovering the injury, or ten years from the wrongful act, whichever period is shorter).[71]

Criminal statutes of limitation in common law and civil jurisdictions typically begin to run from the time that the criminal offense was completed.[72] Unlike civil cases, where the limitations period may begin to run only upon discovery of the injury, criminal statutes of limitation begin to run regardless of when the state or the victim becomes aware of the criminal act.

The Policy Objectives behind Statutes of Limitations

Scholars and courts explain that statutes of limitation are intended to:[73] provide repose for both guilty and innocent defendants by insuring that plaintiffs and the state do not suddenly or arbitrarily revive claims from years in the past;[74] help insure that evidence is authentic by encouraging plaintiffs and the state to bring their cases sooner rather than delaying;[75] discourage plaintiffs from strategically waiting to bring claims after defendants may have lost or discarded exculpatory evidence;[76] and to help courts reduce costs and clear their dockets.[77]

Statutes of limitation primarily benefit defendants. Defendants can take comfort in knowing that they are no longer subject to civil and criminal actions and will not be required to fight a claim long after exculpatory evidence has disappeared.[78] The statutes may also benefit courts, which will not be burdened with sifting through older evidence that is difficult to authenticate and by reducing the court's caseload.

Criticisms of Statutes of Limitation

Statutes of limitation are subject to criticism, especially when meritorious claims are rejected on grounds that they are untimely.[79] Among other things, statutes of limitation, if rigidly applied: deprive plaintiffs of their right of access to the courts;[80] prevent courts from resolving claims on their merits;[81] may unfairly and disproportionately affect disenfranchised persons who rely on the courts to protect their human and civil rights, especially where other branches of governments, such as the legislature are unresponsive;[82] and deny courts the opportunity to develop and to articulate public values by rendering decisions on the merits in connection to important cases of national interest.[83] Jurisdictions must balance the reasonable purposes that statutes of limitation serve against the harm that can result when courts apply statutes of limitation inflexibly.

Rigid Statutes of Limitation Block Justice in Illegal Adoption Cases

South Korea's statutes of limitation pose a significant obstacle to adoptees. Article 766 of South Korea's Civil Code requires a civil action for money damages to be brought within three years of discovery of the injury and no later than ten years from the date of the injury.[84] The Civil Code provides an exception for minors who may commence an action six months from the time they turn nineteen.[85]

Realistically, no one would expect an adoptee to commence a lawsuit within the limitations period imposed by the Civil Code. By way of example, consider Yong-moon, who was sent to the United States when he was six years old (which is actually older than many other adoptees). To bring a timely civil lawsuit under Article 766, he would have had to initiate his case in a South Korean court before his seventeenth birthday.[86] Although the Civil Code extended the statute of limitations to six months after his nineteenth birthday, to file a timely lawsuit Young-moon would have had to initiate a lawsuit in South Korea while still a teenager living in a foreign country.

Criminal statutes of limitation, codified in South Korea's Criminal Procedure Act, would also time bar prosecution of most illegal international adoption cases. Pursuant to the Act, the applicable statute of limitations to prosecute persons who, for example, falsify documents or commit criminal fraud is seven years.[87] No exceptions apply under the Criminal Procedure Act—even murder cases, which are subject to the death penalty, must be prosecuted within twenty-five years.[88]

Assuming that a seven-year criminal statute of limitations applied to an illegal criminal adoption case, only the most recent illegal international adoptions could possibly be subject to criminal prosecution. Thus, South Korea's statutes of limitation effectively preclude both civil and criminal illegal international adoption cases from being decided on their merits.

Exceptions to the Rigid Application of Statutes of Limitation

Although sometimes rigidly applied, courts and legislatures abolish, extend, or toll[89] statutes of limitation where their strict application would unfairly deny victims their right of access to the courts or would be inconsistent with the state's obligation to prosecute crimes. The sections below discuss circumstances where legislatures and courts in different jurisdictions, including South Korea, apply such exceptions.

Exceptional Cases: State Violations of Good Faith and National Interest

Shin Eui Chik: Civil Cases and the State's Breach of the Duty of Good Faith

In two civil cases discussed below, South Korean courts held that the principle of *Shin Eui Chik*—the people's right to trust that their government shall act in good faith, as set forth in Article 2 of the South Korean Civil Code[90]—prohibits the South Korean government from relying on a statute of limitations defense when the state betrays the people's trust.

In 1987, a woman known as "Suzy Kim" was murdered by her husband who then falsely claimed that Ms. Kim was a North Korean spy.[91] Notwithstanding its knowledge that this was a lie, the South Korean government refused to prosecute the husband, insisted that Ms. Kim was a spy, and stated that her death was not a crime.[92]

Years after the statute of limitations expired, Suzy Kim's family sued the South Korean government in a civil suit. Finding that the South Korean government could not rely on a statute of limitations defense, a Seoul district court (a trial-level court) in 2003 awarded Ms. Kim's family 4.2 billion Korean won.[93]

In reaching its decision, the Court reasoned that when the government breaches its duty to act in good faith toward the public, the statute of limitations is tolled.[94] By deceiving Suzy Kim's family and concealing the true circumstances of her death, the government prevented the family from bringing a civil case. As this deception was a breach of the duty of good faith owed to the South Korean people, the Court held that the statute of limitations was suspended.[95]

In 2006, the Seoul High Court (an intermediate appellate-level court) held that the civil statute of limitations did not apply to a lawsuit brought by the family of Professor Jong-Gil Choi, who died following his detention and torture by the South Korean intelligence agency.[96] The Court heard the case on appeal, after a lower court declined to hear the case on its merits and disposed of the case on grounds that the case was time-barred.[97]

Reversing the lower court, the Seoul High Court held that the South Korean government could not rely on a statute of limitations defense for several reasons. First, the Court explained that the South Korean intelligence agency concealed facts from Professor Choi's family by, among other things, fabricating a false document concerning the circumstances of his death.[98] Second, the family was unable to acquire the facts necessary to imitate a lawsuit until after a truth commission (the Presidential Truth Commission on Suspicious Deaths) completed its investigation.[99] Third, relying on the same principle of *Shin Eui Chik* as the Seoul District Court in the Suzy Kim case, the Court held that by (1) committing a serious crime against the victim, (2) concealing the truth from the victim's family, and (3) failing to investigate and prosecute the crime, the government breached its duty of good faith to the people. Having breached its duty of good faith, the South Korean government could not rely on a statute of limitations defense.[100]

Retroactive Criminal Prosecution

At least twice, South Korea's democratic governments enacted legislation to punish activity committed under prior regimes. In both instances, South Korea's Constitutional Court subjected the legislation to judicial review. Whether the state can prosecute criminal cases after the statute of limitations expired is subject to dispute but a reasonable argument can be made that under limited circumstances, states should prosecute crimes after the statute of limitations expired.

South Korea's Special Law about the Return of Pro-Japanese Anti-National Persons' Property[101] provided for the confiscation of property acquired by Korean collaborators during the Japanese colonial occupation.[102] This law was challenged on grounds that (among other things) the state may not retroactively punish conduct that was legal at the time it occurred under the Japanese colonial administration.

South Korea's Constitutional Court agreed that the law applied retroactively to conduct that might have been legal at the time it occurred; however, the Court held that the seizure was constitutional because: (1) the collaborators could have reasonably expected that their property would eventually be confiscated; and (2) retroactive legislation is appropriate in exceptional circumstances of national interest.[103]

In 1995, South Korea enacted the Special Law on the May 18th Democratization Movement which suspended the statute of limitations from running with respect to certain state crimes committed in 1979 and 1980 "during the period in which there existed a cause preventing the nation from exercising its prosecutorial powers."[104] The law was challenged in South Korea's Constitutional Court on grounds that it violated the principle of *ex post facto*[105] because it retroactively revived a criminal case against perpetrators of the Gwangju massacre (in which pro-democracy activists were killed) that otherwise would have expired under the statute of limitations.[106]

Five justices of the Constitutional Court agreed that the law unconstitutionally deprived the defendants of their reliance interest in the expiration of the statute of limitations; however, the justices lacked a supermajority needed to render the law unconstitutional.[107] Four justices held that the law was constitutional because the public interest in meting out justice for those who violated human rights, delayed South Korea's transition to democracy, and suppressed individual freedoms, outweighed any reliance interest of the defendants.[108]

Scholars note that the Special Law on the May 18th Democratization Movement and the Constitutional Court's decision raise issues relevant to "transitional justice."[109] Although there is no single definition,[110] transitional justice refers to the manner in which a nation that undergoes a political transformation from a repressive to a less repressive form of government addresses crimes committed by the prior regime.[111]

Some commentators argue that during the transitional period when an authoritarian regime is replaced by a less autocratic government, statutes of limitation should not shield members of the prior regime that committed serious crimes.[112] Statutes of limitation presuppose that there was a realistic possibility of prosecution at the time the crime was committed and some scholars believe that limitations periods should not immunize state actors who violate human rights knowing that the state will not prosecute them for their crimes.[113] These commentators believe that when a nation transitions to democracy, statutes of limitation for serious crimes committed under the prior regime should be tolled.[114]

Implications of Key Legal Cases and Special Laws in South Korea

The Suzy Kim and Professor Choi cases discussed above support the proposition that the South Korean government may not rely on statute of limitations defense in a *civil* case where the government betrayed the duty of good faith that it owes South Korean citizens, such as when it deceives the public and helps to cover up a crime.[115] However, as reflected in the constitutional dispute over the Special Laws on the return of Collaborators' Property and the May 18th Democratization Movement, South Korea's courts will hesitate to allow the state to prosecute a criminal case once the applicable statute of limitations expires.[116] Some justices may agree that where the state was complicit in serious crimes, and prevented timely prosecutions, rigid application of the statute of limitation is inappropriate.

Common Law Principles Applied to Civil Cases

Below, this chapter discusses equitable principles that common law jurisdictions typically apply to extend or toll statutes of limitation in civil cases.

The Discovery Rule

Since the eighteenth century, common law jurisdictions, including the United States, have applied the discovery rule (sometimes called the "delayed discovery rule") to civil actions where the plaintiff does not know that he has been injured. The discovery rule provides that the statute of limitations does not begin to run until the plaintiff learns (or should have learned) of the injury.[117]

Fraud cases frequently implicate the discovery rule because a plaintiff typically does not know that he was deceived at the time the deception occurred. The US Supreme Court recently explained that the doctrine arose "based on the recognition that 'something different was needed in the case of fraud, where a defendant's deceptive conduct may prevent a plaintiff from even *knowing* that he or she has been defrauded.'"[118] Without the discovery doctrine, a statute of limitations could expire on a plaintiff who "has been injured by fraud and 'remains in ignorance of it without any fault or want of diligence or care on his part.'"[119] The discovery rule, once an equitable doctrine applied by the courts, has been codified in many jurisdictions so that the statute of limitations does not run from the time of the injury, but only when the plaintiff should be aware that he has been injured.[120]

Equitable Tolling and Equitable Estoppel

Two other common law doctrines that extend the time for plaintiffs to file a civil lawsuit are equitable tolling and equitable estoppel (equitable estoppel is sometimes referred to as "fraudulent concealment").[121] Equitable tolling refers to circumstances where a plaintiff knows of his injury but despite his diligence cannot acquire the facts necessary to bring a claim before the statute of limitations expires. The court may toll the statute of limitations—meaning the statute of limitations does not begin to run—during the period in which the plaintiff could not acquire these necessary facts.[122]

A plaintiff may rely on equitable estoppel where a defendant prevents a plaintiff from filing a claim by (1) deliberately concealing facts from the plaintiff;

or (2) threatening or deceiving the plaintiff.[123] As with the discovery rule, many jurisdictions in the United States have now codified principles of equitable estoppel.[124]

Commentators explain that these equitable doctrines are particularly important in cases involving human rights violations.[125] For example, in *Bodner v. Banque Paribas* defendant French banks argued that plaintiffs' lawsuit to recover assets stolen by the Nazis and subsequently converted by the banks in the years following the Second World War was barred by the statute of limitations.[126] Rejecting this defense on several grounds, the Court found that the statute of limitations should not run against plaintiffs where the defendants allegedly engaged in a "policy of systematic and historical denial and misrepresentation concerning the custody of the looted assets to plaintiffs and the public at large."[127]

Similarly, in *Rosner v. United States*, a federal court held that a claim to recover property stolen by Hungary's pro-Nazi government[128] and then seized by the US Army was timely because plaintiffs were not aware of all of the facts necessary to bring their claim until an investigative body released its report on these events in 1999.[129] The Court found that plaintiffs were not at fault for failing to bring their case earlier because the truth was concealed from them for almost sixty years.[130]

The Continuing Violations Doctrine

Courts may apply the continuing violations doctrine if a defendant commits a series of wrongful acts where the earlier acts fell outside the limitation period but the latter acts occurred within the limitations period.[131] Pursuant to this doctrine, the court treats the violations as a single continuous act, all falling within the limitations period.[132]

As with equitable tolling and equitable estoppel, the continuing violations doctrine may apply to claims in connection with human rights abuses.[133] In *Bodner*, the Court found that by (1) continuing to deny the existence of looted assets; and (2) failing to return the assets to their rightful owners, the banks' alleged actions were a continuing violation that fell within the limitations period.[134]

Tolling the Statute of Limitations for Minors

As early as 1623, England provided that statutes of limitation should not run against legally disabled persons—including minors—who typically lack capacity to sue or to be sued in their own name.[135] Most jurisdictions in the United States recognize that a minor would "suffer grievously" if she were required to sue within the statutory limitation period.[136] For that reason, in almost every state in the United States the statute of limitations for a civil action is tolled if the plaintiff is a minor at the time the cause of action accrues. Typically, the action must be brought within a certain number of years after the plaintiff reaches the age of majority.[137]

The tolling doctrine for minors is so important that US courts have declared unconstitutional statutes of limitation that effectively deny minors their right of access to the courts.[138] As one state court explained, statutes of limitation are meant to encourage plaintiffs to bring lawsuits while their claims are fresh—not to punish children who are unable to bring a lawsuit.[139]

Abolishing Criminal Statutes of Limitation for Serious Crimes

Many jurisdictions provide that statutes of limitation should not apply to serious crimes. Canada and the United Kingdom have no statute of limitation for any felony. Germany,[140] Japan,[141] and all jurisdictions in the United States[142] do not impose statutes of limitation for murder. South Korea, which recently extended its statute of limitations for murder, has considered following suit and abolishing it altogether.[143]

Movement to Abolish Limitation Periods for Child Sexual Crimes

The principles described above—the discovery rule, equitable tolling/equitable estoppel, tolling the statute of limitations for minors, and abolishing statutes of limitation for serious crimes—are consistent with a growing movement around the world to abolish criminal and civil statutes of limitations for sexual crimes committed against children.

Children frequently do not know that they are the victims of crimes and are often unable or unwilling to report the crimes committed against them.[144] In the United States, and elsewhere in the world, children's rights advocates, courts, and legislatures have made inroads against the rigid application of statutes of limitation in both civil and criminal cases involving sexual crimes against children.[145]

Beginning in the late 1980s and 1990s, before there were any legislative efforts, courts began extending the time for adults who were sexually abused as children to sue their abusers.[146] In the 1990s, many jurisdictions in the United States passed laws tolling the statute of limitations for civil lawsuits against abusers. For example, California and Delaware enacted laws that applied retroactively, thereby reviving civil claims that had already expired.[147]

But advocates urge lawmakers to go further and completely abolish statutes of limitations in civil and criminal cases.[148] More than half of the states in the United States do not impose criminal statutes of limitation in child sexual abuse cases, and children's rights advocates are working to expand that number.[149]

Efforts to repeal statutes of limitation in child sexual abuse cases are not limited to the United States. In Switzerland, advocates successfully spearheaded a movement to abolish criminal statutes of limitation in response to child sexual abuse.[150] South Korea has also abolished its criminal statute of limitations with respect to serious sexual crimes against children under the age of thirteen.[151] Similarly, in 2011, Germany responded to widespread sexual abuse of children by extending the statute of limitations in civil cases to thirty years after the victim's twenty-first birthday.[152]

Imprescriptibility and Non-Core Human Rights Abuses

Under customary international law, core crimes against humanity, such as genocide and torture, are imprescriptible, meaning states must criminally prosecute these crimes without regard to statutes of limitation.[153] In the past two decades, international courts have consistently held that statutes of limitation do not apply to serious violations of human rights.[154] This principle applies retroactively—even if a claim expired under a nation's domestic statute of limitation, the state must prosecute the defendant.[155]

A number of commentators believe that the principle of imprescriptibility should also apply to human rights claims that do not arise to the level of core crimes against humanity.[156] This position finds support in the Basic Principles and Guidelines on the Right to a Remedy and Reparation for Victims of Gross Violations of International Human Rights Law and Serious Violations of International Humanitarian Law,[157] which provides that where violations do not rise to the level of core crimes against humanity, "domestic statutes of limitations … including those time limitations applicable to civil claims and other procedures, should not be unduly restrictive."[158]

Retroactively Abolishing Limitation Periods for Illegal Adoptions

The principles set forth above in Sections II and III favor South Korea abolishing, tolling, or at a minimum significantly extending its civil and criminal statutes of limitation in connection with international adoptions.

Good Faith Principle Supports Retroactive Abolition in Civil Cases

According to the South Korean Constitution, the people have a right to trust that the government will act toward them with good faith.[159] In the Suzy Kim and Professor Choi cases, the South Korean courts recognized that statutes of limitation should not apply to civil claims against the government where the state betrays its obligation of good faith owed to the public, fails to investigate and prosecute its own crimes, and prevents plaintiffs from filing timely lawsuits.[160]

Advocates believe that the South Korean state and its agents—the international adoption agencies—violated the trust of the South Korean people by engaging in corrupt international adoption practices.[161] Moreover, they allege that the state and the adoption agencies continue to withhold information from adoptees about the circumstances of their adoption and that the state has failed to properly investigate the role of the government in illegal international adoptions.[162]

Adoptees can reasonably allege that the South Korean government breached its duty of good faith to the South Korean people in connection with illegal international adoptions, just as it breached its duty of good faith in the Suzy Kim and Professor Choi cases.[163] Based on these arguments, South Korean courts should hold that the principle of good faith precludes both the government and the adoption agencies, as agents of the state, from relying on a limitations defense in civil cases.[164]

Equitable Principles and Civil Lawsuits

The equitable principles discussed in the third section argue against rigid application of South Korea's civil statute of limitations.

Application of the Discovery Rule to Civil Lawsuits by Adoptees

The discovery rule protects plaintiffs who, though no lack of diligence on their part, are unaware that defendants injured them.[165] Victims of illegal adoption fit precisely within this category. Illegally adopted children may not understand the circumstances of their adoption, or appreciate their injuries until much later in life, well after the time limit to bring civil actions under South Korean law expired.[166]

Application of Equitable Tolling and Equitable Estoppel to Adoptees Civil Lawsuits

Objectively viewed, even the most diligent plaintiffs could not possibly bring an action within the time limits prescribed by South Korea's statute of limitations.[167] Equitable tolling should apply to these circumstances because adoptees from South Korea are typically under two years old and they cannot be expected to initiate a timely action themselves, nor is there anyone who could feasibly bring an action in their name.[168]

In addition, it can take years for an adoptee to understand exactly how her adoption was processed. Among other things, an adoptee may have to locate her family's authentic Hojeok or family registration documents and uncover evidence regarding how her orphan Hojeok was fraudulently prepared.[169] Rigid application of South Korea's statute of limitations to adoptees is unfair if they cannot muster the necessary facts to initiate a lawsuit.

Similarly, pursuant to principles of equitable estoppel, when a defendant prevents a plaintiff from filing a claim within the limitations period, he should not be allowed to benefit from the statute of limitations defense.[170] International adoptees, sent overseas by the defendants, were rendered incapable of bringing their claims in South Korean courts within the limitations period. Furthermore, adoptees have had to struggle to gain access to information concerning their adoption from KAS (and its predecessors) and from adoption agencies.[171]

In fact, South Korea implicitly recognized that adoption authorities withheld critical information from adoptees when it enacted the Special Adoption Law, which provides for greater access to birth records by adoptees.[172] However, even today, adoption agencies are reportedly withholding information with impunity.[173] Based on these circumstances, plaintiff adoptees can reasonably argue that defendants' own actions caused any delay in commencing civil lawsuits and defendants should be estopped from relying on a statute of limitations defense.

Application of the Continuing Violations Doctrine to Adoptees Civil Lawsuits

The doctrine of continuing violations also militates against rigid application of South Korea's statute of limitations to adoptee lawsuits. Although the initial wrongful acts may have occurred outside the limitation period, adoptees can argue that the wrongful acts are ongoing because adoption agencies continue to withhold vital information regarding their birth, relinquishment, and adoption.[174] So long as the offense continues, courts should deem all of defendants' actions as falling within the limitations period.[175]

Flexibility Needed for Victims Who Were Minors

For hundreds of years, courts in other jurisdictions have recognized the equitable principle that when a victim is a minor, statutes of limitations should be tolled until after the minor reaches the age of majority.[176] Where, as here, the victims were literally and legally infants at the time they were adopted, fairness demands that courts apply statutes of limitation more flexibly so that victims may have access to the courts.[177] Although extend statutes of limitation for civil cases to six months after the child's nineteenth birthday, this extension would not meaningfully empower minors who were adopted overseas to bring a timely action.

Illegal Adoption as a Serious Crime beyond Limitation Periods

Many jurisdictions do not apply statutes of limitation to serious crimes because society's interest in punishing defendants who commit serious crimes outweighs the defendants' interest in repose.[178] South Korea should consider treating illegal international adoptions, which may have victimized thousands of children over the course of six decades, as a serious crime for which statutes of limitation are inappropriate.[179]

Parallels with Abolishing Limits for Child Sexual Crimes

The worldwide movement to abolish or extend statutes of limitations with respect to sexual crimes against children is a model for South Korea to similarly abolish, toll, or meaningfully extend its statutes of limitation with respect to illegal international adoptions.[180] In both sexual crimes and illegal international adoptions, the offender committed serious crimes with potential long-term repercussions.[181] Also, just as statutes of limitation can prejudice young victims of sexual abuse and unfairly shield adult perpetrators, South Korea's statutes of limitations render those responsible for carrying out illegal international adoptions against children virtually immune from justice.[182]

Adoptees can reasonably argue that by rigidly enforcing the statute of limitations, South Korea victimizes the plaintiffs twice. First, defendants allegedly sent the children overseas for profit. Second, when the adoptees finally return to South Korea to seek justice, they are told their claims are untimely.

Illegal Adoption as a Violation of Children's Human Rights

Because illegal international adoption is not a core crime against humanity, adoptees cannot argue that under customary international law South Korea is *required* to treat illegal international adoptions as imprescriptible.[183] Possibly, as international law develops and the scope of illegal international adoptions becomes better understood, international law may deem statutes of limitation inapplicable to international adoption cases on grounds that illegal adoption is a human rights crime equivalent to human trafficking.[184]

But courts and legislatures should recognize that even if illegal international adoption is not an imprescriptible crime, it is a violation of children's human rights and rigid application of statutes of limitation to claims by the victims is inappropriate. The Basic Guidelines provide that domestic statutes of limitation as applied to human rights violations, including statutes of limitation governing civil claims, should not be "unduly restrictive."[185] South Korea's statutes of limitation could not be more restrictive—they utterly eliminate any possibility of a court deciding an illegal adoption case on its merits. Consistent with the principles of the Basic Guidelines, at the very least South Korea should significantly extend statutes of limitation applicable to illegal international adoptions.[186]

As to Retroactively Reviving Civil and Criminal Cases

One issue that South Korea will need to address is whether new statutes of limitation can apply retroactively, without violating principles of *ex post facto*.

Reviving civil cases retroactively should not raise constitutional issues for South Korea. Most jurisdictions view civil statutes of limitation as procedural rules, therefore, civil claims may be revived, without violating the constitutional guarantee against *ex post facto* punishment.[187]

But states generally do not revive criminal cases once a statute of limitations has run.[188] In South Korea, reviving criminal cases would require special legislation and even then, it might not be constitutional as evidence by the majority decision (but not a supermajority) by South Korea's Constitutional Court deeming retroactive criminal legislation unconstitutional in the May 18th Democratization case.[189] Consistent with this view, most South Korean scholars believe that the South Korean Constitution prohibits the state from depriving defendants of their purported reliance interest in limitations periods.[190]

South Korean scholars, legislators, and courts should reconsider this perspective for three reasons: First, when a state eliminates a statute of limitation it does not (1) retroactively criminalize conduct that was once legal; nor (2) does it retroactively increase the punishment for a crime after it has been committed.[191] The new statute of limitations only extends the time available to the state to prosecute its case. As four members of South Korea's Constitutional Court held, where there are exceptional cases of national interest, *ex post facto* should not shield state actors who committed serious crimes.[192]

Second, there is a serious dispute as to whether defendants truly have a protected reliance interest in the statute of limitations expiring. As the dissenting justices in the US Supreme Court case *Stogner v. California* explained, "the reliance exists, if at all, because of the circular reason that the Court today says so; it does not exist as part of our traditions or social understanding."[193]

Third, the reliance interest presupposes the possibility that a prosecution was possible. Commentators note that where a regime engages in serious crimes but prevents the police and judiciary from investigating and prosecuting such crimes, statutes of limitation unfairly render the perpetrators immune to prosecution.[194]

These arguments favor South Korea abolishing its statute of limitations in connection with illegal international adoptions, and retroactively applying this change to revive criminal cases that already expired.

In addition, although South Korea transitioned to a democracy several decades ago, there has never been a meaningful accounting with respect to South Korean children who were victims of illegal international adoptions.[195] Viewed in the context of transitional justice, adoptees can reasonably contend that South Korea should allow cases to proceed on their merits as part of a process to address abuses committed under prior regimes.[196]

As one author noted, justice after a government transition might be delayed, but should not be denied.[197] Now that the South Korean government is in the position to investigate and prosecute past crimes in connection with illegal international adoptions, it should do so.

Policy Reasons to Abolish or Extend Limitation Periods

Rigidly applying time limits to civil or criminal cases in connection with illegal international adoptions is inconsistent with the policy objectives of statutes of limitation discussed in the second section of this chapter in two ways:

First, statutes of limitation are intended to encourage plaintiffs and prosecutors to be diligent and to prevent them from unfairly surprising defendants.[198] But as discussed above, statutes of limitation do not encourage adoptees to be more diligent because at the time of the offense they were children. The statutes of limitation applied to illegal adoption accomplish something else entirely—they make illegal international adoptions immune to civil or criminal prosecution. This does not merely grant repose to defendants; it insulates them from any possibility of answering for an alleged crime.

Second, although statutes of limitation are meant to insure the reliability of evidence,[199] the evidence that plaintiffs and prosecutors can bring before a South Korean court today in connection with illegal international adoptions might be *more*—not less—reliable than evidence available decades ago. For years adoptees have struggled to uncover the facts underlying their procurement by adoption agencies and their adoption overseas.[200] Today there may be witnesses, such as birth parents and adoption agency staff, who are more comfortable testifying as to what they experienced. The passage of time might increase the likelihood South Korean courts will be able to adjudicate illegal international adoption cases based on reliable testimonial and documentary evidence that previously was unavailable.[201]

Abolishing statutes of limitation in connection with illegal international adoption may also have at least two other ancillary benefits for South Korea. First, democracy thrives when its political institutions candidly address social and political issues. Allowing litigation to proceed will encourage public discourse and enable South Korean courts to make judicial findings with respect to what happened to thousands of South Korean children. Rejecting adoptees claims on limitations grounds would deny adoptees and the South Korean public an opportunity to confront the truth of what happened to the adoptees.

Second, commentators believe that one factor that spurred South Korean international adoptions was the country's attitude toward single mothers and their children.[202] International adoptions are inextricably linked to social issues within South Korea that may be receiving insufficient attention, such as programs to help families and children in need.

Conclusions and One Possible Alternative

Principles of fairness and precedent from jurisdictions around the world, including South Korea, support eliminating statutes of limitation in connection with illegal international adoptions. Rigid application of the statute of limitations would unfairly deprive adoptees of access to the courts and would unfairly render defendants immune to prosecution. South Korean courts should retroactively revive civil claims, and South Korea's National Assembly should consider special legislation to revive criminal cases.

But one possible alternative to retroactively abolishing statutes of limitation that South Korea could undertake is to establish a truth and reconciliation commission and convene hearings with respect to international adoptions.[203] A truth and reconciliation commission could invite people involved in the adoption process, including adoptive parents, birth parents, adoptees, adoption agencies, and government officials to relate their experiences. Hearings by the truth and reconciliation commission might result in reparations as well as meaningful reforms.

The choice of whether to abolish statutes of limitation and enable courts to decide international adoption cases on their merits or to adopt other measures, such as a truth and reconciliation commission, rests with the South Korean courts and legislature. But South Korea should not ignore the issue of international adoptions on grounds that the cases are untimely. To do so would deny adoptees their chance to be heard, and would also deprive South Korea the opportunity to meaningfully assess how it has treated the most vulnerable members of its society.

Notes

1 The author expresses his deepest appreciation to South Korean attorneys Pillkyu Hwang (Gong-Gam Human Rights Law Foundation) and Jungseon Kim for their thoughtful insights and comments. He also thanks Soongsil University undergraduate students Ji Hun "Regina" Jang and Sang Yong "Andrew" Son for their helpful research and translation work. The author owes special thanks to Jane Jeong Trenka for sharing her views on a controversial topic.

2 Schuster Institute for Investigative Journalism, "Capsule History of International Adoption," *Adoption Law: A History of Fictions*, accessed February 23, 2011, http://www.brandeis.edu/investigate/adoption/history.html; Tobias Hübinette, "Comforting an Orphaned Nation: Representations of International Adoption and Adopted Koreans in Korean Popular Culture" (PhD diss., Stockholm University, 2005), 17.

See Parliamentary Assembly of the Council of Europe, *Recommendation 1443 on International Adoption: Respecting Children's Rights* [hereinafter Recommendation 1443] 2 (2000). For a discussion of how international adoption between the South Korea and the United States took hold in the 1950s and 1960s, *see* Catherine Ceniza Choy, "Institutionalizing International Adoption: The Historical Origins of Korean Adoption in the United States," in *International Korean Adoption: A Fifty-Year History of Policy and Practice*, eds. Kathleen Ja Sook Berquist et al. (New York: Routledge, 2013), Kindle Location 784. Transnational adoptive parents may have different motivations to choose to adopt internationally, including, but not limited to, a preference for children from other countries, a belief that there is an orphan crisis in overseas countries, and/or a wish to religiously indoctrinate children from other countries. *See* Kathryn Joyce, *The Child Catchers: Rescue, Trafficking, and the New Gospel of Adoption* (New York: PublicAffairs, 2013), Kindle Locations 135, 976.

3 *See* Veronica Dagher, "Adopting? Prepare to Be Surprised," *Wall Street Journal*, February 23, 2013, https://www.wsj.com/articles/SB10001424127887323452204578287961483250712?msockid=3a09b86e89ce63fb0291ae2a880562ee; Caryn Fisher, "'Baby Exporter': Taking a Closer Look at Korean Adoptions," *Korea Economic Institute*, February 8, 2012, http://blog.keia.org/2012/02/baby-exporter-taking-a-closer-look-at-korean-adoption; *see also* Matthew Rothschild, "Babies for Sale: South Koreans Make Them, Americans Buy Them," *The Progressive*, January 1988, https://thesearchformothermissing.blogspot.com/2012/03/babies-for-sale-south-koreans-make-them.html.

4 *See* Peter Selman, "Global Trends in Intercountry Adoption, 2000–2010," *Adoption Advocate*, no. 44 (National Council for Adoption, February 2012): 1–17.

5 *See, e.g.*, Elizabeth Bartholet, "International Adoption: Thoughts on the Human Rights Issues," *Buffalo Human Rights Law Review* 13 (2007): 151, 178–9, 185–7; Richard Carlson, "Seeking the Better Interests of Children with a New International Law of Adoption," *New York Law School Law Review* 55 (2010/2011): 733, 765–6; *see also* Elizabeth Bartholet, "Permanency Is Not Enough: Children Need the Nurturing Parents Found in International Adoption," *New York Law School Law Review* 55 (2010/11): 781.

6 *See, e.g.*, David Smolin, "Child Laundering: How the Intercountry Adoption System Legitimizes and Incentivizes the Practices of Buying, Trafficking, Kidnapping, and Stealing Children," *Wayne Law Review* 52 (2006): 113; *see also* Recommendation 1443, *supra* note 2, at 2–3.

7 Professor David Smolin uses this term to describe the process whereby children are falsely represented to be orphans for purposes of international adoption, just as money from illegitimate enterprises is "laundered" to appear to come from legitimate sources. *See* David Smolin, "Child Laundering and the Hague Convention on Intercountry Adoption: The Future and Past of Intercountry Adoption," *University of Louisville Law Review* 48 (2010): 441, 445.

8 *See* Joyce, *supra* note 2, at Kindle Locations 2893–905; Karen S. Rotabi, "From Guatemala to Ethiopia: Shifts in Intercountry Adoption Leave Ethiopia Vulnerable for Child Sales and Other Unethical Practices," *Social Work and Society News Magazine*, June 8, 2010, https://unc.academia.edu/KarenSmithRotabi.

9 *See generally* Michelle Goodwin, "The Free Market Approach to Baby Adoption: The Value of a Baby," *Boston College Third World Law Journal* 26 (2006): 61.

10 *See* David Smolin and Desiree Smolin, "The Aftermath of Abusive Adoption Practices in the Lives of Adoption Triad Members: Responding to Adoption Triad Members Victimized by Abusive Adoption Practices," *Fleas Biting*, effective April 20, 2012, https://fleasbiting.blogspot.com/2012/04/aftermath-of-abusive-adoption-practices.html.

11 United Convention on the Rights of the Child, 1588 UNTS 530 (entered into force Jan. 16 1991), Article 21 (a)–(d); *see generally* Commissioner for Human Rights, "Adoption and Children: A Human Rights Perspective," *Issue Papers* (2011): 1–23, https://rm.coe.int/adoption-and-children-a-human-rights-perspective-issue-paper-commissio/16806dac00.

12 *See* "Child Trafficking and Australia's Intercountry Adoption System," Siobahn Clair, effective February 13, 2013, https://siobhanclair.wordpress.com/2013/02/13/child-trafficking-and-australias-intercountry-adoption-system; *See* David Smolin, "Adoption as Child Trafficking," *Valparaiso University Law Review* 39 (2004): 281, 323. *But see* Bartholet, *supra* note 5, at 187.

13 General Assembly Resolution 49/166 of December 23, 1994.

14 According to Tobias Hübinette, advocate and lecturer at Södertörn University in Sweden, the South Korean Ministry of Health and Welfare calculated that between 1953 and 2004 there were 158,343 international adoptions. *See* http://www.tobiashubinette.se/korean_adoptions.pdf. Jane Jeong Trenka, co-founder of Truth and Reconciliation for the Adoption Community of Korea ("TRACK") believes that by 2012 the official number of international adoptions from South Korea is around 166,565 (email from Jane Jeong Trenka, November 5, 2013). TRACK is a South Korean organization that, among other things, advocates for adoption reform in South Korea. On its website (www.adoptionjustice.com) TRACK explains that it "advocate[es] full knowledge of past and present Korean adoption practices to protect the human rights of adult adoptees, children, and families."

15 Commentators believe that the real number of adoptees might be closer to 200,000 because some children were adopted overseas without any records. *See* Shawna O'Reilly, "Korean Adoption Program Changes Are Examined by Korean Adoptee," *Examiner.com*, accessed February 28, 2013, http://www.examiner.com/article/korea-adoption-program-changes-are-analyzed-by-korean-adoptee.

16 *See* Smolin, *supra* note 6, at 125. Illegal adoptions also usually violate the laws of receiving countries, although criminal prosecution in a receiving country would be challenging. For a discussion of possible criminal violations and potential remedies, *see* Katie Rasor et al., "Imperfect Remedies: The Arsenal of Criminal Statutes Available to Prosecute International Adoption Fraud in the United States," *New York Law School Law Review* 55 (2010): 801, 802.

17 *See* Shuster Institute of Investigative Journalism at Brandeis University, collecting articles about international adoption from Cambodia, available at http://www.brandeis.edu/investigate/adoption/CambodiaNews.html. Cambodia halted all international adoptions in 2009 in response to widespread abuses. *See* Denise Hubry, "Cambodia Tries to Solve Its Baby-Stealing Problem," *Global Post*, effective July 31, 2016, https://theworld.org/stories/2016/07/31/cambodia-tries-solve-its-baby-stealing-problem. Although Cambodia has since lifted its ban, the United States does not allow adoptions from Cambodia because of persistent trafficking abuses.

18 *See* Rasor et al., *supra* note 16, at 802.
19 *See* Arun Dohle, "Inside Story of an Adoption Scandal," *Cumberland Law Review* 39 (2009): 131, 147–8.
20 *See* Smolin, *supra* note 7, at 477–8.
21 Kristi Brian, "Marketing Korea: Marketing 'Multiculturalism' to Choosy Adopters," in *International Korean Adoption: A Fifty-Year History of Policy and Practice*, eds. Kathleen Ja Sook Berquist et al. (New York: Routledge, 2013), Kindle Location 1563. For an interesting historical perspective on how international adoption agencies commenced operations in South Korea and promoted international adoption from South Korea in the United States, *see* Choy, *supra* note 2, at Kindle Location 784.
22 *See* Carlson, *supra* note 5, at 766 (commenting that South Korea "seems to have avoided the corruption" of Cambodia and India). Smolin, *supra* note 6, at 134.
23 *See, e.g.*, Patricia Meier and Xiaole Zhang, "Sold into Adoption: The Hunan Baby Trafficking Scandal Exposes Vulnerabilities in Chinese Adoptions to the United States," *Cumberland Law Review* 39 (2009): 87–9; Charlie Custer, "Kidnapped and Sold: Inside the Dark World of Child Trafficking in China," *The Atlantic*, July 25, 2013, http://www.theatlantic.com/china/archive/2013/07/kidnapped-and-sold-inside-the-dark-world-of-child-trafficking-in-china/278107/.
24 *See* Trenka, "My Adoption File" (emphasis in original).
25 *See* South Korea Act on Adoption, Article 6 and the Amended Special Adoption Law, Article 9(b). The law was recently amended in response to abuses in the South Korean adoption system.
26 The following seven bullet points are based on examples discussed in the TRACK's *Report to the Ombudsman of Korea*, (2008) at 10–11 (hereinafter "TRACK Report") (file on copy with the author). TRACK is discussed in greater detail, *supra* note 14.
27 Commentators, including both detractors and supporters of international adoption, seem to agree that pressure on single mothers was the primary cause for South Korean women to relinquish their children. Adoption agencies in South Korea had financial incentives to encourage mothers to relinquish their children for overseas adoption. *See* Joyce, *supra* note 2, at Kindle Location 5702. *See also* Brian, *supra* note 21, at Kindle Locations 1586–611. Brian quotes one adoption "facilitator" who explained to potential clients that "Korea is brave for participating in international adoption. Over all these years she has been saving her children. These are children born out of wedlock, so they would have that stigma to live with, so it's better they are adopted. The mothers are brave because they have not chosen abortion but adoption. How wonderful for these kids." *Ibid.* at Kindle Location 1613.
28 Some of the practices described above are consistent with information the author of this chapter received from a woman who worked for one of South Korea's major international adoption agencies in the 1980s. To protect her confidentiality the chapter refers to her as "AE." AE recalls that adoption agencies competed to find children for international adoption. Employees of adoption agencies told her that their agencies paid obstetricians and midwives who notified their agencies when there were children available for adoption. She believes that financial incentives motivated adoption agencies to, at times, not act in the best interests of children and their birth mothers.

29 Based on information provided by Holt International Child Services (an international adoption agency) on its website at http://www.holtinternational.org/adoption/criteria.php.

30 Jane Jeong Trenka, "Draft Report on South Korean International Adoption," August 2013, 2–3 (on file with author); *see also* Youn-joo Sang, "Fears of Unintended Consequences as Adoption Tightened," *The Korea Herald*, October 10, 2012, https://www.koreaherald.com/article/10374336.

31 Trenka, *supra* note 30, at 2. There is no internationally accepted single definition of "orphan." UNICEF defines orphans as children who lost one or both parents. UNICEF Press Centre, *Press Release* (May 25, 2012) http://www.unicef.org/media/media_45279.html. UNICEF believes that by its definition of orphan, the "evidence clearly shows that the vast majority of orphans are living with a surviving parent, grandparent, or other family member." *Ibid.*

32 Until recently, family registries in Korean were called Hojeok Deungbon. The registries were kept at municipal offices. The names were usually written in Chinese ideographic characters. Wives were placed on their husband's family registries as were their children. Orphans were assigned special Hojeok Deungbon on which only their names appear (with neither parent nor other ancestry listed). Under the Korean system, child laundering usually depends on falsifying documents to create a fake orphan Hojeok Deungbon. In Yong-moon's case his name was rendered on a false Hojeok Deungbon with different Chinese ideographic characters, read phonetically the same as his birth name. Trenka, *supra* note 30, at 2–3. South Korea recently abolished the family registry, with its archaic placement of the father as the head of the household.

33 Trenka, *supra* note 30, at 2.

34 TRACK Report, *supra* note 26, at 11. AE (*supra* note 28), a former employee of a major international adoption agency in South Korea, confirmed that it was standard practice for international adoption agencies to furnish adoptees with documentation that erased any mention of their birth family. Based on her discussions with knowledgeable sources, AE believes that in many cases agencies eliminated references to birth families to protect the anonymity of mothers, particularly unmarried women who feared that they would be ostracized for having children out of marriage. But AE is also aware of circumstances where agencies created orphan Hojeok Deungbon for children who would otherwise not be eligible for international adoption. At least one commentator argues that fraudulent documentation may be excusable, in cases of urgent need. Carlson, *supra* note 5, at 765. The author of this chapter suggests that in cases where there an adoptee was furnished with fraudulent documentation, it may be appropriate for the burden of proof to fall on the adoption agency to prove that the adoption was otherwise legitimate, as opposed to the burden of proof falling on the adoptee to prove that the adoption was illegal.

35 Rothschild, *supra* note 3. The number of adoption agencies operating in Korea was limited to four (and had to be Korean institutions) pursuant to reforms in the mid-1970s at the direction of military dictator President Chun Hee Park. Following President Park's assassination, the military regime of President Doo Hwan Chun promoted international adoption, and allowed the four international agencies to compete with each other to export children. *See* Hübinette, *supra* note 2, at 71. AE (*supra* note 28) is aware that in the early 1980s an individual associated with the government was appointed director of a major international adoption agency, and

that the new director brought with him about thirty employees, most of whom were given newly created positions at a supervisory level.

36 *See* Rothschild, *supra* note 36; Joyce, *supra* note 2, at Kindle Location 5720; Bong Joo Lee, "Recent Trends in Child Welfare and Adoption in Korea: Challenges and Future Directions," in *International Korean Adoption: A Fifty-Year History of Policy and Practice*, eds. Kathleen Ja Sook Berquist et al. (New York: Routledge, 2013), Kindle Locations 4113–15.

37 *See* Do-hyun Kim, "Overseas Adoption: Child Welfare or Abuse?" *The Korea Times*, December 30, 2011, https://www.koreatimes.co.kr/opinion/20111230/overseas-adoption-child-welfare-or-abuse; Rothschild, *supra* note 3; Joyce, *supra* note 2, at Kindle Location 5697. *Ibid.* at Kindle Location 5711. It is difficult to imagine the South Korean government as anything other than actively endorsing international adoptions given the large number of adoptions that took place.

38 *See* Hübinette, *supra* note 2, at 87 citing *The Korea Times*, October 13, 1989.

39 *See* Dong Soo Kim, "A Country Divided: Contextualizing Adoption from a Korean Perspective," in *International Korean Adoption: A Fifty-Year History of Policy and Practice*, eds. Kathleen Ja Sook Berquist et al. (New York: Routledge, 2013), Kindle Location 618.

40 Elena Kim, "Remembering Loss: The Koreanness of Overseas Koreans," in *International Korean Adoption: A Fifty-Year History of Policy and Practice*, eds. Kathleen Ja Sook Berquist et al. (New York: Routledge, 2013), Kindle Location 2487. For an interesting discussion of President Kim and his concern regarding South Korean adoptees, *see* "President Kim Dae Jung and the Adoption Issue," Tobias Hübinette, accessed August 10, 2025, https://www.tobiashubinette.se/kim_dae_jung_and_adoption.pdf.

41 Joyce, *supra* note 2, at Kindle Location 5723; Hübinette, *supra* note 2, at 17.

42 *See* Andrew Wolman, "Looking Back While Moving Forward: The Evolution of Truth Commissions in Korea," *Asian-Pacific Law and Policy Journal* 27 (2013): 51.

43 Jane Jeong Trenka, "Internationally Adopted Koreans and the Movement to Revise the Korean Adoption Law," *Ewha Journal of Gender and Law* (2011) (manuscript on file with author).

44 *Ibid.* Australia offers an interesting comparison. *See* "Commonwealth Contribution to Former Forced Adoption Policies and Practices," Australian Senate Community Affairs References Committee, accessed February 29, 2012, http://www.aph.gov.au/Parliamentary_Business/Committees/Senate/Community_Affairs/Completed_inquiries/2010-13/commcontribformerforcedadoption/report/index. *See* Australian Senate Report at 9.58 and 9.76. On March 21, 2013, the Australian government delivered an apology to birth mothers, their children, and the children's fathers. The transcript of the apology can be found on Australia's Department of the Prime Minister and Cabinet's website, http://pmtranscripts.dpmc.gov.au.

45 Jane Jeong Trenka, "Over Two Years after the Special Adoption Law Was Amended, Adoptees Still Waiting for Enforcement: How Can the Hague Convention Be Ratified without Enforcing the Special Adoption Law?" (unpublished manuscript).

46 TRACK is described *supra* note 14.

47 Special Law on Adoption Promotion and Procedure (Act No. 11007, August 4, 2011).

48 KAS is the new name of the government agency, KCARE (Korean Central Adoption Resources), established in 2009. KCARE replaced South Korea's earlier central adoption resource agency GAIPS (Global Adoption Information and Post Adoption

Services, established by the adoption agencies.) Under South Korean law, the Ministry of Health and Welfare established and operates KAS "for the sake of the promotion of domestic adoption and post-adoption services." Special Adoption Law Article 26.1.

49 Trenka, *supra* note 45, at 3–7.

50 *Ibid.* at 2. Among other things, TRACK describes KAS as understaffed and its employees as often unwilling or unable to assist adoptees. *Ibid.* at 3–7.

51 *Ibid.* at 2. South Korea's failure to provide information to adoptees is not a new development. Adoptees and commentators explained for years that KCARE—the predecessor to KAS—failed to provide information to adoptees and did not receive full and complete information from Korea's four main adoption agencies. *See* Shinwoo Kang, "South Korea's Central Authority on Adoption Lacks Information," *The Hankyoreh*, April 10, 2009, http://english.hani.co.kr/arti/english_edition/e_national/367603.html.These are the same criticisms adoptees have with respect to KAS.

52 *See, e.g.*, Jane Jeong Trenka, "My Adoption File," *Jane's Blog*, accessed (n.d.), http://jjtrenka.wordpress.com/about/adoption-file.

53 Smolin, *supra* note 7, at 481.

54 *Ibid.*

55 "FY 2011 Annual Report on Intercountry Adoption, November 2011," Bureau of Consular Affairs, U.S. Department of State, accessed August 10, 2025, https://travel.state.gov/content/dam/aa/pdfs/fy2011_annual_report.pdf.

56 "Intercountry Adoption, Adoption Notice: The Republic of Korea Signs the Hague Adoption Convention," U.S. Department of State, accessed May 28, 2013, http://adoption.state.gov/country_information/country_specific_alerts_notices.php?alert_notice_type=notices&alert_notice_file=south_korea_2.

57 Smolin, *supra* note 7, at 451–2. Professor Smolin argues that the Hague Convention is not comprehensive "but is primarily an anti-trafficking treaty, and a very incomplete anti-trafficking treaty at that." *Ibid.* at 452.

58 Commentators believe that KAS (*supra* note 48) is likely to be designated the central authority.

59 *See* Elizabeth Long, "Where Are They Coming From, Where Are They Going: Demanding Accountability in International Adoption," *Cardozo Journal of Law & Gender* 18, no. 3 (2012): 827, 835–7.

60 *Supra* note 47.

61 *Ibid.* article 19.1.

62 *Ibid.* articles 7–8.

63 *Ibid.* article 36. *See* article 36.1.

64 *Ibid.* article 41.

65 *See Kavanagh v. Noble*, 332 U.S. 535, 539 (1947)

66 *See United States v. Marion*, 404 U.S. 307, 324 (1971); The Harvard Law Review Association, "Developments in the Law: Statutes of Limitations," *Harvard Law Review* 63, no. 7 (1950): 1177, 1185.

67 Scholars trace statutes of limitation to Roman law, consequently, limitations are more common in civil law systems, such as Germany, than in common law systems. *See* Jan Arno Hessbruegge, "Justice Delayed, Not Denied: Statutory Limitations and Human Rights Crimes," *Georgetown Journal of International Law* 43 (2012): 335, 338.

68 In the United States, actions for breach of a sales contract usually must be brought within a certain number of years from the time that the contract was breached,

irrespective of whether the plaintiff knew that the breach occurred. *See, e.g.*, New York U.C.C. Section 2–725(2).

69 For example, under California law, and some other states a cause of action generally accrues "upon the occurrence of the last element essential to the cause of action." *See Neel v. Magana, Olney, Levy, Cathcart, & Gelfand*, 6 Cal. 3d 176, 182–83 (Cal. 1971). But this general rule is subject to exceptions, as discussed in Section III.

70 The South Korean legal system in many respects is modeled after Germany and Japan, as a result of Japan's colonial occupation. *See* Marie Seong-Hak Kim, "Customary Law and Colonial Jurisprudence in Korea," *American Journal of Comparative Law* 57 (2009): 205, 210–12; Sang-Hyun Song, "Legal Education in Korea and the Asian Region," *Journal of Legal Education* 51, no. 3 (2001): 398, 401.

71 *See* German Civil Code 199(2)-(3); "Developments in the Law," *supra* note 66, at 1178.

72 *See, e.g.*, German Criminal Code, 78(a); Korean Code of Criminal Procedure 252(1); *see* James West, "Martial Lawlessness: The Legal Aftermath of Kwangju," *Pacific Rim Law & Policy Journal* 6 (1997): 85, 117; "Statutes of Limitation in Federal Cases: An Overview," Charles Doyle, Congressional Research Service, accessed August 10, 2025, http://www.fas.org/sgp/crs/misc/RL31253.pdf; *see also Gabelli v. SEC*, 133 S.Ct. 1216, 1223–24 (2013).

73 For a more comprehensive discussion, *see* Suzette M. Malveaux, "Statutes of Limitation: A Policy Analysis in the Context of Reparations Litigation," *George Washington Law Review* 74 (2005): 68, 75–82. Also recommended is "Developments in the Law," *supra* note 66. Readers may also benefit from an online report prepared by "Limitations, Final Report No. 55," Alberta Law Reform Institute, accessed August 10, 2025, https://www.alri.ualberta.ca/1989/12/limitations/.

74 The Supreme Court has gone so far as to praise statutes of limitations because "[t] hey provide 'security and stability to human affairs'" and concluded that "'even wrong doers are entitled to assume that their sins may be forgotten.'" Gabelli, *supra* note 72, 133 S.Ct., at 1221 quoting *Wood v. Carpenter*, 101 U.S. 135, 139 (1879) and Wilson v. Garcia, 471 U.S. 261, 271 (1985).

75 Malveaux, *supra* note 73, at 75–82.

76 *Railroad Telegraphers v. Railway Express Agency, Inc.*, 321 U.S. 342, 348–9 (1944) (stating that statutes of limitation "promote justice by preventing surprises through the revival of claims that have been allowed to slumber until evidence has been lost, memories have faded, and witnesses have disappeared"). More recently, the Supreme Court stated that the goals of limitations periods are: "repose, elimination of stale claims, and certainty about a plaintiff's opportunity for recovery and a defendant's potential liabilities." Gabelli, *supra* note 72, 133 S.Ct., at 1221 quoting *Rotella v. Wood*, 528 U.S. 549, 555 (2000).

77 Malveaux, *supra* note 73, at 82–6 (2005) (providing a comprehensive analysis of why rigid application of statutes of limitation deprive plaintiffs and victims of their right to access the courts and other undesirable consequences).

78 *Ibid.*

79 *Ibid.*

80 *Ibid.*

81 *Ibid.*

82 *Ibid.*

83 *Ibid.*

84 *See* the Civil Procedure Act of Korea, Article 766.
85 Civil Procedure Act of Korea, Article 179.
86 *Ibid.*
87 *See* Criminal Procedure Act of Korea, Articles 225 and 347.
88 Criminal Procedure Act of Korea Article 249(1).
89 To toll the statute of limitations is to delay the date from when the limitations period begins to run.
90 South Korean Civil Code, Article 2.
91 Suzy Kim Case, 2002 Ga Hap 32467, Seoul District Court (2011); Kuk Cho, "Transitional Justice in Korea," in *Law and Society in Korea*, ed. Hyunah Yang (Cheltanham: Edward Elgar Publishing, 2013), 189, 194.
92 Suzy Kim Case, *ibid.*
93 *Ibid.*
94 *Ibid.*
95 *Ibid. See* In Sup Han, "Dealing with Wrongful Trials under the Authoritarian Regime," *Seoul National University Law Review* 46 (2005): 84.
96 Jong-Gil Choi Case, 2005 Na 27906, Seoul High Court (2006).
97 *Ibid.*
98 *Ibid.*
99 *Ibid.*
100 *Ibid. See* Pyeong Woo Kim, "Demurrer Based on the Statute of Limitations and the Principle of Good Faith," *Sogang University Journal of Law* 8 (2006): 175.
101 Act No. 7769, December 29, 2005.
102 *See* Wolman, *supra* note 42, at 41.
103 Confiscation of Property Awarded for Pro-Japanese Collaboration during Japanese Occupation Case, 2008 Hun-Ba 141, at pgs.47, 51 Constitutional Court of Korea (2011); *see also* Sang Wook Daniel Han, "Transitional Justice: When Justice Strikes Back—Case Studies of Delayed Justice in Argentina and South Korea," *Houston Journal of International Law* 30 (2008): 653, 672. *See* Si-Woo Park, "Seizing Wealth of Pro-Japanese Collaborators Ruled Constitutional," *The Korea Times*, March 31, 2011, http://www.koreatimes.co.kr/www/news/nation/2013/01/117_84250.html.
104 *See* West, *supra* note 72, at 121–2.
105 In most jurisdictions, *ex post facto* prohibits a state from either (i) retroactively criminalizing conduct that was once legal; or (ii) retroactively increasing the punishment for a crime after it has been committed. This principle is set forth in Article 13(1) of the South Korean Constitution.
106 *See* Davie M. Waters, "Korean Constitutionalism and the 'Special Act' to Prosecute Former Presidents Chun Doo-Hwan and Roh Tae-Woo," *Columbia Journal of Asian Law* 10 (1996): 461, 469.
107 Yi-Li Yee, "The Korean Constitutional Court and the Kwangju Massacre: Note on the Special Act Concerning the May Democratization Movement," *National Taiwan University Law Review* 4 (2009): 227, 239; Waters, *ibid.* at 474.
108 May 18 Pro-Democracy Movement Case, 96 Hun Ka 2 (Korea Constitutional Court 1996); Waters, *ibid.* at 474; Han, *supra* note 103, at 672; Kuk Cho, "Transitional Justice in Korea: Legally Coping with Past Wrongs after Democratization," *Pacific Rim Law & Policy Journal* 16 (2007): 579, 584; Yi-Li Yee, *ibid.* at 239.
109 *See, e.g.*, Han, *ibid.* at 672; Cho, *ibid.* at 584; Yi-Li Yee, *ibid.* at 239.

110 *See* Tricia D. Olsen, Leigh A. Payne, and Andrew G. Reiter, eds., *Transitional Justice in Balance: Comparing Processes, Weighing Efficacy* (Washington: U.S. Institute of Peace Press, 2013), Kindle Location 2621.
111 *See* Ruti G. Teitel, *Transitional Justice* (New York: Oxford University Press, 2000).
112 *See* Cho, *supra* note 109, at 588.
113 *See* "Legal Opinion Submitted to the Ministry of Turkey: Lifting the Statute of Limitations for Violations of the Right to Life and Torture by Suspected State Perpetrators," Human Rights Watch, accessed August 10, 2025, http://www.hrw.org/news/2013/03/25/january-2013-legal-opinion-submitted-minister-justice-turkey.
114 Han, *supra* note 103, at 691; *see* Cho, *supra* note 98, at 588.
115 *See* Suzy Kim Case, *supra* note 92; Jong-Gil Choi Case, *supra* note 97.
116 *Supra* notes 101–8 and accompanying text.
117 *See* Gabelli, *supra* note 72, 133 S.Ct., at 1221.
118 *Ibid.* quoting *Merck & Co. v. Reynolds*, 130 S.Ct. 1784, 1793 (2010) (emphasis in original).
119 *Holmberg v. Armbrecht*, 327 U.S. 392, 397 (1946). Courts also apply the discovery rule in cases that do not involve fraud. For example, if a surgeon leaves a foreign object in a plaintiff causing a latent injury or a plaintiff was unaware of latent defects in construction the statute of limitations might not begin to run until the plaintiff becomes aware (or should have been aware) that he/she was harmed. *See Smith v. Johnston*, 591 P.2d 1260 (Okla. 1978).
120 *See, e.g.*, N.Y. C.P.L.R. sec. 214–c.
121 Some courts in the United States use these terms interchangeably and readers should be mindful that these terms are sometimes defined differently depending on the jurisdiction. *See Cada v. Baxter Healthcare Corp.*, 920 F.2d 446, 450–1 (7th Cir. 1990); *Pearl v. City of Long Beach*, 296 F.3d 76 (2d. Cir. 2002).
122 *Ibid.*
123 *Ibid.* By way of example, if an employer fires a woman but tells her she was fired because there was not enough work as opposed to her gender there may be grounds to argue that the company has fraudulently concealed that she has a potential lawsuit based on discrimination. Likewise, if the company promises her that the company will not rely on the statute of limitations if she delays her lawsuit for a few years while they negotiate a settlement, a court might find that the company may not raise a limitations defense.
124 For example, Connecticut codified the doctrine of fraudulent concealment (CSGA Section 52–595) to provide that where a defendant knowingly conceals the facts necessary for a plaintiff to commence his lawsuit, the statute of limitations does not begin to run until the plaintiff learns that he/she has a cause of action against the defendant.
125 Morris Ratner, "Factors Impacting the Selection and Positioning of Human Rights Class Actions in U.S. Courts: A Practical Overview," *New York University Annual Survey of American Law* 58 (2003): 623, 626–7; Joseph Kinnicut Angell and John Wilder May, *A Treatise on the Limitations of Actions at Law and Suits in Equity and Admiralty*, 6th ed. (Boston: Little, Brown, 1861), 192; Zach Zagger, "Japan Abolishes Its Statute of Limitations for Murder," *Jurist*, April 28, 2010, http://jurist.org/paperchase/2010/04/japan-abolishes-statute-of-limitations.php.

126 *Bodner v. Banque Paribas*, 114 F.Supp.2d 117, 135 (E.D.N.Y. 2003); *see also* Ratner, *ibid.* at 626–7; Malveaux, *supra* note 73, at 104–7.
127 Bodner, *ibid.* 114 F.Supp.2d at 135; *see also* Ratner, *ibid.* at 627.
128 Frequently referred to as the Hungarian Gold Train.
129 *Rosner v. United States*, 231 F.Supp.2d 1202, 1205 (S.D. Fla. 2002); *see* Malveaux, *supra* note 73, at 105. This reasoning is also consistent with the decision of the Seoul High Court in the Professor Choi case, *supra* notes 96–100 and accompanying text.
130 Rosner, *ibid.* 231 F.Supp.2d at 1205.
131 Malveaux, *supra* note 73, at 88; Bodner, *supra* note 126, 114 F. Supp. 2d at 134–6.
132 *Ibid.*
133 Ratner, *supra* note 125, at 626–7.
134 Bodner, *supra* note 126, 114 F. Supp. 2d at 134–5.
135 "Developments in the Law," *supra* note 66, at 1178; Angell and May, *supra* note 125, at 192.
136 Thomas A. Jacobs, 2 Children & the Law: Rights and Obligations Section 11:14 (2013).
137 *See, e.g.*, Wisc. Stat. 893.16.
138 *Barrio v. San Manuel Division Hospital*, 692 P.2d 280, 284 (Ariz. 1984); *Strahler v. St. Luke's Hospital*, 706. S.W.2d 7, 9 (Miss. 1986).
139 Barrio, *ibid.* 692 P.2d at 284. The Arizona Supreme Court found that the statute violated Article 18 section 6 of the Arizona Constitution by abrogating the rights of citizens to sue for damages. *See* Ariz. Con. article 18 Section 6. *Ibid.* (internal citations omitted). In a case presenting similar facts, the Missouri Supreme Court held that a statute of limitations deprived a plaintiff her right of access to the courts in violation of Missouri Constitution article I, Section 14, which guarantees "that the courts of justice shall be open to every person, and certain remedy afforded for every injury to person." *Strahler v. St. Luke's Hospital*, 706 S.W.2d 7, 9 (Miss. 1986).
140 German Crim. Code Ch. 5 Section 78 (2). Germany abolished its statute of limitations because it would have rendered the German state incapable of prosecuting persons responsible for genocide during the Holocaust. Urging the German Parliament to not allow the limitations period to expire, one parliamentarian explained that "the sense of a justice of an entire people would be corrupted in an unbearable manner if there was no retribution for murder, even though retribution would be possible." Hessbruegge, *supra* note 67, at 336 (quoting Ernst Benda).
141 *See* Zagger, *supra* note 125.
142 A growing number of states in the United States do not have a statute of limitations for the crime of rape. For example, recently Kansas joined around twenty other states by abolishing its statute of limitations for rape. Shaun Hittle, "Rape Survivor Works to Change Law, Abolish the Statute of Limitations in Rape Case," *The Lawrence Journal-World*, March 3, 2013, http://www2.ljworld.com/news/2013/mar/03/rqe-victin; *see also* Conn. Gen. Stat. 54–193; N.Y. Crim. Proc. Section 30.10 (same). Among those states that do have a limitations period for prosecution of rape, many provide an exception in cases where there is DNA evidence of the crime and allow prosecution at any time. *See, e.g.*, Colo. Rev. Stat. Section 16–5–401.
143 "Legislating the Abolition of Statute of Limitations on Homicide," Human Rights Monitor South Korea, accessed June 26, 2012, http://www.humanrightskorea.org/2012/legislating-the-abolition-of-statute-of-limitations-on-homicide/.

144 Jessica Mindlin, *Child Sexual Abuse and Criminal Statutes of Limitation: A Model for Reform*, 65 Wash. L. Rev. 189, 189 (1990). Experts explain that child victims of sexual abuse frequently do not acknowledge or report the abuse for many years for the following reasons: the perpetrators are family members and victims do not want to hurt their own family; the victims feel shame and embarrassment effects of the abuse, such as depression, drug or alcohol addiction, and suicidal tendencies might not manifest themselves until years after the abuse ended; the victim is so preoccupied dealing with the negative effects of the abuse (such as depression) that she may not have the inclination to file a lawsuit; and the abuser intentionally shames or threatens the child victim into silence. Gregory Gordon, "Adult Survivors of Child Sexual Abuse and the Statute of Limitations: The Need for Consistent Application of the Discovery Rule," *Pepperdine Law Review* 20 (1993): 1359, 1364–5 citing Kelli L. Nabors, "The Statute of Limitations: A Procedural Stumbling Block in Civil Incestuous Abuse Suits," *Law & Psychology Law Review* 14 (1990): 153, 159; Jenna Miller, "The Constitutionality of and Need for Retroactive Civil Legislation Related to Sexual Abuse," *Cardozo Journal of Law and Gender* 17 (2011): 599, 603–4; "Facts About Childhood Sexual Abuse," Marci A. Hamilton and Paul R. Verkuil, accessed August 10, 2025, http://sol-reform.com/images/FactsAboutCSA.pdf.

145 Despite lobbying efforts by their opponents, advocacy groups continue to urge jurisdictions to expand or abolish statutes of limitation so that victims may seek restitution and persons who exploited children may be punished for their crimes.

146 Gordon, *supra* note 144, at 1379–80. In these cases, where a statute of limitations would otherwise apply, victims asked that the statute of limitations be tolled under a number of theories, including the discovery rule, estoppel, and other theories. *Ibid.* Of these theories, the discovery rule was the most widely accepted. *Ibid.*; *see generally*, Russell Donaldson, "Running of Limitations against Action for Civil Damages for Sexual Abuse of Child," *American Law Reports, 5th* 9 (2013): 321. For example, in an early case from 1990, a California appellate court held that a trial court, rigidly applying California's then three-year statute of limitation, improperly dismissed a civil lawsuit by plaintiffs against their alleged abusers without allowing the plaintiffs to replead. *Evans v. Eckelman*, 216 Cal.App.3d 1609, 1620 (Cal. Ct. App. 1990). In holding that plaintiffs should be allowed to replead to allege facts showing why the discovery rule should apply to toll the statute of limitations the Court reasoned that the discovery rule should apply in cases where "in actions in which it will generally be difficult for plaintiffs to immediately detect or comprehend the breach of the resulting injuries" and where there is a "confidential or fiduciary relationship" between the plaintiff and the defendant. *Ibid.* at 1614–15. Some courts held that defendants should be equitably estopped from relying on a statute of limitations defense or that the limitations period should be tolled pursuant to a doctrine of fraudulent concealment. *See Hildebrand v. Hildebrand*, 73 F. Supp 1512 (S.D. Ind. 1990); *Hammer v. Hammer*, 142 Wis.2d 257 (Wis. App. 1987).

147 Cal. Civ. Proc. Code Section 3401.1; Del. Code. Ann tit. 10 Section 8145(b); *see* Miller, *supra* note 144, at 607–11.

148 "Bill to Eliminate Civil Statute on Sex Abuse Cases Clears Judiciary Panel," NJ Today, accessed June 22, 2012, http://www.abolishsexabuse.org/index.php?option=com_content&view=article&id=1608:bill-to-eliminate-civil-statute-of-limitations-on-sex-abuse-cases-clears-judiciary-panel&catid=54:latest-news&Itemid=179.

149 "Summary of Statutes of Limitation Reform across the United States," Marci Hamilton, accessed June 28, 2013, http://sol-reform.com/SNAPSHOT_OF_SOL_STATUTES_AND_2013_PENDING_BILLS_ACROSS_THE_US.pdf. For example, in 2010, overcoming lobbying efforts by the Catholic Church, Florida abolished its criminal statute of limitations for most sexual crimes against children. John Frank, "No Time Limits on Sex Crimes," *Tampa Bay Times*, April 27, 2010, accessed December 6, 2025, https://www.tampabay.com/archive/2010/04/27/no-time-limits-on-sex-crimes.

150 These efforts culminated in a nationwide referendum in 2008 in which the Swiss voted to abolish the statute of limitations for criminal prosecution of acts of child abuse against children under the age of twelve. Clare O'Dea, "Child Abusers Face Life-Long Prosecution," *SWI swissinfo.ch*, January 2, 2013, https://www.swissinfo.ch/eng/swiss-politics/child-abusers-face-life-long-prosecution/34557754.

151 South Korea Act on the Protection of Children and Juveniles from Sexual Abuse (No. 11574, December 18, 2012).

152 Associated Press, "Germany Extends Statute of Limitations on Abuse," The Honolulu Star-Advertiser, March 23, 2011, https://www.staradvertiser.com/2011/03/23/breaking-news/germany-extends-statute-of-limitations-on-abuse. Similarly, the Council of Europe recognized that children sexually abused by tourists from countries other than their own are often unable to come forward and identify offenders before the statute of limitations expire in the offender's home. For that reason, the Council of Europe's Convention on the Protection of Children against Sexual Exploitation and Abuse requires that the statute of limitations in each ratifying country to "continue for a period of time sufficient to allow the efficient starting of proceedings *after the victim has reached the age of majority* and which is commensurate with the gravity of the crime in question." Council of Europe's Convention on the Protection of Children against Sexual Exploitation and Abuse (CETS no. 201), article 33. (Emphasis added); Karen Fredette, "International Legislative Efforts to Combat Child Sex Tourism: Evaluating the Council of Europe Convention on Commercial Child Sexual Exploitation," *Boston College International and Comparative Law Review* 32 (2009): 1, 38.

153 *See generally* Hessbruegge, *supra* note 67; Convention on the Non-Applicability of Statutory Limitations to War Crimes and Crimes Against Humanity, G.A. res. 2391 (XXIII), annex, 23 U.N. GAOR Supp. (No. 18) at 40, U.N. Doc. A/7218 (November 11, 1970).

154 *See* Barrios *Altos v. Peru*, Inter-Am. Ct. H.R., No. 75, 41 (March 14, 2001) available at http://www.corteidh.or.cr/docs/casos/articulos/seriec_75_ing.pdf. In the Czech Republic, Germany, and Poland, serious crimes committed during the Communist-era were deemed imprescriptible. *See* Teitel, *supra* note 111, at 40–1. Some experts believe that international treaty law also renders statutes of limitation inapplicable to civil claims by victims of human rights abuses. Hessbruegge, *supra* note 67, at 373–4.

155 Convention on the Non-Applicability of Statutory Limitations to War Crimes and Crimes against Humanity, G.A. res. 2391 (XXIII), annex, 23 U.N. GAOR Supp. (No. 18) at 40, U.N. Doc. A/7218 (November 11, 1970). Consistent with this principle, the Human Rights and Equal Opportunity Commission of Australia recommended that compensation for aboriginals forcibly removed from their families should not be subject to a civil statute of limitations. Hessbruegge, *supra* note 67, at 374

citing Human Rights & Equal Opportunity Comm'n, *Bringing Them Home: Report of The National Inquiry into the Separation of Aboriginal and Torres Strait Islander Children from Their Families* 270–5 (1997). In addition, the Committee against Racial Discrimination criticized Japan for dismissing claims brought by "comfort women" based on the statute of limitations. *Ibid.* at 375 citing the Comm. Against Torture, Consideration of Reports Submitted by States Parties Under Article 19 of the Convention, Conclusions and Recommendations of the Comm. Against Torture: Japan, 38th Sess., April 30–May 18, 2007 12, U.N. Doc. CAT/C/JPN/CO/1 (August 3, 2007).

156 Hessbruegge, *supra* note 67, at 356. Crimes against humanity other than genocide include torture, deportation, and forced disappearances. *See, e.g.*, *Rome Statute of the International Criminal Court*, 2187 U.N.T.S. 90, *entered into force* July 1, 2002, Article 7.

157 G.A. Res. 60/147, U.N. Doc. A/RES/60/147 (December 16, 2005).

158 *Ibid.* at IV (7).

159 *Supra* note 90 and accompanying text.

160 *Supra* notes 90–100 and accompanying text.

161 *Supra* notes 35–44 and accompanying text.

162 *Supra* notes 42–52 and accompanying text.

163 *Supra* notes 90–100 and accompanying text.

164 *Ibid.*

165 *Supra* notes 117–20 and accompanying text.

166 *See ibid. supra* notes 84–8 and accompanying text.

167 *Ibid.*

168 *Supra* notes 121–3 and accompanying text.

169 *Supra* notes 45–52 and accompanying text.

170 *Supra* notes 124–5 and accompanying text.

171 *Supra* notes 45–52 and accompanying text.

172 *Supra* notes 47–8 and accompanying text.

173 *Ibid.*

174 *Supra* notes 45–52 and accompanying text.

175 *Supra* notes 132–5 and accompanying text.

176 *Supra* notes 135–9 and accompanying text.

177 *Ibid.*

178 *Supra* notes 140–3 and accompanying text.

179 *See ibid.*

180 *Supra* notes 144–52 and accompanying text.

181 *See supra* note 10 and accompanying text.

182 *See supra* notes 84–8 and accompanying text.

183 *Supra* notes 153–5 and accompanying text.

184 *See supra* notes 11–13 and accompanying text.

185 *Supra* notes 157–8 and accompanying text.

186 *C.f.* Hessbruegge, *supra* note 67, at 385.

187 Most jurisdictions view civil statutes of limitation as merely procedural rules; therefore, civil claims may be revived, without violating *ex post facto*. *See* Marci Hamilton, "The Supreme Court Renders Another Decision Interpreting the Ex Post Facto Clause That Makes It More Difficult to Incarcerate Sex Offenders," *Justia*, June

14, 2013, http://verdict.justia.com/2013/06/14/the-supreme-court-renders-another-decision-interpreting-the-ex-post-facto-clause.

188 "The Validity of Extending the Statute of Limitations for Cambodian National Crimes Tried before the Extraordinary Chambers and the Implications of Ex Post Facto, Documentation Center of Cambodia," Margarita Clarens, accessed August 10, 2025, https://vt.ldc-eccc.gov.kh/storage/6590/00333216-00333221_E9_8.14_EN.pdf; *Stogner v. California*, 539 U.S. 607 (2003).

189 *Supra* notes 105–6 and accompanying text.

190 Cho, *supra* note 108, at 586.

191 *See* Stogner, *supra* note 188, 539 U.S., at 633 (Kennedy, J. dissenting).

192 *Supra* note 108 and accompanying text.

193 Stogner, *supra* note 188, 539 U.S., at 633.

194 *Supra* notes 112–13 and accompanying text.

195 *Supra* note 42 and accompanying text.

196 South Korean courts should view international adoptions in the context of serious crimes that occurred under prior autocratic regimes, such as the Gwangju massacre, which could not have been prosecuted at the time they occurred. *Supra* notes 104–8 and accompanying text.

197 *See generally* Hessbruegge, *supra* note 67.

198 *Supra* notes 74, 76 and accompanying text.

199 *Supra* note 75 and accompanying text.

200 *Supra* notes 45–52 and accompanying text.

201 *See ibid.* See Malveaux, *supra* note 73, at 106, 116–17.

202 *Supra* note 28.

203 *See* Cho, *supra* note 109, at Kindle Locations 631–707.

Bibliography

Alberta Law Reform Institute. "Limitations, Final Report No. 55." Accessed August 10, 2025. https://www.alri.ualberta.ca/1989/12/limitations/.

Angell, Joseph Kinnicut, and John Wilder May. *A Treatise on the Limitations of Actions at Law and Suits in Equity and Admiralty*. 6th ed. Boston: Little, Brown, 1861.

Associated Press. "Germany Extends Statute of Limitations on Abuse." *The Honolulu Star-Advertiser*, March 23, 2011. https://www.staradvertiser.com/2011/03/23/breaking-news/germany-extends-statute-of-limitations-on-abuse/.

Australian Senate Community Affairs References Committee. "Commonwealth Contribution to Former Forced Adoption Policies and Practices." Accessed February 29, 2012. http://www.aph.gov.au/Parliamentary_Business/Committees/Senate/Community_Affairs/Completed_inquiries/2010-13/commcontribformerforcedadoption/report/index.

Bartholet, Elizabeth. "International Adoption: Thoughts on the Human Rights Issues." *Buffalo Human Rights Law Review* 13 (2007): 151–203.

Bartholet, Elizabeth. "Permanency Is Not Enough: Children Need the Nurturing Parents Found in International Adoption." *New York Law School Law Review* 55 (2010/2011): 781.

Brian, Kristi. "Marketing Korea: Marketing 'Multiculturalism' to Choosy Adopters." In *International Korean Adoption: A Fifty-Year History of Policy and Practice*, edited by Kathleen Ja Sook Berquist et al., 61–78 New York: Routledge, 2013.

Bureau of Consular Affairs, U.S. Department of State. "FY 2011 Annual Report on Intercountry Adoption, November 2011." Accessed August 10, 2025. https://travel.state.gov/content/dam/aa/pdfs/fy2011_annual_report.pdf.

Carlson, Richard. "Seeking the Better Interests of Children with a New International Law of Adoption." *New York Law School Law Review* 55 (2010/2011): 733–79.

Cho, Kuk. "Transitional Justice in Korea." In *Law and Society in Korea*, edited by Hyunah Yang, 189, 194. Cheltenham: Edward Elgar Publishing, 2013.

Cho, Kuk. "Transitional Justice in Korea: Legally Coping with Past Wrongs after Democratization." *Pacific Rim Law & Policy Journal* 16 (2007): 579–611.

Choy, Catherine Ceniza. "Institutionalizing International Adoption: The Historical Origins of Korean Adoption in the United States." In *International Korean Adoption: A Fifty-Year History of Policy and Practice*, edited by Kathleen Ja Sook Berquist et al., 25–42 New York: Routledge, 2013.

Clair, Siobahn. "Child Trafficking and Australia's Intercountry Adoption System." February 13, 2013. https://siobhanclair.wordpress.com/2013/02/13/child-trafficking-and-australias-intercountry-adoption-system.

Clarens, Margarita. "The Validity of Extending the Statute of Limitations for Cambodian National Crimes Tried before the Extraordinary Chambers and the Implications of Ex Post Facto." Documentation Center of Cambodia. Accessed August 10, 2025. https://vt.ldc-eccc.gov.kh/storage/6590/00333216-00333221_E9_8.14_EN.pdf.

Commissioner for Human Rights. "Adoption and Children: A Human Rights Perspective." *Issue Papers* (2011): 1–23. https://rm.coe.int/adoption-and-children-a-human-rights-perspective-issue-paper-commissio/16806dac00.

Custer, Charlie. "Kidnapped and Sold: Inside the Dark World of Child Trafficking in China." *The Atlantic*, July 25, 2013. http://www.theatlantic.com/china/archive/2013/07/kidnapped-and-sold-inside-the-dark-world-of-child-trafficking-in-china/278107/.

Dagher, Veronica. "Adopting? Prepare to Be Surprised." *Wall Street Journal*, February 23, 2013. https://www.wsj.com/articles/SB100014241278873234522045782879614832507l2?msockid=3a09b86e89ce63fb0291ae2a880562ee.

Dohle, Arun. "Inside Story of an Adoption Scandal." *Cumberland Law Review* 39 (2009): 131–85.

Donaldson, Russell. "Running of Limitations against Action for Civil Damages for Sexual Abuse of Child." *American Law Reports*, 5th ser., 9 (2013): 321–34.

Doyle, Charles. "Statutes of Limitation in Federal Cases: An Overview." *Congressional Research Service*. Accessed August 10, 2025. http://www.fas.org/sgp/crs/misc/RL31253.pdf.

Fisher, Caryn. "'Baby Exporter': Taking a Closer Look at Korean Adoptions." Korea Economic Institute. Accessed February 8, 2012. http://blog.keia.org/2012/02/baby-exporter-taking-a-closer-look-at-korean-adoption.

Frank, John. "No Time Limits on Sex Crimes." *Tampa Bay Times*, April 27, 2010. Accessed December 6, 2025. https://www.tampabay.com/archive/2010/04/27/no-time-limits-on-sex-crimes.

Fredette, Karen. "International Legislative Efforts to Combat Child Sex Tourism: Evaluating the Council of Europe Convention on Commercial Child Sexual Exploitation." *Boston College International and Comparative Law Review* 32 (2009): 1–43.

Goodwin, Michelle. "The Free Market Approach to Baby Adoption: The Value of a Baby." *Boston College Third World Law Journal* 26 (2006): 61–79.

Gordon, Gregory. "Adult Survivors of Child Sexual Abuse and the Statute of Limitations: The Need for Consistent Application of the Discovery Rule." *Pepperdine Law Review* 20 (1993): 1359, 1364–5.

Hamilton, Marci. "Summary of Statutes of Limitation Reform across the United States." Accessed June 28, 2013. http://sol-reform.com/SNAPSHOT_OF_SOL_STATUTES_AND_2013_PENDING_BILLS_ACROSS_THE_US.pdf.

Hamilton, Marci. "The Supreme Court Renders Another Decision Interpreting the Ex Post Facto Clause That Makes It More Difficult to Incarcerate Sex Offenders." *Justia*, June 14, 2013. http://verdict.justia.com/2013/06/14/the-supreme-court-renders-another-decision-interpreting-the-ex-post-facto-clause.

Hamilton, Marci A., and Paul R. Verkuil. "Facts about Childhood Sexual Abuse." Accessed August 10, 2025. http://sol-reform.com/images/FactsAboutCSA.pdf.

Han, In Sup. "Dealing with Wrongful Trials under the Authoritarian Regime." *Seoul National University Law Review* 46 (2005): 84–120.

Han, Sang Wook Daniel. "Transitional Justice: When Justice Strikes Back—Case Studies of Delayed Justice in Argentina and South Korea." *Houston Journal of International Law* 30 (2008): 653–702.

Hessbruegge, Jan Arno. "Justice Delayed, Not Denied: Statutory Limitations and Human Rights Crimes." *Georgetown Journal of International Law* 43 (2012): 335–75.

Hittle, Shaun. "Rape Survivor Works to Change Law, Abolish the Statute of Limitations in Rape Case." *The Lawrence Journal-World*, March 3, 2013. http://www2.ljworld.com/news/2013/mar/03/rqe-victin.

Hübinette, Tobias. "Comforting an Orphaned Nation: Representations of International Adoption and Adopted Koreans in Korean Popular Culture." PhD diss., Stockholm University, 2005.

Hübinette, Tobias. "President Kim Dae Jung and the Adoption Issue." Accessed August 10, 2025. https://www.tobiashubinette.se/kim_dae_jung_and_adoption.pdf.

Hubry, Denise. "Cambodia Tries to Solve Its Baby-Stealing Problem." *Global Post*, July 31, 2016. https://theworld.org/stories/2016/07/31/cambodia-tries-solve-its-baby-stealing-problem.

Human Rights Monitor South Korea. "Legislating the Abolition of Statute of Limitations on Homicide." Accessed June 26, 2012. http://www.humanrightskorea.org/2012/legislating-the-abolition-of-statute-of-limitations-on-homicide/.

Human Rights Watch. "Legal Opinion Submitted to the Ministry of Turkey: Lifting the Statute of Limitations for Violations of the Right to Life and Torture by Suspected State Perpetrators." Accessed August 10, 2025. http://www.hrw.org/news/2013/03/25/january-2013-legal-opinion-submitted-minister-justice-turkey.

Joyce, Kathryn. *The Child Catchers: Rescue, Trafficking, and the New Gospel of Adoption*. New York: PublicAffairs, 2013.

Kang, Shinwoo. "South Korea's Central Authority on Adoption Lacks Information." *The Hankyoreh*, April 10, 2009. http://english.hani.co.kr/arti/english_edition/e_national/367603.html.

Kim, Do-hyun. "Overseas Adoption: Child Welfare or Abuse?" *The Korea Times*, December 30, 2011. https://www.koreatimes.co.kr/opinion/20111230/overseas-adoption-child-welfare-or-abuse.

Kim, Dong Soo. "A Country Divided: Contextualizing Adoption from a Korean Perspective." In *International Korean Adoption: A Fifty-Year History of Policy and Practice*, edited by Kathleen Ja Sook Berquist et al., 3–23 New York: Routledge, 2013.

Kim, Elena. "Remembering Loss: The Koreanness of Overseas Koreans." In *International Korean Adoption: A Fifty-Year History of Policy and Practice*, edited by Kathleen Ja Sook Berquist et al., 115–30 New York: Routledge, 2013.

Kim, Marie Seong-Hak. "Customary Law and Colonial Jurisprudence in Korea." *American Journal of Comparative Law* 57 (2009): 205–48.

Kim, Pyeong Woo. "Demurrer Based on the Statute of Limitations and the Principle of Good Faith." *Sogang University Journal of Law* 8 (2006): 175–87.

Lee, Bong Joo. "Recent Trends in Child Welfare and Adoption in Korea: Challenges and Future Directions." In *International Korean Adoption: A Fifty-Year History of Policy and Practice*, edited by Kathleen Ja Sook Berquist et al., 189–206 New York: Routledge, 2013.

Long, Elizabeth. "Where Are They Coming From, Where Are They Going: Demanding Accountability in International Adoption." *Cardozo Journal of Law & Gender* 18, no. 3 (2012): 827–53.

Malveaux, Suzette M. "Statutes of Limitation: A Policy Analysis in the Context of Reparations Litigation." *George Washington Law Review* 74 (2005): 68–122.

Meier, Patricia, and Xiaole Zhang. "Sold into Adoption: The Hunan Baby Trafficking Scandal Exposes Vulnerabilities in Chinese Adoptions to the United States." *Cumberland Law Review* 39 (2009): 87–130.

Miller, Jenna. "The Constitutionality of and Need for Retroactive Civil Legislation Related to Sexual Abuse." *Cardozo Journal of Law and Gender* 17 (2011): 599–626.

NJ Today. "Bill to Eliminate Civil Statute on Sex Abuse Cases Clears Judiciary Panel." Accessed June 22, 2012. http://www.abolishsexabuse.org/index.php?option=com_content&view=article&id=1608:bill-to-eliminate-civil-statute-of-limitations-on-sex-abuse-cases-clears-judiciary-panel&catid=54:latest-news&Itemid=179.

O'Dea, Clare. "Child Abusers Face Life-Long Prosecution." *SWI swissinfo.ch*, January 2, 2013. https://www.swissinfo.ch/eng/swiss-politics/child-abusers-face-life-long-prosecution/34557754.

O'Reilly, Shawna. "Korean Adoption Program Changes Are Examined by Korean Adoptee." Examiner.com. Accessed February 28, 2013. http://www.examiner.com/article/korea-adoption-program-changes-are-analyzed-by-korean-adoptee.

Olsen, Tricia D., Leigh A. Payne, and Andrew G. Reiter, eds. *Transitional Justice in Balance: Comparing Processes, Weighing Efficacy*. Washington: United States Institute of Peace Press, 2013.

Park, Si-Woo. "Seizing Wealth of Pro-Japanese Collaborators Ruled Constitutional." *The Korea Times*, March 31, 2011. http://www.koreatimes.co.kr/www/news/nation/2013/01/117_84250.html.

Rasor, Katie, Richard M. Rothblatt, Elizabeth A. Russo, and Julie A. Turner. "Imperfect Remedies: The Arsenal of Criminal Statutes Available to Prosecute International Adoption Fraud in the United States." *New York Law School Law Review* 55 (2010): 801–22.

Ratner, Morris. "Factors Impacting the Selection and Positioning of Human Rights Class Actions in United States Courts: A Practical Overview." *New York University Annual Survey of American Law* 58 (2003): 623–50.

Rotabi, Karen S. "From Guatemala to Ethiopia: Shifts in Intercountry Adoption Leave Ethiopia Vulnerable for Child Sales and Other Unethical Practices." *Social Work and Society News Magazine*, June 8, 2010. https://unc.academia.edu/KarenSmithRotabi.

Rothschild, Matthew. "Babies for Sale: South Koreans Make Them, Americans Buy Them." *The Progressive*, January 1988. https://thesearchformothermissing.blogspot.com/2012/03/babies-for-sale-south-koreans-make-them.html.

Sang, Youn-joo. "Fears of Unintended Consequences as Adoption Tightened." *The Korea Herald*, October 10, 2012. https://www.koreaherald.com/article/10374336.

Schuster Institute for Investigative Journalism. "Capsule History of International Adoption." *Adoption Law: A History of Fictions*. Accessed February 23, 2011. http://www.brandeis.edu/investigate/adoption/history.html.

Selman, Peter. "Global Trends in Intercountry Adoption, 2000–2010." *Adoption Advocate*, no. 44 (National Council for Adoption, February 2012): 1–17.

Smolin, David. "Adoption as Child Trafficking." *Valparaiso University Law Review* 39 (2004): 281–325.

Smolin, David. "Child Laundering: How the Intercountry Adoption System Legitimizes and Incentivizes the Practices of Buying, Trafficking, Kidnapping, and Stealing Children." *Wayne Law Review* 52 (2006): 113–200.

Smolin, David. "Child Laundering and the Hague Convention on Intercountry Adoption: The Future and Past of Intercountry Adoption." *University of Louisville Law Review* 48 (2010): 441–98.

Smolin, David, and Desiree Smolin. "The Aftermath of Abusive Adoption Practices in the Lives of Adoption Triad Members: Responding to Adoption Triad Members Victimized by Abusive Adoption Practices." *Fleas Biting*, April 20, 2012. https://fleasbiting.blogspot.com/2012/04/aftermath-of-abusive-adoption-practices.html.

Song, Sang-Hyun. "Legal Education in Korea and the Asian Region." *Journal of Legal Education* 51, no. 3 (2001): 398–402.

Teitel, Ruti G. *Transitional Justice*. New York: Oxford University Press, 2000.

The Harvard Law Review Association. "Developments in the Law: Statutes of Limitations." *Harvard Law Review* 63, no. 7 (1950): 1170–270.

Trenka, Jane Jeong. "Draft Report on South Korean International Adoption." August 2013, 2–3. On file with author.

Trenka, Jane Jeong. "Internationally Adopted Koreans and the Movement to Revise the Korean Adoption Law." *Ewha Journal of Gender and Law* (2011). Manuscript on file with author.

Trenka, Jane Jeong. "My Adoption File." *Jane's Blog*. Accessed n.d. http://jjtrenka.wordpress.com/about/adoption-file.

Trenka, Jane Jeong. "Over Two Years after the Special Adoption Law Was Amended, Adoptees Still Waiting for Enforcement: How Can the Hague Convention Be Ratified without Enforcing the Special Adoption Law?" Unpublished manuscript.

United States Department of State. "Intercountry Adoption, Adoption Notice: The Republic of Korea Signs the Hague Adoption Convention." Accessed May 28, 2013. http://adoption.state.gov/country_information/country_specific_alerts_notices.php?alert_notice_type=notices&alert_notice_file=south_korea_2.

Waters, Davie M. "Korean Constitutionalism and the 'Special Act' to Prosecute Former Presidents Chun Doo-Hwan and Roh Tae-Woo." *Columbia Journal of Asian Law* 10 (1996): 461–88.

West, James. "Martial Lawlessness: The Legal Aftermath of Kwangju." *Pacific Rim Law & Policy Journal* 6 (1997): 85–168.

Wolman, Andrew. "Looking Back While Moving Forward: The Evolution of Truth Commissions in Korea." *Asian-Pacific Law and Policy Journal* 27 (2013): 51.
Yee, Yi-Li. "The Korean Constitutional Court and the Kwangju Massacre: Note on the Special Act Concerning the May Democratization Movement." *National Taiwan University Law Review* 4 (2009): 227–51.
Zagger, Zach. "Japan Abolishes Its Statute of Limitations for Murder." *Jurist*, April 28, 2010. http://jurist.org/paperchase/2010/04/japan-abolishes-statute-of-limitations.php.
The Harvard Law Review Association. "Developments in the Law: Statutes of Limitations." *Harvard Law Review* 63, no. 7 (1950): 1170–270.

This chapter was previously published under the same title in Yonsei Law Journal 5, no. 2 (2014): 117–162.

Index

About the Contributors

Joon-Kyu Choi is Professor at Seoul National University School of Law. He co-authored *Legal Theory and Interpretation in a Dynamic Society*, published by Nomos Verlagsgesellschaft in 2021. He holds an LL.B., an LL.M., and a JD from Seoul National University School of Law.

Daniel A. Edelson is Assistant Professor of Legal Practice at Seton Hall Law School and an attorney licensed to practice in New York and New Jersey. Prior to joining Seton Hall, he specialized in business litigation and taught US law and legal English both online and internationally.

Jeong-Chul Kim holds a PhD in Sociology from Northwestern University. He is an independent researcher and also works as a civil servant at the Dong-gu Office in Gwangju, South Korea. His work has been published in several peer-reviewed journals, including the *International Journal of the Legal Profession* and the *Annual Review of Sociology*. He also has a forthcoming monograph titled *Korean Collaboration in the Shadow of Japanese Rule: Negotiating Nationhood* (Lexington Books, in press).

Rosa Kim is Professor of Legal Writing at Suffolk University Law School, where she teaches Legal Practice Skills, Global Lawyering, and Advanced Legal Writing. She earned a BA from Tufts University, an MA from the Johns Hopkins University School of Advanced International Studies, and a JD from Boston College Law School. Before joining the legal academy, she served as Assistant Attorney General of the Commonwealth of Massachusetts Civil Trial Division litigating cases in the areas of civil rights and employment law. She is a Fulbright Scholar and past Chair of the Association of American Law Schools' Legal Writing, Reasoning, and Research Section.

Michelle Kwon is Assistant Professor at Inha University Law School. She holds a BA from the University of Illinois, a JD from the Indiana University Maurer School of Law, and an LL.M. from the University of Washington School of Law. Before joining Inha University, she worked as Legal Counsel for Korea's Ministry of Foreign Affairs and Trade, served as Legal Counsel for Samsung Electro-Mechanics, and was Adjunct Professor at Kyung Hee University in Korea.

Jae-Hyup Lee is Professor at Seoul National University School of Law and the author of *Dynamics of Ethnic Identity: Three Asian Communities in Philadelphia* (Routledge, 1998). He holds a BA from Seoul National University, a PhD in Anthropology from the University of Pennsylvania, and a JD from Northwestern University in Chicago.

John Sanghyun Lee is Professor at Soongsil University College of Law. He is the author of *Strategies to Achieve a Binding International Agreement on Regulating Cartels: Overcoming Doha Standstill* (Springer, 2017) and *Current Legal Issues in South Korea* (Korea Legislation Research Institute, 2017). He holds an LL.B. from Seoul National University School of Law, an LL.M. from both Korea University and New York University School of Law, and an S.J.D. from Golden Gate University School of Law.

Justin D. Levinson is the Cades Foundation Professor of Law at the University of Hawai'i at Mānoa, where he also serves as Director of the Culture and Jury Project, and Deputy Director of the Institute of Asian-Pacific Business Law. He holds a BA from the University of Michigan, a JD from the University of California, Los Angeles, and an LL.M. from Harvard Law School.

Jaewan Moon is Professor at the Law School of Hankuk University of Foreign Studies. He co-authored *Law Crossing Eurasia: From Korea to the Czech Republic* (rw&w Science & New Media Passau-Berlin-Prague, 2015). He holds an LL.B. from Seoul National University School of Law, as well as an LL.M. and a JD from Indiana University Maurer School of Law in Bloomington.

Joong-Hwan Oh is Professor of Sociology at Hunter College of The City University of New York. He is the author of *A Public Encounter in New York City: A Phenomenological View on a Sobering Experience* (Palgrave Macmillan, 2023), *Examining the Use of Online Social Networks by Korean Graduate Students: Navigating Intercultural Academic Experiences* (Routledge, 2019), and *Immigration and Social Capital in the Age of Social Media: Messages of the American Social Institutions on a Korean-American Women's Online Community* (Lexington Books, 2016), as well as the coauthor of five edited books about Korean communities around the world. His work has also appeared in more than twenty peer-reviewed journals, such as *International Migration Review*, *Urban Studies*, *New Media & Society*, *Social Science & Medicine*, *American Journal of Economics and Sociology*, and *Sociological Inquiry*.

Jisuk Woo is Professor at the Graduate School of Public Administration at Seoul National University. She is the author of *Copyright Law and Computer Programs: The Role of Communication in Legal Structure*, published by Garland Publishing in 2000. She holds a BA from Yonsei University, a PhD from the Annenberg School for Communication at the University of Pennsylvania, and a JD from New York University School of Law.

www.ingramcontent.com/pod-product-compliance
Ingram Content Group UK Ltd.
Pitfield, Milton Keynes, MK11 3LW, UK
UKHW020214290926
15470UKWH00001B/187

9 798216 277699